T0164548

THE
VALEDICTION

THREE NIGHTS OF DESMOND

Paul Fitzgerald
Elizabeth Gould

Published by:
Trine Day LLC
PO Box 577
Walterville, OR 97489
1-800-556-2012
www.TrineDay.com
trineday@icloud.com

Library of Congress Control Number: 2021943881

Fitzgerald, Paul & Gould, Elizabeth,
VALEDICTION—1st ed.
p. cm.
Epub (ISBN-13) 978-1-63424-395-7
Trade Paper (ISBN-13) 978-1-63424-394-0
Cloth: (ISBN-13) 978-1-63424-393-3
1. Memoir -- Fitzgerald, Paul -- 1951- . 2. Memoir -- Gould, Elizabeth -- 1948. 3. Afghan Wars. 4. Civil-military relations -- Afghanistan. . 5. World politics. 6. Fitzgerald family history. I. Title

FIRST EDITION
10 9 8 7 6 5 4 3 2 1

Printed in the USA
Distribution to the Trade by:
Independent Publishers Group (IPG)
814 North Franklin Street
Chicago, Illinois 60610
312.337.0747
www.ipgbook.com

PUBLISHER'S FOREWORD

Pussy cat, pussy cat, where have you been?
I've been to London to visit the Queen.
Pussy cat, pussy cat, what did you do there?
I frightened a little mouse under her chair.
              – Songs for the Nursery (1805)

The wheel of the world swings through the same phases again and again.
  – Rudyard Kipling, *The Man Who Would Be King* (1888)

Somehow it was not the fault of the born adventurers, of those who by
their very nature dwelt outside society and outside all political bodies,
that they found in imperialism a political game that was endless by
definition; they were not supposed to know that in politics an endless
game can end only in catastrophe and that political secrecy hardly ever
ends in anything nobler than the vulgar duplicity of a spy. The joke on
these players of the Great Game was that their employers knew what
they wanted and used their passion for anonymity for ordinary spying.
But this triumph of the profit-hungry investors was temporary, and they
were duly cheated when a few decades later they met the player of the
game of totalitarianism, a game played without ulterior motives like
profit and therefore played with such murderous efficiency that it de-
voured even those who financed it.
  – Hannah Arendt, *The Origins of Totalitarianism* (1967)

A ccording to the latest research, time flows differently atop
mountains than at sea level. Scientists installed "two extremely
precise atomic clocks, one placed 33 centimeters higher than the
other ... time moved slower for the clock closer to Earth." Not a huge
difference, but measurable. All relative, correct? Does *it* matter?

Mountains are autonomous zones, you can pretty much do what you
want there until someone with a gun, comes up and says not to. Afghanistan is most definitely a mountainous area. It comprises most of the Hindu Kush mountain range, and more than 50% of the land area is above

6,500 feet, with the highest peak over 25,000 feet. Remote tribal populations overlain with centuries of international imperialist intrigues.

In 2017, Rod Norland noted in the *New York Times*: "Afghanistan has long been called the 'graveyard of empires' – for so long that it is unclear who coined that disputable term. In truth, no great empires perished solely because of Afghanistan. Perhaps a better way to put it is that Afghanistan is the battleground of empires."

As an "American Empire" departs Afghanistan, Paul Fitzgerald and Elizabeth Gould's timely memoir, *Valediction – Three Nights of Desmond* gives us a different perspective: a viewpoint developed through deep research, critical analysis, and years of actually living history – a more proper narrative.

Valediction explores the real, behind-the-scenes' reasons of the American foray, and how events and people were set on a course of inevitability. How journalism is twisted in service of goals hidden from the American people, and stilted information is then used to push political agendas, pecuniary profits and pernicious outcomes.

Paul and Liz worked hard to tell the American people of their shocking finds. They are published authors, have written screen plays, produced documentary films, gathered news and appeared on national TV in the effort. *Valediction* shows how the mainstream media shunts aside authentic reportage for prepackaged rhetoric – leaving our nation beggared in spirit, prestige and honor. Does "Empire" checkmate the "shining city on a hill"?

But there is more to this tale than meets the eye, Paul traces his Fitzgerald line back to the 11th century, they helped the Normans subdue Ireland, later becoming enemies of the Monarchy. He began having dreams of his ancestors, of knights and castles. *They* were talking to him!

Something's afoot! Paul is related to "Honey Fitz," JFK's grandfather, who was a mayor of Boston. In the early 1970s Paul was in the Boston production of *Hair*, and later, *Jesus, Christ Superstar* – he played Jesus. Will the hopes of generations for a better world come forth?

Time … will tell.

Let The sunshine in!

Onward to the Utmosts of Futures,
Peace,
R.A. "Kris" Millegan
Publisher
TrineDay
August 22, 2021

There are more things in heaven and earth, Horatio,
Than are dreamt of in your philosophy.
— *Hamlet*, William Shaespeare

Now listen to me, you benighted muckers! We're going to teach you soldiering, The world's noblest profession! When we're done with you, you'll be able to stand up and slaughter your foes like civilized men! But first, you will have to learn to march in step. And do the manual of arms without even having to think! Good soldiers don't think, they just obey! Do you suppose that if a man thought twice, he'd give his life for Queen and Country? Not bloody likely! He wouldn't go near the battlefield!
— Sean Connery as Daniel Dravot, *The Man Who Would Be King*

And what rough beast, its hour come round at last,
Slouches towards Bethlehem to be born?
— *The Second Coming*, William Butler Yeats

PREVIOUSLY PUBLISHED BOOKS AND PRAISE

Invisible History: Afghanistan's Untold Story published by City Lights in 2009.

Crossing Zero: The AfPak War at the Turning Point of American Empire published by City Lights in 2011.

The Voice published first in 2000 and republished in 2012.

Readers with a serious interest in U.S. foreign policy or military strategy will find it helpful ... Bob Woodward's recent Obama's War focuses on the administration's AfPak deliberations, but this book provides a wider perspective.

> – Marcia L. Sprules, Council on Foreign Relations Lib.,
> *NY Library Journal*

Journalists Fitzgerald and Gould do yeoman's labor in clearing the fog and laying bare American failures in Afghanistan in this deeply researched, cogently argued and enormously important book.

> – *Publishers Weekly* (starred review)

A probing history of the country and a critical evaluation of American involvement in recent decades.... A fresh perspective on a little-understood nation.

> —*Kirkus*

Paul Fitzgerald and Elizabeth Gould have seen the importance of the "Great Game" in Afghanistan since the early 1980s. They have been most courageous in their commitment to telling the truth – and have paid a steep price for it.

> – Oliver Stone

Fitzgerald and Gould have consistently raised the difficult questions and inconvenient truths about western engagement in Afghanistan. While many analysts and observers have attempted to wish a reality on a grim and tragic situation in Afghanistan, Fitzgerald and Gould have systematically dug through the archives and historical record with integrity and foresight to reveal a series of misguided strategies and approaches that have contributed to what has become a tragic quagmire in Afghanistan.

> – Professor Thomas Johnson, Department of National Security Affairs and Director, Program for Culture and Conflict Studies,
> Naval Postgraduate School, Monterey California

A ferocious, iron-clad argument about the institutional failure of American foreign policy in Afghanistan and Pakistan.

– Daniel Ellsberg

Crossing Zero is much more than a devastating indictment of the folly of U.S. military intervention in Afghanistan. Paul Fitzgerald and Elizabeth Gould demonstrate that the U.S. debacle in Afghanistan is the predictable climax of U.S. imperial overreach on a global scale. Like their earlier work documenting the origins of U.S. involvement in Afghanistan during the Cold War, *Crossing Zero* deserves the attention of all serious students of U.S. foreign policy."
—Selig S. Harrison, Co-author with Diego Cordovez of *Out of Afghanistan: The Inside Story of the Soviet Withdrawal*

I loved it. An extraordinary contribution to understanding war and geo-politics in Afghanistan that will shock most Americans by its revelations of official American government complicity in using, shielding, sponsoring and supporting terrorism. A devastating indictment on the behind-the-scenes shenanigans by some of America's most respected statesmen.

– Daniel Estulin, author of *The True Story of the Bilderberg Club*

Americans are now beginning to grasp the scope of the mess their leaders made while pursuing misguided military adventures into regions of Central Asia we once called "remote." How this happened – and what the US can do to extricate itself from its entanglements in Pakistan and Afghanistan – is the story of *Crossing Zero*. Based on decades of study and research, this book draws lines and connects dots in ways few others do."
—Stephen Kinzer, author of *All the Shah's Men and Reset: Iran, Turkey and America's Future*

In this penetrating inquiry, based on careful study of an intricate web of political, cultural, and historical factors that lie in the immediate background, and enriched by unique direct observation at crucial moments, Fitzgerald and Gould tell "the real story of how they came to be there and what we can expect next." Invocation of Armageddon is no mere literary device.

– Noam Chomsky

A serious, sobering study ... illuminates a critical point of view rarely discussed by our media ... results of this willful ignorance have been disastrous to our national well-being.

– Oliver Stone

Authors' Foreword

Few people are given the opportunity to witness the making of history. Even fewer have had the honor of following and interacting with that history as it unfolds and plays out over four decades. It has been our good fortune as a husband and wife team to have done both and in that process to have made the memory of something as impersonal and distant as Afghanistan's role in ending the Cold War – personal and human.

Getting to that point was not easy. In retrospect, growing up during the Cold War was just a reality we learned to accept. Unlike our parents we grew up as children under the constant threat that our lives could be wiped away by a surprise nuclear attack at any moment. As a consequence our sense of identity evolved in a detached twilight zone between war and peace. Through a succession of undeclared wars and "police actions" in the 1950s and 60s we were numbed to the meaning of real war, of ruined cities and devastated families. Only when the irrationality of Vietnam began to be felt at home, did America's leadership finally move to lessen the tension.

From 1968 until the end of the Vietnam War in 1975, the first real steps to end the Cold War with the Soviet Union were taken through a process known as détente and by 1979 the effort was approaching its third decade. During that time a series of negotiations aimed at limiting strategic nuclear weapons was embarked upon called the Strategic Arms Limitation Talks, SALT. But as the time approached for the ratification of a second arms control treaty between the United States and the Soviet Union, resistance grew. Following the Soviet invasion of Afghanistan in December of 1979 relations snapped back to the coldest of Cold War levels and it is during this time that our story begins.

This memoir tells the tale of how we came to be drawn to the war in Afghanistan and into what is known as the Great Game for Central Asia. It tells of the dangers and hardships we faced by going against the grain of a revived Cold War narrative; of crossing the line and returning with an eyewitness account that certain powerful interests did not want revealed.

One of the most important of those who did not want to hear that story was our CBS News sponsor. In agreeing to send us to Afghanistan in the spring of 1981 they provided the backing to open up a mysterious front-line state that had been closed to western eyes since the Soviet invasion sixteen months before. Having CBS News as a backer gave us the credibility of America's Tiffany News Network as it stood at the height of its reputation.

At the time we expected that CBS had an institutional interest in controlling a story of this magnitude having set the tone for international broadcast journalism since World War II. What we did not know was that for CBS's Vietnam War-weary brass, the story was as personal as it was institutional and that making Afghanistan look like "Russia's Vietnam" was part of our assignment.

A year earlier *CBS Evening News* anchor Dan Rather had staked his reputation on a furtive venture into Afghanistan by trekking over the mountains, and was mocked with the nickname "Gunga Dan" as a reward. The Afghan government had accused him of numerous crimes and tried him in absentia. Anything we brought back from Kabul was therefore viewed with deep suspicion.

In the end CBS News did air a limited, unsatisfactory news story of our trip, but for us the adventure had just begun. A second trip followed two years later with international negotiator Roger Fisher for a presentation on ABC's *Nightline*. The story that time was the possibility of getting the Soviet Union to end the war in Afghanistan and what we found confirmed our suspicions that the Soviets were desperate to get out.

Our story was a blockbuster and completely invalidated the official Washington narrative which under normal circumstances should have been front page news. But with the Reagan White House bent on keeping the Soviet Union trapped in their own Vietnam, the story was swept under the rug.

From our unique vantage over the years, we came to see the U.S. position on Afghanistan as a contradiction of historic proportions which on the one hand claimed the Soviets had invaded Afghanistan to launch a conquest of the Middle East while at the same time undermining their efforts to withdraw – preferring instead to keep them bogged down in a Vietnam-style quagmire.

We are accustomed as Americans to viewing history through the eyes of powerful "experts" whom we assume know more than we do about any given situation. But our personal experience opened our eyes to the limits of focusing only on facts which in many cases were arbitrarily selected or bent to conform – by these "experts" – to an ideological narrative.

This revelation provoked us in the late 1980s to move from journalism to screenwriting which resulted in Oliver Stone asking us to interpret our experience for the screen. As writers we could finally impact the ongoing narrative on Afghanistan and put our personal motivations into the story. But with the first bombing of the World Trade Towers in 1993 we came to realize that our personal Afghan story had been brought home to America.

What followed broadened our experience into an epic adventure in which we encountered enough Afghan royals, CIA operatives, American ambassadors and religious fanatics to populate a spy novel. This memoir, in sum, is our journey through that experience from the perspective of two Americans from very different backgrounds who came together on an unconventional course and discovered a hidden history that continues to shape our present day.

Paul Fitzgerald and Elizabeth Gould

MAJOR CHARACTERS

Ambassador Adolph Dubs – was a career diplomat who served in Germany, Liberia, and the Soviet Union. He became a noted Soviet expert, and in 1973-1974 he served as charge d'affaires at U.S. Embassy in Moscow. In 1978 he was appointed Ambassador to Afghanistan. On February 14, 1979, Dubs was kidnapped and assassinated. His death remains a mystery to this day.

Ambassador Theodore Eliot – served in the American embassy in Moscow in the mid-1950s; in the American embassy in Tehran in the mid-1960s and from 1973-1978 was Ambassador to Afghanistan. He then became Inspector General of the State Department and was named Dean of the Fletcher School of Law and Diplomacy at Tufts University. He also served as General Secretary for the U.S. to the Bilderberg meetings.

Roger Fisher – was a pioneer in the field of international law and negotiation and co-founder of the Harvard Negotiation Project. As a professor at Harvard Law School, Fisher established negotiation and conflict resolution as a field deserving of academic study. He was a co-author of the 1981 best seller *Getting to Yes*. His expertise in resolving conflicts led to a role in drafting the Camp David accords between Egypt and Israel and in ending apartheid in South Africa.

John Kenneth Galbraith – was an economist, teacher, diplomat and a liberal member of the political and academic establishment. He was a revered lecturer for generations of Harvard students. Galbraith was one of the most widely read authors in the history of economics and was consulted frequently by national leaders.

Farid Zarif – was Council and then charge d'affaires of the Permanent Mission of Afghanistan to the UN, 1980-1981. He then became the permanent representative of Afghanistan to the UN as ambassador in 1981. Following that he became Special Representative of the Secretary-General, UN Mission in Liberia and continues to work for the UN.

Peter Larkin – started as a foreign correspondent for UPI and CBS News in Vietnam and during the Indo-Pakistani war. He continued to work for

CBS News; first with anchor Walter Cronkite and later with Dan Rather. Larkin rose from foreign correspondent to become Foreign Editor of CBS News until he retired.

Allard Lowenstein – was a liberal Democratic politician whose work on civil rights and the antiwar movement inspired many public figures including John Kerry, Barney Frank, William F. Buckley, Jr., Warren Beatty and Peter Yarrow. Lowenstein was a vocal critic of the Federal authority's refusal to reopen the investigation into RFK's assassination. He created the National Student Association (NSA) and served as its first President in 1950. It was suspected that Lowenstein had a relationship to the CIA since its main vehicle for recruiting student leaders from around the world throughout the 1950s and 1960s was the NSA.

Colonel Alexander Gardner (1785-1877) – was an American soldier and mercenary who travelled to Afghanistan and Punjab and served in various military positions in the region. Gardner's exploits have been identified as inspiration for George MacDonald Fraser's novel *Flashman* and Rudyard Kipling's *The Man Who Would Be King*.

Selig Harrison – was a journalist, scholar and author who specialized in US relations with South and East Asia. He was the *Washington Post* Bureau Chief in New Delhi and Tokyo in the 1960s and 1970s and also worked for the Associated Press, *New Republic*, Carnegie Endowment, Brookings Institution and Center for International Policy. His books included *India: The Most Dangerous Decades, Out of Afghanistan: The Inside Story of the Soviet Withdrawal, Korean Endgame* and he was credited with helping to arrange the 1994 nuclear deal with North Korea called the "Agreed Framework."

Zbigniew Brzezinski – was the hawkish strategic theorist who was President Jimmy Carter's national security adviser from 1977-1981. Brzezinski guided most of Carter's foreign policy for four years to thwart the Soviets at any cost. He delayed implementation of the SALT II arms treaty in 1979 and supported billions in military aid for Islamic militants to fight the Soviet troops in Afghanistan. He tacitly encouraged China to continue backing the murderous regime of Pol Pot in Cambodia to stop the Soviet-backed Vietnamese from taking over that country. From the start of his tenure Brzezinski gave Carter his daily intelligence briefings, which had previously been the prerogative of the CIA. He frequently called journalists to his office for secret briefings in which he would put his own spin on events.

The Novelized Memoir Defined

A memoir is defined as any nonfiction narrative writing based in the author's personal memories. The assertions made in a memoir are understood to be factual. Our purpose in describing *The Valediction* as a novelized memoir is to differentiate from a traditional memoir in this way. It became clear that we could not express the multi-dimensional quality of our story using the straight chronological order in which it occurred. Although the order of events has been rearranged when needed, exchanges with our cast of characters are factual. There is one exception, Desmond Fitzmaurice. Although he is a composite character it would be inaccurate to describe him as fictional. Fitzmaurice is a combination of both worldly and other worldly encounters we had along the way through our forty year adventure.

PROLOGUE

February 14, 1979. Cold, medieval Kabul Afghanistan under clear blue skies. St. Valentine's Day. Police stop American ambassador Adolph Dubs' big beige Oldsmobile.

Diplomatic immunity ignored. Car door opens from the inside. Three men show up. Guns drawn. Orders barked – drive to the Kabul Hotel. Kidnappers march ambassador through the lobby up to room 117. Embassy political officer Bruce Flatin responds. Shouts from the hall outside the door. Dubs tries to explain. Everything was going according to plan. Somebody threw a monkey wrench into the deal.

Tehran: Iranian Students storm the U.S. embassy. Carter and Vance out of town. Under Secretary takes the call. Are Iran and Afghanistan connected? Hesitates. Sends mixed signals to embassy Kabul – stalling. Contacts national security advisor Brzezinski: "We have a problem."

Kabul: Russians and Afghans pledge not to storm room 117. So why are Kabul police storming the room? Automatic gun fire tears through the windows from the bank building across the street. Barrage of bullets riddle the room for forty seconds before Kabul police chief Mohammed Lal forces his way in. Flatin held back. Four more shots ring out. Lal opens the door. Dubs and two kidnappers are dead.

Headline *Washington Post*: SOVIET ROLE ALLEGED IN DUBS' DEATH

Washington: Brzezinski accuses Afghans and Russians of murder. Secretary of State's hands are tied. Slams phone down in frustration. Brzezinski sends written memo to President Carter, "Now we can lure the Russians into the Afghan trap."

The clock ticks. Brezhnev acts.

KABUL, DECEMBER 27, 1979

Bloody Christmas. Soviets Spetsnaz special forces crush Kabul's palace guard. Western press has a field day making up stories. Afghan government kicks them out – total news blackout. Détente falls apart, SALT put on hold. The Western peace movement collapses; disillusion, Carter "betrayed." Can't trust the Russians. Communist thugs. Brzezinski claims Soviets want warm water port and the Persian Gulf. Carter sinks in the polls. Reagan becomes a shoo-in.

Chapter 1

Boston: Parker House Hotel opposite the old Puritan graveyard – December 12, 1981.

If only my father could see me now he'd have understood me better. This was the place where his father Michael had made his union deals with his cousin John Francis "Honey Fitz" Fitzgerald in the basement bar; a Last Hurrah. Fitz's grandson Jack had announced for President right here in the press room. Walnut paneling, cut glass chandeliers, haunted echoes of the New Jerusalem. Saturday Club; Yankee moralists Emerson, Hawthorne, Longfellow building their shining city on a hill. I could almost smell their wet wool and worn shoe leather after walking twenty-five miles from Concord. Mine eyes have seen the glory. Charles Dickens chose it for his first reading of *A Christmas Carol* in 1867. John Wilkes Booth, Sarah Bernhardt, Judy Garland and James Dean stayed here when starring at nearby theatres. Malcolm X and Ho Chi Minh worked the wait staff. *"Such guests!"* wrote Oliver Wendell Homes. *"What famous names its record boasts, whose owners wander in the mob of ghosts!"*

The Dunfey brothers saved the ghosts from the wrecking ball and built a little empire led by World War II fighter pilot brother Jack. Hospitaller hospitality. Tough, Catholic Irish bulldog. Dropped French-fries from his plane to the family's clam stand at Hampton beach on the Fourth of July. Left the competition stuck in traffic. Now over cocktails and shrimp he's invited me to drop a bombshell called Afghanistan on the local cognoscenti.

Jack smiled from behind the podium. The Dunfeys took their political activism seriously. Sheltered Coretta Scott King at the family compound when MLK was assassinated. Jack liked a good fight and he expected one tonight. "Ladies and Gentlemen, I'd now like to introduce the man behind the film you have just seen, *Afghanistan Between Three Worlds* – Paul Fitzgerald."

Jack took a seat in the front row and smiled while he waited for the show to begin. I stared back at the audience, wondering what to expect. Not bad. He and his brother Jerry had assembled a crop of national news reporters, talk show hosts and diplomats. They'd even bagged Theodore

Eliot, a former U.S. ambassador to Afghanistan and dean of the Fletcher School of Law and Diplomacy at Tufts University. The first and only time I'd seen Eliot was with Harvard Professor Richard Pipes on the *MacNeil/Lehrer NewsHour* a couple of days after the Soviets invaded Afghanistan the year before. Jerry said they'd invited him in the past but he hadn't come. So why had he shown up tonight?

"Who gave you the permission to do this?" Eliot demanded after repeatedly standing up and intercepting questions addressed to me. I could hear the audience gasp. Gloves off. No formalities. He'd come at me right out of the box.

At six foot, eight inches, Theodore Lyman Eliot was the voice of a deeper agenda – arrogant, imperious and self-righteous. Descended from a 17th century Salem witch trial judge and a long line of Puritan demonizers, Theodore Eliot was a Knight Templar guarding the gates of Jerusalem and I was a prying "Inquisitor" in dire need of comeuppance.

"I did this for CBS News. And I didn't need permission. There are no travel restrictions on Afghanistan."

Shock. Confusion gripped the guests. People began to mutter under their breath. Shouldn't the dean know this? Isn't a free press supposed to be a constitutional right? The ambassador was over the line for a guest. But for a diplomat and a lawyer he'd broken every rule in the book. And he was not stopping.

"I hope you realize that you are treading very close to being a conduit for Soviet disinformation," he threatened, stretching up to his full height.

So this was how the "free" press was controlled. The Soviet army invaded Afghanistan in December 1979. It was now December 1981. Jimmy Carter had got on the tube and called Afghanistan the greatest threat to peace since the Second World War. Fantastic claims were being made about Soviet intentions. The U.S. military had moved into the Middle East. Nobody had been inside Afghanistan but me, and the audience had come to see what was going on. But the dean of the Fletcher School was ordering everyone to ignore what they just saw, and stop me from talking about it.

I responded diplomatically but diplomat Eliot wasn't being diplomatic. Jack Dunfey smiled from his front row seat, clenched his fists and mouthed the words "give it to him."

Eliot had come for blood – my blood. The Irish who'd come to Boston had a long history with old Yankees like him, the Fitzgeralds especially. Traced back to the 11th century, my family was English before they were Irish and French before they were English and synonymous with Catholic Rome. They had fought against the Protestant Reformation until the bitter end when in 1583 they'd lost their lands and their heads. The Puritans knew the name Fitzgerald would be trouble and it was. Local folklore held that the Lowells spoke only to Cabots and the Cabots only to God. Thanks to Jack and Jerry I now had a chance to talk to God so I took a deep breath and responded to Theodore Eliot with appropriate indignation.

"There was a time in the U.S. called the McCarthy era when the press was intimidated from reporting the truth about the world they lived in," I said. "The black list was a very dark time for the United States. I was too young to have known that era personally but I do know the damage it caused our democracy and the fear it created. To return to it now by stopping Americans from judging for themselves what's going on in Afghanistan and by threatening others to close their eyes, would bring on a danger to our country that we cannot afford."

There it was. If the dean of the Tufts Fletcher School of Law and Diplomacy was squelching a journalist's right to report a story then he was no different than a Soviet commissar and the audience knew it.

The shocked look on Eliot's face said it all as his 6'8" frame slumped into his chair. His breach of protocol had backfired. Eliot's attempt to seize the floor and stop me from speaking called attention to how out of line American policy had become. He'd left me no choice but to challenge him, and based on the reaction of the crowd I'd succeeded as they rose to their feet in a standing ovation.

Everything blurred. Mumbled congrats, back slaps. Was I in a dream? Now what? Jack was back at the podium, big smile on his face. "I want to thank everyone for coming out tonight. The night is still young. There's a lot to talk about. Coffee and refreshments are being served at the back of the room, so let's get started."

It was almost 1982. I'd been on the story since the summer of 1979. But everything had flipped. Détente was over, Strategic Arms Limitation on hold. Carter had mismanaged everything. Or had he? Reagan sent him packing. Limiting nuclear arms made us weak. Afghanistan proved we must be strong. It was a right-wing dream come true.

So now what?

I had entered my third decade and was on the verge of being thirty-one. CBS News was history. Somebody had hung a big *no trespass* sign around Afghanistan and I'd ignored it. Along the way I'd run into something seamy about the way the American media did its job. Now I had to decide what I was going to do about it. The answer didn't take long.

The man introduced himself as Roger Fisher – 60ish, tall. Not as tall as Theodore Eliot, but tall enough I had to squint against the yellow glare of the chandeliers. "You have to forgive Ted," he said. "When it comes to Afghanistan it's personal. He was there for six years as ambassador but he's really O.K., a good guy."

Oh really? Was he serious? I was too startled to answer, so I nodded warily.

"Ted and I work together at Harvard Law School on the negotiation project. What you're doing is exactly what I want the project to do. Go to those places where negotiation has failed and find a way to make it work." Fisher reached into his pocket and pulled out a card. "I did a series for PBS back in 1975 called *Arabs and Israelis*. Showed both sides of the argument. Only television can do that. Put yourself in the other guy's shoes the way you just did. Let the audience see it from their perspective. If I can help you, just let me know."

I already knew something was wrong with Afghanistan. There were huge blank spots in the official narrative. But now because of Eliot I knew the problem came straight from the top. Why would the highest level point man for the official narrative go public with an attack on me? And why would his colleague rush to apologize for him?

My wife Liz struggled through the crowd, excited. "That was really something. Did you see the look on his face?"

"I really didn't want to do that."

"You heard the audience. He left you no choice."

I pulled out Roger Fisher's card and showed it to her. "This guy came over and apologized for him." Liz stared at the embossed Harvard Law School emblem. Three sheaves of wheat under the word Veritas (Truth). "He offered any help we need."

"And we're going to take it, right?"

I smiled. "What else can we do? Of course."

Liz looked relieved for the first time since this whole thing had begun. I'd gone looking for trouble and found it. Now I had to deal with the consequences. There was something very wrong with the Afghanistan story and the former U.S. ambassador just confirmed it. The death of his successor Adolph Dubs only added to the mystery. Eliot should have wanted answers. Instead he showed up at the Parker House to attack me. Was it just Afghanistan or was it me? The Fitzgerald legacy was like being involuntarily enlisted in some phantom army. The coincidences surrounding JFK had been piling up. Now it was serious. What did it mean? That wouldn't be easy to explain. Not unless I went back to the beginning and rethought how it all came about.

CHAPTER 2

Elizabeth – Liz. If ever two people were born opposites it was us. We'd met as students in 1970. She was the beautiful, artsy-intellectual New York Jew from Emerson College. I was the Irish Catholic jock from Boston University (BU) whose faculty advisor had pegged for a career in intelligence. Not exactly a match made in heaven for a detached nihilist like me, but then I'd learned that God worked in mysterious ways. Looking back, my advisor was spot on given my father's recent death and the dire consequences the son of a widow was destined to face. I needed a job but I also wanted a partner who'd help me carve a new path away from the dark arts I was apparently cut out for. Liz was a big part of the reason I'd gone to Afghanistan as a journalist and I doubt that I would ever have done so without her. I'd gone looking for answers and found more questions instead. Now I had to deal with the consequences.

There was something about *Afghanistan* that had trouble written all over it. Why? Because the Soviet invasion thing just didn't add up.

Well, it did add up if you bought into the official narrative. Based on a bogus 1977 CIA study, the Soviet Union was running out of oil and needed Afghanistan as a base to invade the Middle East and seize *our* oil fields. As far as just about everyone was concerned it was an open and shut case. But it wasn't an open and shut case if you'd been following it closely. And I had. Call it pattern recognition. Or better yet – divine insight.

Believe it or not, I had come to the Soviet invasion of Afghanistan via an act of God. Well, maybe not God directly, but certainly by one of his messengers. Following my work in a successful congressional campaign in 1976 I'd sought out a job in television. Any job. The Vietnam War was behind us. Jimmy Carter had just been elected to heal the nation, to rid the world of nuclear weapons, and I had a handful of IOUs. A few phone calls later and out of the blue arrived a job as the host of a public affairs program at the local affiliate of the Christian Broadcasting Network (CBN) WXNE.

WXNE, Channel 25 was not your normal TV station. WXNE, which stood for Christ in New England, was technically a hybrid ministry and forward operating base for CBN's fanatical founder Pat Robertson. Robertson was known worldwide as a *televangelist* for his popular *700 Club* talk show. But for much of the day his station operated as a commercial venture supported by advertising revenue from reruns and children's cartoons. By anybody's standards Channel 25 was a bizarre, under-funded operation housed in an old warehouse in a nondescript Boston suburb. It consisted of two obsolete RCA studio cameras, a dozen or so cubicles from which to raise money and a variety of dedicated born-again believers to man them. Each taping session began with the crew joining hands in prayer in the hopes that Jesus would prevent the camera tubes from exploding in the middle of a show. And so far it had worked.

Finding opposing points of view to a Southern Baptist in liberal Boston was not difficult, and during the first two years I managed to squeeze some interesting guests between myself and the two plastic plants that served as a set. But when it came to talking about the Cold War with the Soviet Union things got a little funny. The Vietnam catastrophe had caused all kinds of problems. With defeat came inflation, economic stagnation and the humiliation of détente and strategic arms limitation – SALT. The basic problem was that the people who benefited most from the arms race – the Pentagon, arms manufacturers, scientists and academics – didn't want to be limited at all. And neither did Pat Robertson, whose contribution to the debate was to take biblical prophecies and apply them to the evils of Soviet communism.

Robertson's unabashed promotion of right wing causes violated every rule issued by the Federal Communications Commission (FCC). But airing *The SALT SYNDROME*, a documentary attacking President Carter and the treaty process, three times a day put him over the top and it was my job to provide an opposing opinion. America needed to prepare for a "MILITARY INVASION," one ad for the program screamed. The President was disarming America and surrendering to the commies without firing a shot.

It was crazy stuff, not to mention that the group behind the documentary – the American Security Council – was sponsored by a Who's Who of America's military industrial complex. They'd organized during the McCarthy-era to smear any effort at limiting war spending as a communist conspiracy and done one heck of a job driving the U.S. to defeat in Vietnam. By the time the U.S limped out of Saigon in 1975 their credibility was zero. But here they were, back again and pushing like madmen for World War III. When I'd first seen the film running on the control room monitors I'd thought it was a 1950s science fiction movie with unsuspecting Americans about to be devoured by hundred-foot-tall aliens. But it wasn't a joke.

"You don't really believe this stuff, do you?" I asked the control room engineer.

"I was in the Navy and all I know is *we* cheat," he said, looking up at the monitor as a cartoon Soviet laser beam zapped an American satellite. "We do lots of things we don't tell the Russians. And if we're the good guys and we cheat, what do you think they do?"

At that moment it didn't matter whether the Russians or the Americans were cheating. *WXNE was cheating* by airing a right wing political fantasy as a "public service" without offering equal time for an opposing point of view.

"It's Pat's station, he bought it, and he can air anything he likes on it," said Bill Knight, the general manager. Knight was a doughy, overweight and aging local TV guy with a lot of experience and a lot of old-time traditional conservative values. Looking back, 1955 was probably the best year of Bill's life and he lived it every day, over and over again. Brown suit, brown tie, brown wingtips and a brown Ford Crown Vic in the general manager's parking spot. I didn't even know they made them in brown. Like most of the people who worked at Channel 25 Bill had accepted Jesus Christ as his personal lord and savior and there was nothing more to say about it. He should have known better than to run afoul of federal rules, but since joining CBN he answered only to a higher authority.

"The federal government does not own the airwaves," he told me. "God owns the airwaves, and we can do whatever we want with them."

"Bill," I told him with all the sincerity I could muster, "I know how you feel but we're in violation of the Fairness Doctrine and we need to do something about it." After a brief discussion he agreed to let me answer with my own documentary and shortly thereafter I began. I had no idea at the time that I had stepped into the rarified and medieval world of the defense intellectual, never to return.

CHAPTER 3

AND THAT WAS WHEN THE PHONE CALL CAME IN. "Hey, Paul. We're hosting a rally for the Americans for SALT this week end and wondered if you might like to come. Ted Kennedy will be there and Cabot Lodge. Ken Galbraith and Paul Warnke might show up, too. Maybe you could bring your camera and get some interviews!"

Cambridge was still packed with Manhattan Project alumni and Roosevelt New Dealers trying to show support for Jimmy Carter, but his indecision on SALT and détente was a cause for concern. It seemed to me as I interviewed Kennedy that weekend he was suspicious of Carter's commitment while the old irascible Henry Cabot Lodge put up a good front. But with those two heavyweights on board, getting some of the local stars of arms control was easy and within a few weeks I'd met everybody.

Manhattan Project team leader Philip Morrison and his wife Phyllis explained how easy it would be to trigger Mutual Assured Destruction. SALT II chief negotiator Paul Warnke invited me to Washington for a briefing on what would happen *without* Strategic Arms Limitation. Economist John Kenneth Galbraith invited me into his home for hours of discussion, and that's where my answer to *The SALT SYNDROME* came together.

"We're at a crossroads," Galbraith said with a deep frown as he stretched out his long legs trying to find a comfortable position. "We've got to turn America's resources away from military spending back to the civilian sector before we destroy ourselves. SALT is simply a case against reciprocal suicide."

I'd come upon *The SALT SYNDROME* not knowing much about nuclear weapons. Who did? It even came with its own language and a glossary of arcane acronyms which you had to learn to understand anything. My favorite was MAD for Mutual Assured Destruction. According to theory, MAD was the only thing stopping the U.S. and the Soviets from wiping each other out. The problem with MAD was that not everyone accepted the theory. There was a struggle between the believers and the non-believers. And that's when I realized what had been going on for thirty-five years really *was* mad.

"Roosevelt asked me to help manage prices during World War II. So I saw the beginnings of the military industrial complex firsthand. I juggled the financial demands of generals, admirals and civilians. I even convinced some Republicans to go along until they realized how deeply subversive I was to the established orthodoxy," Galbraith said dryly.

"They actually found your ideas subversive?" I offered, somewhat shocked by the admission.

"I always saw the economy as the product of society and culture, not as a gambling casino for Wall Street," he said, grinning scornfully. "My critics of course did not agree. Because of that they branded me an economic socialist."

Galbraith shrugged the way I imagined the wizard Gandalf would shrug; a thoughtful giant of a man, of course without the hat and the staff.

"So what happens if you detach the economy from society?" I wondered.

"Main Street starves while Wall Street gets rich on war."

"And that's being repeated now, isn't it?"

Galbraith could barely contain his frustration. "Thirty-five years of economic warfare against the Soviet Union and China have produced a vast arsenal of nuclear weapons that are proving useless even as threats. These expenditures have come at a massive expense to the civilian economy."

"But your critics claim defense spending is good for the economy."

"That's my old friend Paul Nitze speaking."

"Nitze? Mr. Team B, Paul Nitze?"

"I worked with him on the Strategic bombing survey after the war. Team B is just his latest venture into military Keynesianism."

"Military Keynesianism?"

Galbraith settled into his Harvard instructor mode.

"Paul was a stock broker on Wall Street in 1929. He went to Germany after Hitler came to power and saw how he had driven the economy out of depression with military spending. He thought the Germans had done it right."

"But they didn't do it right."

"FDR was doing it right by rebuilding the Main Street economy. But that wasn't good enough for the Wall Street gang. World War II set the stage for the happy marriage of war production to business. Cost plus profit. In one year it pulled the U.S. out of the depression by doubling the Gross National Product. But of course it all went for war production not Main Street."

I'd heard the stories told around the kitchen table. "Workers had money in their pockets but there was nothing to buy."

"The Cold War extended the financial benefits but permanently transformed the economy into a command economy. In addition, America's best and brightest were lured away from the civilian economy and even the real world of guns, tanks and armies into a world detached from time, space and money."

"And that's where we are now."

"America's military Keynesianism has been the unseen hand of government behind the economy since World War II. The Pentagon budget was 16 percent of the Gross Domestic Product in the 1950s. By 1963 defense spending accounted for 52 percent of all the research and development done in the United States. But Vietnam exposed the weakness in the system. Inflation took off. As German and Japanese manufacturers battered their American competition, the economy had nowhere to turn."

"And that's where Paul Nitze and his friends at Team B come in."

"It's a self-fulfilling prophecy. They make up a threat and challenge you to prove that it isn't. In the 1950s it was the Bomber Gap, then when Sputnik appeared it mysteriously became the missile gap. When McNamara became defense secretary he went over to the national reconnaissance office and asked to see the proof and discovered there wasn't any."

"And now it's the threat of a first strike."

Galbraith ruminated for a moment before continuing.

"They don't have to fight a nuclear war. All they need is the threat to get them what they want. The irony is they claim to be saving the capitalist system but instead they're transforming it into a Soviet-style 'planned economy.' To make it even larger will create a force too seductive to resist."

Galbraith was an enormously influential figure. He'd warned a senate committee in 1955 that another great economic crash was inevitable and that day the stock market dropped like a stone. But as I sat in his living room listening I could sense his growing fear that he knew this time the country was changing for the worse.

"So where do you put the blame? On Nitze?"

"Paul Nitze sealed his grip on the levers of power by marrying a Standard Oil heiress and he's never let go. Before World War II he testified to Congress that if given a choice the U.S. should back the Nazis and not the British, and I think he can rightfully be called the father of the Cold War. His "Committee on the Present Danger" has successfully lobbied for bigger defense budgets for thirty years. But his effort at forging Team B from a handpicked group of right wing ideologues may go down as his crowning achievement."

"How so?"

"The ingeniousness of Team B is in the mindset. First they claim the Soviets are planning a first strike which they don't bother to prove. Then they reverse the burden of proof from themselves onto those who question them. Whatever they claim to be the truth about Soviet intentions becomes the truth no matter what. It's the *sine qua non* of excuses and virtually fool-proof because it's all self-fulfilling from beginning to end."

It seemed so impersonal when it began that summer of 1979. Galbraith, Lodge and Nitze were just abstract characters out of a history book. Now suddenly they were quickly becoming personal. In my capacity as a lowly talk show host all I could do was try to understand the paradigm shift that was taking place. But it was clear something profound had happened with the loss of Vietnam and I had found myself squarely in the middle of it.

"Nitze is one of a handful of elite officials who have moved back and forth from finance to government and shaped the military industrial complex," Galbraith said. "But the big difference this time is whether the U.S. is going to continue talking to the Soviets about strategic arms limitation or mortgage America for a new arms race and risk World War III."

And that was the question our documentary *Arms Race and the Economy, A Delicate Balance* posed as the year came to a close. And that was when the Soviet Union did exactly what Team B and *The SALT SYNDROME* said they would do, by invading a little known country on their southern border called Afghanistan on December 27, 1979. And that was when the scales fell from my eyes and I realized my time at Pat Robertson's New England outpost was coming to an end.

Chapter 4

Robin MacNeil gave the details on the nightly *MacNeil/Lehrer News-Hour* the day after New Year's, 1980. "Soviet forces using tanks and helicopter gunships were reported battling Muslim guerrillas throughout Afghanistan today, as President Carter considered what actions to take. Good evening."

Good evening? How about good morning, America, and wake the hell up. Your life is about to change in ways you could never imagine. If Paul Nitze had personally called up the Kremlin and ordered a move that would cancel détente, remove the last of Roosevelt's New Deal Democrats from power and roll back U.S./Soviet relations to 1950, it would have looked exactly like the Soviet invasion of Afghanistan. The United States had seen its Middle East policy collapse only months before when followers of the Ayatollah Khomeini ousted the Shah of Iran and took the entire U.S. embassy staff hostage. Now the Soviets were occupying the country next door and President Carter couldn't do anything but whimper that he'd been betrayed.

It was the end of the Carter administration and the beginning of a descent into right-wing madness. The door was wide open for Reagan's World War II-size arms push now. There would be no way to stop him. The so-called left had been driven from the field and none of it made sense.

SALT had been negotiated over ten years under three Presidents – two Republicans and one Democrat. Warnke, Galbraith and all the rest had made it clear the Soviets wanted better relations because they needed it even more than the U.S. Why had they chosen to end it this way when it was clearly not in their interest to do so?

I had worked for two full years at a faith-based broadcasting outfit whose owner framed every issue imaginable to serve his ideology. Now here was America's official government network PBS behaving the same way. Were they nuts or was I? But the real kicker came when anchor Robin MacNeil introduced Ambassador Theodore Eliot and Team B leader Richard Pipes, who laid out an in depth narrative as if it had already been scripted by a biblical prophet and bound in leather.

MacNeil: "People are wondering whether the Soviet intervention in Afghanistan means an end of the relationship that for several years has been called détente. Some Soviet experts have had a pessimistic view of détente for those same several years. One of them is Professor Richard Pipes of Harvard University. Professor Pipes headed the task force which wrote the so-called 'B Team' report on Soviet intentions, sponsored by the CIA, three years ago."

I could see it all clearly now. End of détente? Richard Pipes? "B Team" report on Soviet intentions? Here was the windup and the pitch. HOME RUN! The Carter administration had been strangely inept when it came to defending détente. Now, the death notice was being delivered live by the leader of the team that had been assigned to kill it: Team B.

What was this all about? Ambassador Theodore Eliot, Boston Brahmin, Dean of Tufts Fletcher School of Law and Diplomacy and Inspector General at the State Department teamed up with a Russophobic Harvard Professor? Eliot was supposed to be about finding diplomatic solutions, not undermining them. Pipes was an ideologue that had spent his life hating Russians. How did they come together to declare the death of détente only days after the invasion? It was just too convenient.

MacNeil: "And what do you see as the danger for us and our interests in this action?"

Pipes evoked the nervousness of a displaced outsider who'd been trying to rebrand his Eastern European ethnic grudges as sane foreign policy all his life.

Pipes: "This is a historic moment. It is the first time since the revolution of 1917 that the Russians have felt bold enough to send their forces to conquer a sovereign country not in the communist bloc. They have meddled but they have never dared to engage in a direct *blitzkrieg*. So if they get away with it in Afghanistan, there'll not only be great danger to our Middle Eastern position but we will have encouraged them to engage in this sort of actions in Southeastern Europe or possibly even Western Europe."

There it was – the essence of Richard Pipes and Team B and the message of *The SALT SYNDROME*. The Russians *were* coming with "a direct blitzkrieg," threatening Western Europe just like the Nazis. The right wing was now vindicated, Vietnam had been a *noble cause*, and we could get back to the business of war posthaste.

It seemed so simple and all too familiar. Just like the official version of the JFK assassination.

I turned to Liz. "Forgive me but I'm in awe. This is exactly what Team B was set up to do. Kill SALT *and* détente, and the Russians just gave it to them. How did they do that?"

Liz gave me one of those *I told you so* looks. "Well maybe I was right about Carter."

"What about Carter?" I said, now deeply intrigued.

"He's a fraud. Name me one thing he promised that he actually delivered. He was recommended to David Rockefeller for president by Zbigniew Brzezinski then brings Brzezinski in as his national security advisor? Brzezinski and Pipes are both foreign born Polish Nationals. They are well known Russophobes. One works for the Democrats, the other works for the Republicans, and they both despise the Soviet Union. Either way they win," she said, smirking.

I had to admit she was right. "So Carter is a Trojan Horse. I actually hadn't thought of that. But what's Theodore Eliot doing sitting there with Mr. Team B? The Deputy Director at the CIA labeled them a Kangaroo Court.'"

"Well I guess the kangaroos have taken over," Liz said, trying not to grimace at the TV screen.

I wasn't despondent but I was close. By the day after New Year's 1980 it was over for Carter and limiting the nuclear arms race, and all because of a place nobody ever heard of. There were too many questions. But it would only be a few weeks before I realized that my little documentary had opened up a window on a global transition and that it came with a history that was deeper and older than I could ever have imagined.

***

Despite the invasion, Channel 25 aired the documentary when scheduled. I continued my weekly program but the fun was gone. I hadn't joined the station to tweak Pat Robertson's nose. Getting my own TV show was the break of a lifetime, but as I entered my third year at CBN, with the Soviet Union occupying Afghanistan, I could read the handwriting on the wall. America had changed and the Soviet invasion of Afghanistan had done it. By February of 1980 Jimmy Carter was a pariah within his own party. The former Georgia governor had once seemed a brilliant choice, but as President he'd proved indecisive and easily misled by his national security advisor, Zbigniew Brzezinski. Ted Kennedy and Governor Jerry Brown of California were doing the unthinkable and challenging him for the nomination. Liz and I were invited to the University of New Hampshire to hear Kennedy speak about it, where we were introduced back-stage to a close Kennedy political insider named Allard Lowenstein.

Lowenstein had been the driving force behind Robert Kennedy's election campaign in 1968. He'd carried on after RFK's death and spent most of the 1970s researching the murders of both Kennedys. Just being a Fitzgerald suddenly made me a confidante and he made his intentions clear. Get Ted elected and we'll finally bring those CIA sons of bitches that killed Jack and Bobby to justice.

"Since you're family I can tell you this. We know who did it and people are willing to talk," he said. "But we need the presidency to protect them."

Ted Kennedy was inspired that night as he railed at the Carter adminis-tration from the podium atop a makeshift stage in the UNH gym.

Kennedy's challenge to Carter was closer to being a north/south civil war than a presidential campaign and even closer to being a bitter holy war between southern Baptists and northern Catholics. Growing up as a Fitzgerald and a northern Catholic I knew the feeling well. I also knew there was a darker legacy that my encounter with Lowenstein had just shoved in my face.

My mind kept flashing back to Lowenstein's words as we drove the dark lonely highway from New Hampshire to home that frigid night. John Kennedy's murder had left a mark on everybody but I never accepted the official story. Now here I was at twenty-nine getting an inside look that confirmed my suspicions.

CHAPTER 5

L iz finally broke the silence. "You never said anything about being related to the Kennedys."

"I'm not related to the Kennedys, I'm related to their grandfather, John Francis Fitzgerald – Honey Fitz. My grandfather Mike was a union boss and met with him when he was mayor of Boston. They knew they were related but that's as far as it went."

"That's too bad."

"Oh, I don't know. I think there were issues back in the old country."

"Issues? What kind of issues?"

"The usual stuff; land, inheritance, history. This struggle with the British ate into everything. It still does. My aunt Mary used to say we'd all come to Ireland in the 12th century from England with Strongbow, the Earl of Pembroke. The family had millions of acres. They went to war with the Tudors over taxes and religion – Henry the VIII, Queen Elizabeth I. But they lost most of it. Family feuds, backstabbing? You know, the usual intrigues."

"What were they doing in England in the first place?" Liz asked.

"Robbing the poor to help the rich. What do you think Norman-French mercenaries do?"

"Norman-French? Wait a minute. I thought you were Irish."

"*Fitz* is Norman-French for son of. The son of Gerald, constable of the King's castle at Windsor. They're in the *Battle Abbey Book*, 1066. They hired out to royal families all over Europe but they wanted Ireland for themselves so they took it. London accused them of creating a race of their own and sent in a succession of Protestant armies to wipe them out."

"I've never heard of such a thing. Creating a race of your own?" Liz said, bemused.

"Breeding out a subject race and replacing it with your own is the part of history they don't teach you in high school," I responded. "The Tudors waged a flat-out genocide against the Fitzgeralds. Eventually my own family got to reclaim some property because they had a land grant signed by an English king. At least that's the way the story goes."

"And you think the motives for killing JFK go that far back?" she offered skeptically.

"The grudge lived on in my family. Why shouldn't it live on in theirs?"

The history of Ireland was cold, cruel and confusing. The Irish *were* different from other people in the way they remembered. I think it was the way they stored the hurt in their heart. I knew I remembered that way, anyway. Just talking about JFK and Ireland brought out the defensiveness in me. I knew I had to protect myself and remembered exactly how to do it.

My father could have gone back to those Irish acres, claimed the farm and probably lived another thirty years, but he'd wanted nothing to do with the legacy. I doubted anyone else but me would have tied the Kennedy assassinations to this forgotten genocide but for some reason it was all connected to my feelings and it wouldn't let me go.

I wished I could have interrogated Lowenstein further. His boast sounded reckless. But he'd know better than me what reckless was. Wouldn't he?

The year 1980 was feeling a lot like 1968 only this time on the other side of the mirror. This time the war was in Afghanistan and not Vietnam, and it was the Russians not the Americans who were dying. But I couldn't shake the sickening sense of déjà vu, and a few weeks later it came home when Liz picked up the morning newspaper and read aloud in disbelief that Al Lowenstein had been assassinated.

"An old colleague walked into his office in New York yesterday and shot him seven times, then put the gun down on his desk and waited for the police. He's dead."

I'd sensed danger lurking in Lowenstein's boast that night in Dover, New Hampshire. But now the closeness sent a chill down my spine.

"Why did he choose to involve you personally in this?" Liz asked.

"Because he was getting scared and he thought it would ward off the danger."

"Why do you say that?"

"I just feel it. Like laying off a bet or sharing a burden. He needed somebody else to know it. Calling me family like that – it was getting too heavy for him to carry alone."

It didn't take much for Liz to agree we needed to know more about the guy, and so we began digging into Al Lowenstein's background for clues. What we found straight away was that Lowenstein wrote the instruction manual for 1960s campus activism.

"Lowenstein campaigned tirelessly for civil rights, the Kennedys, Martin Luther King and against the Vietnam War," Liz said, reading from her notes. "Very close to Eleanor Roosevelt, organized the *Dump Johnson* movement, and lived to tell the tale."

"That would put him pretty high up on the Democratic party food chain."

Liz smiled. "He functioned as a guru to the New Left, created the National Student Association (NSA) and served as its first President in 1950. That's what the press reported. *But*, what the press didn't report was Lowenstein's suspected relationship to the CIA or how his creation – the NSA – had been used as the CIA's main vehicle for recruiting student leaders from around the world throughout the 1950s and 60s."

"Oh, I get it. So the major organizer of the New Left and the student movement is working for the CIA?" I asked.

Liz responded, "Think about it. The cultural Cold War? The left moves from the workers to the students? They get to control the Vietnam anti-war movement?"

Liz had me thinking. "I met some of those 'leftists' at B.U. SDS – Students for a Democratic Society. Violent bourgeois revolutionaries. Wanted to tear the whole thing down to get back at daddy."

"Al Lowenstein didn't want them to tear it down. He opposed SDS. He wanted the student movement to take it over from within peacefully."

Liz located a series of *Ramparts Magazine* articles from 1967 and that's where things went off the road.

"The CIA used Lowenstein's NSA to control the politics of the international student movement," she read, standing by the window in the kitchen of our drafty New England home. "The whole project was aimed at assessing 'the political tendencies of prospective political leaders in critical areas of the world.' One of those critical areas targeted for control was Afghanistan and Iran."

"Can I see that?" I asked, searching for clues as I read further down the page.

"It says a number of key Afghan officials, including cabinet members who studied in the U.S., were 'either CIA trained or indoctrinated. Some are cabinet-level people.'"

Liz followed up. "What an amazing coincidence."

"Coincidence or something else?" I mumbled, trying to grasp what we'd stumbled onto. "It also says the CIA tried to recruit the President of the Afghan Student Association in 1961 'to work for the CIA after his return to Afghanistan.'"

Liz was on top of it. "Didn't we read where the Afghans claimed the guy the Soviets overthrew, Hafizullah Amin, was President of the Afghan Student Association when he was at Columbia back in 1963?"

"Yeah, we did. But that makes sense. What doesn't make sense is that we meet Al Lowenstein then find his National Student Association is directly connected to Afghanistan. We'll probably find Team B in there, too, if we keep looking," I said, half-joking.

"We probably will," Liz said seriously as she took back the magazine. "Maybe we've found the common denominator."

Team B as the common denominator. I liked it. Something powerful was twisting reality to extend the Cold War by using Afghanistan. It wasn't magic so why wouldn't it be Team B? A short time later the *Boston Globe* published an op-ed by President Eisenhower's science advisor and a former deputy director of the CIA strongly suggesting we were right.

It wasn't American military weakness that caused the Soviet invasion of Afghanistan, they wrote. It was Carter's efforts to appease his Team B critics. His sharp drift to the right, his failure to support SALT II, and his total embrace of Brzezinski's Russophobia. Despite appearances, the administration did everything it could to convince Soviet hawks inside the Kremlin that détente and SALT were dead. In other words they wanted the Soviets to invade and the Soviet hawks complied.

***

That spring Liz and I were invited to M.I.T. to present *Arms Race and the Economy*. The audience seemed supportive of our position until a young man named Sherman Teichman rose from the audience during the Q and A.

"Why didn't you discuss the plight of Soviet Jews in your documentary?" he asked pointedly.

"Because the documentary isn't about Soviet Jews," I responded.

"You can't talk about easing the pressure on the Soviet Union until Soviet Jews are allowed to emigrate to Israel," he demanded stridently, trying to flip my presentation on its head. "In fact nobody should be talking to the Soviet Union about anything until they comply with the 1974 Jackson-Vanik Amendment. We have to take a hard line."

A hard line; Teichman said it himself. This was how the neoconservatives worked. Transform compromise into appeasement and appeasement into surrender. Before you even knew it you'd been turned into Neville Chamberlain and were setting the stage for Adolph Hitler and the holocaust. I assumed Teichman had meant to stop me in my tracks but his mention of Senator Henry "Scoop" Jackson's 1974 amendment only set me to thinking. Why was Israel influencing U.S./Soviet arms control?

"Your suspicion about Teichman was right," Liz said, reading from her notes. "Teichman is on the neocon fast track at the Fletcher School where Theodore Eliot is dean. Nixon and Kissinger wanted détente to work. The Jewish community supported it. Jackson and his assistant Richard Perle created Jackson-Vanik to torpedo it but couldn't get the votes. Then came the 1973 Yom Kippur war. Perle used Israel to rally American Jews against the Soviet Union and a year later it passed. "

That was the connection I'd been looking for. "So the beginning of the end for détente was right there in 1973."

"Almost before it began. Richard Perle goes back to Paul Nitze when he was trying to stop the Anti-Ballistic Missile (ABM) Treaty in 1969. It fails so Perle then goes to work for Jackson, the senator from Boeing, and becomes the bridge between the defense industry and the neoconservative political movement which acts as a front for the Israel lobby."

"And who is Perle?" I asked.

"A protégé of Albert Wohlstetter. RAND Corporation? *Delicate Balance of Terror*? Dr. Strangelove?"

It was almost making sense. I tried to reconcile the twisted version of reality that seemed to have taken hold of Washington's psyche and for the next few months Liz and I talked about little else. Instead of holding the line on détente and arms control as he'd promised in 1976, America's Bible belt president Jimmy Carter was acting as midwife to a whole new era of religious holy war. And by the summer of 1980 it was becoming clear that my time at the Christian Broadcasting Network had given me an inside view of what that era would look like.

CHAPTER 6

Aside from the predictable suspects surrounding the arms race I kept encountering something that just shouldn't be there. The final revelation came while wandering the book stores of Harvard Square looking for inspiration. The place had been a second home when I was a kid. My aunt had an apartment there. My father's pharmacy was down the street, replete with soda fountain, three decker ice cream cones and Hershey bars. Elsie's roast beef sandwiches. Lunches at the Wursthaus. Old French films at the Brattle. Jean Gabin and Poetic Realism – irony. Harvard Square was cool.

And then the nostalgia caught up with me. The Cold War was present in my house. My two brothers had been called up for the Cuban missile crisis in 1962. My sister worked at a Harvard lab where they developed dosimeters for the army. She brought some home for me to take to school – army-green metal boxes you clipped to your belt with glass vials inside. They changed color when exposed to radiation to let you know you were going to die.

I'd been prepping myself at Out of Town News and Reading International since high school. I learned a lot there. Angry young Dr. Strangeloves crossing "the yard" on their way to the top. A commune run by a guy named Mel Lyman (Ted Eliot's middle name) put out an underground magazine called *Avatar*. Gave you a feel for the manic depressive counter-culture percolating behind the thin ties and Harris Tweeds. LSD, cults and foreign policy all mixed together and served up to rock music – the cult of intelligence. It was the 1960s. Radical politics. A make-believe revolution in the air. Vietnam, Vietnam, Vietnam. You couldn't buy a cup of coffee and not get into an argument about the war. Trotsky singing the upper-middle class blues at Club 47 – high on himself. Acid fascists liked to brag about how smart they were and put it in print. The Students for a Democratic Society (SDS), left red flags and dirty diapers wherever they went. I'd seen their handiwork at BU. Broken chairs in Hayden Hall – blood on the wall. The right had countered with their own brand of campus crazies, but then came the 1980s and America's foreign policy periodicals revealed where Harvard's Best and Brightest had gone.

I'd been driven to searching the rational academic journals to counter the irrational apocalyptic programming at CBN. Instead, to my dismay, I found the irrational cries for a nuclear Holy War leaping from Pat Robertson's TV pulpit into the mainstream.

"Surely no one can be comfortable with the claim that a strategy that would kill millions of Soviet citizens and would invite a strategic response that could kill tens of millions of U.S. citizens would be politically acceptable," Colin Gray and Keith Payne wrote in their *Foreign Policy* article titled *Victory Is Possible*. "However, it is worth recalling the six guidelines for the use of force provided by the 'just war' doctrine of the Catholic Church."

President Carter had exchanged Mutual Assured Destruction (MAD) for nuclear warfighting without anybody really noticing. Then two academics, Gray and Payne, come along calling for the annihilation of tens of millions of Russians and Americans and justifying it with a medieval Catholic doctrine. "If American nuclear power is to support U.S. foreign policy objectives, the United States must possess the ability to wage nuclear war rationally."

Wage nuclear war *rationally*? This was better than Orwell. I staggered out of the bookstore in disbelief. That summer, Gray and Payne weren't just challenging the thirty year old assumption that nuclear war was irrational. The two nuclear strategists were arguing the opposite; that *not* preparing to fight a nuclear war was irrational.

The failure of high technology to win out over the North Vietnamese had done something to the heads of the nuclear theologians that plotted America's wars, and you didn't need to be one of them to understand what it was. Vietnam had made them crazy, and then tipped them over the edge into lunacy. Nuclear war could not be waged rationally because nuclear war wasn't rational. Vietnam proved that "rational" formulas, basing theories, and force projections were useless even when you had overwhelming superiority, unlimited resources, and ample time to apply them. Technology couldn't win a conventional war in Vietnam and Washington's reliance on it had only delegitimized the concept of fighting a nuclear one.

So how could this be? I thought about it as I steered my beat up old car towards home in the light summer traffic. Had America's Cold War intelligentsia fled back through the gates of their ivy covered walls and simply pretended Vietnam never happened? Or had they just decided to inflict the Russians with the same kind of head trauma they'd suffered and prayed that nobody would notice America's nuclear priesthood were a bunch of psychopaths?

I grappled with the insanity of the plan. Suck everybody into the delusion by pretending we really won in Vietnam and an anti-American media had made it appear we'd lost. Failure had never really occurred, *Victory is Possible*, and everyone would eventually believe nothing had gone wrong at all.

I drove through Kendall Square past Draper Labs where they designed the nuclear warheads. M.I.T. wizard Charles Stark Draper had once boasted that with enough time and money he could put a missile through Khrushchev's bathroom window. Hell, with enough time and money I could put a missile through Khrushchev's bathroom window, but why would I want to?

I drove down Broadway past my father's old drug store, the one he'd had to shutter because the neighborhood went to shit. I was sure Charlie Draper never dreamed of getting out of bed on a freezing January night and driving ten miles to fill a prescription for the desperate father of a sick child.

"I've never heard you sound bitter like this," Liz told me when I got home.

"Bitter? I'm disgusted. Afghanistan is being used to push for nuclear war," I said.

Liz thought for a moment. "They've been talking about getting back at the Soviets for Vietnam for years. Remember that party we went to where the Navy guy claimed to have coined the term Russia's Vietnam?" She mulled it over some more. "Senator Henry Jackson was pushing that claim about the Russian brigade in Cuba. He doesn't need it with the Soviets in Afghanistan."

From the time we'd begun the documentary on the arms race, we'd gone from SALT and détente to preparing for nuclear war. Having run out of pretexts the neocons had now turned to Rome for permission to commit what John Kenneth Galbraith told us would be mutual suicide.

Up until that day I hadn't quite realized making war on the Soviet Union had always been Holy War or that free market capitalism was the religion. But a clear picture was emerging. War was the means by which America spread the faith, and by the end of that summer it was becoming obvious to the folks at Channel 25 that I was a heretic for not accepting it.

It wasn't hard to get out of line in Pat Robertson's church of the looming apocalypse, so by the late summer of 1980 my days there were numbered. I'd made a bet with Liz what it would take to get me fired from Christ's New England outpost of free market Calvinism, and my effort to bring Ralph Nader onto "God's airwaves" finally did the trick.

Just as I had many times before I'd pushed the envelope, but this time the envelope closed. By the fall of 1980 I'd walked away from a half dozen careers but I was damned if I was going to walk away from this one. So what would I do now that I was back at ground zero? Public affairs programming was a wasteland sandwiched between "Bowling for Dollars" and insipid news coverage of every three alarm fire between Providence, Rhode Island and Bangor, Maine. I'd gone as far as I could with the local intelligentsia. The brilliant scientists who'd helped me understand what was at stake with the arms race and the economy were left high and dry by the Soviet invasion. But looking back it should have come as no surprise. Without getting to the core problem of the deeply entrenched ethnic hatreds behind the ideology, no agreement on limiting weapons was ever going to work for very long.

I realized then that if anything was going to work I'd have to start digging behind the Cold War, and much to my surprise my best source turned out to be in the most unexpected of places.

CHAPTER 7

As I came to grips with my post-CBN fate that fall of 1980, President Carter's description of the Soviet invasion of Afghanistan kept rattling around in my head. Was the Soviet move into Afghanistan really on a scale with the Second World War? Was Jimmy Carter really *that* oblivious to compare the Soviet's invasion of a tiny mountainous country on their southern border to the biggest war in history? World War II was a fairly conspicuous affair; 27 million Russians, 6 million Jews, 3 million German soldiers killed on the Eastern front alone. Everybody saw it coming for years. So where did this Afghanistan thing come from? And if it was so important why hadn't we heard anything about it?

The Soviets or somebody had blacked out the country, expelling the entire Western media a month after the invasion. News reports were vague and laced with rumors from soldiers of fortune and unnamed U.S. government sources. The whole thing appeared to be a classic rerun of the old Red scare. Carter's 1980 State of the Union speech transforming the Soviet move into an historic threat set a new standard for exaggeration. It was well known that Carter's national security advisor Brzezinski and Team B leader Richard Pipes had been scheming against the Soviet Union at least since their days at Harvard. In their mission to liberate Eastern Europe from Moscow, both men had come to identify with a right wing political faction known as neoconservativism. And that was where it all got very interesting.

Liz spent some time reading up on RAND analyst Albert Wohlstetter and soon discovered my wild guess about the influence of Team B wasn't so wild.

"The neoconservatives learned their tactics from Wohlstetter," Liz said, combing through her notes. "He's known for changing the nature of American politics with game theory and systems analysis. And who do you think he got the ideas to develop game theory and systems analysis from?"

"I'm all ears."

"The military organizational techniques of Leon Trotsky. Wohlstetter was a follower of Trotsky – founder of the Red Army."

"You're kidding."

"Over a period of thirty years Wohlstetter moved from communism to capitalism and nobody ever challenged him. Trotsky apparently influenced a whole generation of American New Left political activists, including Wohlstetter. It was Wohlstetter who got the ball moving on Team B by passing classified information to Paul Nitze who denounced Kissinger and the CIA to the House Armed Services Committee as soft on communism."

"But Wohlstetter was a communist himself."

"Wohlstetter wasn't just any kind of communist. He was a Trotskyist. Most of the neoconservatives were Trotskyists. My father was a union organizer back in the 1930s and all he ever talked about was the Trotskyists and how they infiltrated the labor movement and left it in chaos."

"I don't get it," I said, trying to get my head around it. "So the core of America's New Right, Judeo-Christian flag-waving patriots are apostles of the founder of the Red Army?"

Liz smiled. "They're political chameleons. The Vietnam War made Washington desperate for answers and they provided them."

"And now we can't get rid of them. So your father had a personal experience with them?" I asked.

"Yes, my father knows a lot about the Trotskyists and their subversion. Do you think we should talk to him about it?"

"I'm just waiting for you to make the call."

***

Not many people outside a handful of intellectuals from the 1930s and 40s understood how all this had happened. But you couldn't really understand the Carter administration or the Reagan agenda until you understood the path of the neoconservatives. When I brought the issue up to Liz's father all I had to do was say the magic words and I got an earful.

"Leon Trotsky was not a communist," Bill said, growing suddenly imperious. "He was an opportunist, a Menshevik, a member of the minority party. He only joined the Bolsheviks, the majority faction, when he saw they were going to win the revolution in 1917."

The depth of Bill's passion was something to see after so many years. "So Trotsky was just an opportunist? I don't understand," I said.

Bill paused a moment, gathering his thoughts, then calmly began a routine he must have recited a thousand times in his mind.

"Russia was a poor country, agrarian. Stalin wanted to secure the revolution in Russia first by industrializing like Germany and England. The workers agreed. Socialism in one country he called it. Trotsky believed that only by spreading world revolution could socialism be achieved."

"And he was banished."

The memory made Bill even more determined. "Trotsky was backed by the bankers. He really represented them. Not the workers. When he left, his political followers came over here. I was still organizing then. They used tricks to get you on their side. Then they'd flip everything around. The French turn they called it. I confronted them over their tactics. When World War II came some of them opposed Stalin at the same time they opposed Hitler. They liked to cover all the bases."

"So how did they come to be so powerful?" I asked.

"Their leadership sold out. Sidney Hook and James Burnham, Trotsky's secretary. They were the point men. They compromised the union movement. Hook informed to the FBI, gave them everything – names, addresses, phone numbers. But it was Burnham, James Burnham who was the mastermind, the intellectual. When he joined the OSS in 1941 I knew we'd all been had."

"Trotsky's secretary joined the Office of Strategic Services?"

"And later the CIA. He invented the whole neoconservative movement with his books *Managerial Revolution* and *The Machiavellians: Defenders of Freedom.*"

I repeated, "*Defenders of Freedom*?"

"Defenders of slavery is more like it," Bill responded with a snort. "Burnham championed the Nazi takeover in Germany and Italy then he switched his admiration from Trotsky to Stalin. Read Burnham's resignation letter in 1940. He calls Trotsky's Fourth International 'arrant nonsense' – as it was. The only true communist leader was Stalin. Even Burnham called him Lenin's heir. George Orwell criticized Burnham as a cynical elitist justifying fascism by force and fraud. Orwell is said to have modeled his novel *1984* on Burnham's vision of the coming totalitarian state. He described it as 'a new kind of society, neither capitalist nor socialist, and probably based on slavery.' But the key to Burnham was this. He didn't separate the managerial class from the working class. That was happening anyway in both capitalism and communism. What he did was articulate how the managers could take control. That one thing laid the foundation for the rise of a new ruling class by Trotsky's followers – the neoconservatives."

"The neocons as a new ruling class? But it sounds as if they don't really have an ideology at all. All they have is a process."

"Exactly," Bill said, pleased with my understanding. "And that's why they're so dangerous. They don't believe in anything. Their only ideology is to gain power and take total control. Once they get it they never give it up. James Burnham blazed the trail for them from Trotsky's Fourth International to right-wing conservativism. They all started out as Trotskyists and they still are."

"Jesus. No wonder things are so messed up."

Bill went on to explain in great detail how the banished Trotskyists evolved from radical Marxists to New York Intellectuals and then on to becoming the Pentagon's Defense Intellectuals.

"Burnham's timing was perfect," Bill admitted. "He graduated from Oxford University and came to City College in New York just in time for the Wall Street crash in 1929. Everybody thought 'Capitalism' was dead. Just like after Vietnam, everybody was looking for answers and he had all the credentials. He liked hanging out with these tough, street-wise Bolsheviks and they both despised the weakness of the liberals. The depression radicalized everybody so he made himself useful. He finds Trotsky's political analysis to be brilliant. His review of Trotsky's book brings them together and he winds up as his secretary."

And so began Burnham's six-year odyssey through America's Communist left that ultimately transformed him into the agent of its destruction. I thought I was beginning to get it.

"So that's why they revile the Soviet Union so much."

"Exactly," Bill said, nodding. "It was Stalin who defeated Nazism. Stalin who was Burnham's 'great man' of history. Stalin who was the one to fear, and Burnham made it clear. The marriage of the Trotskyists to the Pentagon was inevitable," Bill said in a low growl. "They hated Stalin and they believed in endless war. After World War II the Pentagon couldn't have functioned without them. They were made for each other."

Bill was right. Burnham had brokered Trotsky's formula for endless war and provided it with a philosophy it was missing.

"For them it's a crusade," Bill said, completing my education. "Just like this Afghanistan war. With Brzezinski in the White House something was bound to happen. He's always been their agent. The Soviets are very predictable. The fact that they acted against their own interests says to me that something is fishy. Brzezinski or somebody did something to provoke it. They had to."

Of course they had to. Bill knew that I thought the invasion was stupid. But *how* did the Trotskyists get them to do it? And why Afghanistan? Nobody could find out because the road to Afghanistan had been closed for the last nine months. No mainstream media had been able to get in or get out with a story since the Soviet invasion. But if somebody did go in and find the answer, now that would be a scoop of major proportions – maybe the scoop of a lifetime. But how would one go about it?

CHAPTER 8

How could you gain entry to a country occupied by seventy-five thousand Soviet troops and referred to by the President of the United States as the "greatest threat to peace since the second world war?" You looked in the phone book under United Nations and found the listing for Afghanistan. No John Le Carré or Robert Ludlum cloak and dagger there. Finding out who to talk to was easy. His name was Mohammed Farid Zarif and he was the chargé d'affaires for the government of the Democratic Republic of Afghanistan, the DRA. Convincing him to let me be the first to bring a television news crew into his country since the entire western media had been kicked out was another matter entirely. The challenge was all in the pitch, and I thought I had it figured out.

Afghanistan broke down to three separate stories. American policy hinged on the first two. Father of the Cold War George Kennan had come out after the invasion and claimed that Moscow had acted in defense of its southern border. That was one of the few voices coming out of Washington that sounded logical to me. The Washington consensus bought the radical neocon line put out by the CIA that frozen-cold-isolated Russia was on a centuries-long march to capture warm water ports and Middle East oil fields. The third story, the *Afghan* story, was left to ivory tower romantics and their British imperial obsession with Rudyard Kipling. In their view Afghanistan was a backward, feudal no-man's-land populated by tribal warlords, Sufi mystics, and religious fanatics and would remain that way until the end of time.

I wanted to see Afghanistan out from under the Cold War blanket it came wrapped in, and that meant seeing it from the Afghans' eyes, not Washington's or Moscow's. So that was the route I took.

It was a quiet Saturday morning in Manhattan. The sun was shining brightly and the traffic on the East side was light. Liz and the receptionist exchanged pleasantries while I paged through a brochure from a rack near the door of the UN's Embassy of Afghanistan. In it were pictures of Afghanistan from a happier time, of farmers harvesting wheat, snowcapped mountain passes and men whacking at a goat carcass on horseback. For a second I thought going to Afghanistan might not be as bad as I'd imagined until I noticed that someone had scrawled *Death to the infidels* in red letters on the inside page.

I braced at the warning of things to come just as a small but muscular Afghan security man with oriental features came in and ushered us into a conference area overlooking the East River. There we were greeted by a handsome young man who introduced himself with a warm smile as Mohammed Farid Zarif.

Zarif didn't look much older than me. In fact he was only two days older. I imagined that the political shakeup in Afghanistan had probably opened the door for younger, more ambitious revolutionaries, but I soon learned that Zarif's father had served the king as an army general. The fact that he hadn't taken more than a minute to greet us from the moment we'd walked through the door was a pleasant surprise. And after we'd settled down around a coffee table, he listened to my pitch with rapt attention.

"The Soviets have been in your country for almost a year now and nobody knows what they're doing," I said. "You're getting killed in the press and the administration is having a field day with you. Poison gas, butterfly bombs, mass executions? With the door closed you can't refute it. They don't have to do anything. You're winning the war *for* them."

Zarif nodded slowly in agreement and then spoke in the soft, measured tones of a seasoned diplomat.

"I know what you're saying is true," he said, reaching into an inside pocket for a cigarette as a second security man quietly placed a tray of tea and cookies on the table before us.

"They're going to criticize you no matter what you do. That's their job. So when you shut them out it looks like you're hiding something and it makes their job easier."

Zarif gestured toward the cookies as the tea was poured.

"The media is controlled in our country," Zarif said, taking a deep drag on the cigarette, "but it is controlled here also, just in different, more subtle ways. We know what the Western media will do if we let them back in. They will go looking for trouble,s and if they don't find it they will invent some. They ask for permission regularly for this thing or that. Or they send somebody to ask for permission."

Zarif looked at me askance. "You're not one of those are you?"

"No," I said flatly, looking to Liz for assurance as I broached what I knew would be a delicate subject. "But I would have to go to them if you gave me the permission. There's really no other way to get the story out. We need a network, but I would be the one telling the story."

Zarif paused to consider, then nodded to himself as if answering his own question. "I cannot just grant you permission, you understand. Kabul must do that. But if I make the request, what is it you would say about Afghanistan?"

What *would* I say? What *wouldn't* I say? *Here we are in a land that the President of the United States called the greatest threat to peace since World War II? No one's seen the place since 75,000 Soviet soldiers invaded? Where are they going, what are they doing and how do the Afghan people feel about it?*

I'd gone over it in my mind again and again. What was missing from the coverage? Well, everything was missing. Nobody even knew where Afghanistan was let alone why it was important. You could say just about anything and nobody would know the difference. Who cared about this and why? Why were the Russians so desperate to occupy the country they'd risked détente and SALT and the start of a whole new Cold War? I tried to stop my mind from racing.

"We know what the U.S. is telling the world. We know what the Soviets are saying about the invasion. What we don't know is how the Afghans feel about it. What happened that brought the Russians in, and what kind of country is your government trying to create? That's a story that needs to be told, and that's the one I want to tell."

Zarif nodded thoughtfully. "When I was a student at Oxford I heard a report on the BBC that said something or other was good news for Afghanistan and I knew if the BBC was saying it, it was probably good for Britain and bad for us."

The muffled sound of a helicopter could be heard in the distance. Zarif rose from his chair and walked toward the windows overlooking the East River, waiting for the sound to come into view. He stood for a moment, gazing at it as it buzzed down the East River and then he turned towards me.

"We need to open up and tell the world what we are doing," he said. "It would be irresponsible not to." He glanced at Liz. "But the view from this office and the view from Kabul are quite a different thing."

He took a deep breath. "Put everything you have told me in writing. Make it clear that you are independent. It may take some time to get them to see things my way in Kabul, but I assure you that I will do everything in my power to persuade them."

Zarif shook my hand. I looked into his eyes and at that moment the Afghan story became personal. Here was a man representing a country occupied by 75,000 Soviet troops. He needed a very special kind of help. As I had guessed, reality had him trapped between the superpowers. Was he a true believer and die hard Communist or was he something else? At that moment what that something *else* might be I didn't have a clue. But if he wasn't an ideologue it could change everything.

From the moment we left Zarif's office that Saturday morning, I knew that my life would never be the same. The first chill came only moments after we'd stepped into the abandoned corridor and crossed paths with a technician working the wires on the telephone patch-panel. Liz grinned at the cloak and dagger, but from that moment on I found myself giving every stranger the once over and edited my telephone conversations assuming I was being bugged. I tried turning it into a game, wondering who might be listening on the other end, but I knew it was no game. If I'd asked to climb Mt. Everest, it couldn't have been more dangerous. But while conquering Everest might have brought praise and adulation, I knew Afghanistan would bring only controversy and suspicion.

I ran the narrative through my mind over and over. "You want to go where?" someone would say, or "Whatever for?" Or just simply, "Afghanistan? Why?" So I decided that sharing the plan with anybody was not worth the effort. Who'd understand? After all, what exactly was there to share without the actual permission or without knowing whether the permission would ever be granted? No, I would have to be quiet about it and go it alone. And so for the next several months I told no one, settled into our very old and very drafty New England house on the side of hill for the winter and cracked open one of the few books I could find about the struggle to modernize the ancient country and discovered my suspicions were correct. Nobody had a clue about Afghanistan at all.

CHAPTER 9

Dear Mr. Fitzgerald,

With reference to your letter of April 21, 1981, please be informed that permission has been granted on your request by the relevant authorities of the Democratic Republic of Afghanistan.

Sincerely,
M. Farid Zarif, Charge d'Affaires
Democratic Republic of Afghanistan

April 1981: When I called my friend Kate at a local TV station and told her I had permission to bring a film crew to Afghanistan, she said, "Give me an hour." She called back after fifteen minutes and said, "They all want the story, but CBS wants to fly you to New York right now." I should have turned to Liz and screamed, "We did it. Now let's run away."

But I didn't. I figured somebody would jump at the chance to get inside what Jimmy Carter called the greatest threat to peace since the Second World War. The Western media had been kicked out of the country following the December 1979 Soviet invasion and sixteen months later still hadn't been allowed back in. To breach the blackout, CBS News anchor Dan Rather himself had gone over the mountains in disguise for a cloak-and-dagger coast-to-coast broadcast which had ultimately shed no light on the subject.

In the five months since we'd appealed to the Afghan chargé for visas our lives had changed. Liz and I were now expecting our first child so my team was down to one. And that wasn't all. Taking on Afghanistan was one thing. Taking on CBS was quite another. I took the fact they'd jumped out ahead of everybody else as a warning. I couldn't stop thinking about *The Godfather* when Don Corleone warns Michael about falling into a fatal trap. *"Barzini won't move against you first. He'll set up a meeting with someone you absolutely trust, guaranteeing your safety and at that meeting you'll be assassinated."*

Assassinated? I wasn't worried about CBS assassinating me. I hadn't done anything *yet*. But if CBS wanted my story it was because I was about to do something they wanted to control. That had trouble written all over it. And that was where Kate came in.

"I talked to the CBS foreign editor," she said in that cool-headed professional tone. "He wants you to call him. His name is Larkin, Peter Larkin. Here's his number."

I thanked her and hung up, then took a deep breath and dialed the heavy old rotary telephone parked like a large black frog on the dining room table. Peter Larkin answered on the first ring.

"I want your story," he said without even asking for the details. "Can you get down here this afternoon? We can talk face to face."

"No. I can't come today," I said. "But my wife and I will come down tomorrow."

"I'd really like you to come down today," Larkin pressed.

I shook off his reply and changed the subject. "I've got things to straighten out first. Is ten o'clock tomorrow morning alright for you?"

There was a tone in Larkin's voice I'd heard only a few times before. It reminded me of a border guard; a narrow line of questioning that was at once emotionless, steady and insistent.

I repeated his words as he responded. "Ten o'clock at West 57th? Yes, I know where it is. It's just off the West side highway. We'll be there."

I sat back in the chair and put the receiver back on its cradle. I'd done it. For months I'd been wondering what this phone call would sound like and it was over in about a minute. I wondered why Larkin had offered no details over the phone. I supposed it was because you never knew who was listening. Still, I was surprised when within an hour a telephone truck showed up across the street from the house and a lineman went up the pole. I pointed it out to Liz. She laughed.

"They don't need to bug the telephone pole to tap your line," she said. "I think they're more sophisticated than that."

Of course the U.S. government was more sophisticated than that but what if this was a rush job? Or better yet, what if this wasn't the U.S. government?

I took some deep breaths and tried to get a grip. I wanted to believe Liz, to dismiss the telephone lineman as a coincidence. That was until later in the day when I happened to wind up behind a car on a road less than thirty yards from my house with CBS NEWS license plates, headed toward the town hall.

Kate was right. They really did want this story. It was already getting hard to swallow around the lump in my throat and this was only the first day. I'd sent out the signal. The ship had come in and I'd stepped off the pier. Now the time had come to really see what I'd committed to doing.

***

Peter Larkin was everything you'd expect from America's premier news network; cool, professional and direct. At my request Zarif had provided me with an exquisitely diplomatic letter that could not have said less and still been more to the point, but Larkin never even asked to see it.

A friend recommended an old line New York law firm named Debevoise & Plimpton and through a number of frantic meetings with the lawyers and technicians, Liz and I hammered out an agreement that would give CBS an exclusive news story inside Afghanistan. If I was given the opportunity to stay and travel around Afghanistan by the government, that was alright with them, too. Of course that wasn't alright with Liz and she let me know it on the spot. Everything now had to be balanced against the demands of our unborn child. The freedom I'd had when I'd thought this up six months before was gone. Whatever notions of do or die I might have entertained were reduced to simply, *do*. Adding to the intensity of the moment was the attempted assassination of the very political and Polish Pope John Paul II on May 13, which reverberated through the CBS newsroom like an apocalyptic warning shot. Like his fellow Pole Zbigniew Brzezinski, John Paul had put himself on the front line in the renewed Cold War against the Soviet Union and I was about to step into the middle of it.

Damn, I kept thinking to myself. Pulling this thing off was going to be difficult enough. Now, I just didn't know. With my credentials accepted by the Afghans and the legalities out of the way with the CBS brass, the time had come to move on to the grilling. Who was I to tell this story and what was I doing it for? And this is where Peter Larkin came into his own.

The Cold War was already thirty-five years old by the time I'd returned alone to sit across from him at his desk at West 57th that final night before my departure. I remember realizing that his office was really more like a command center than a newsroom with Peter, his eyes straining, barking out orders over the phone to his man in Beirut while he nervously ran his hand through his slicked-back brown hair. Tense, driven; obsessed. "Did you get the pictures, Benny? Did you get the SAMS?"

SAMS – Surface to Air Missiles. The communists had used SAMS to shoot down American planes over Vietnam. If the Syrians were using

SAMS then the Syrians were getting help from the Kremlin. And if the Syrians were getting help from the Kremlin and using it against America's ally Israel, then the gloves could come off.

I'd negotiated a deal with CBS News for an exclusive on Afghanistan and suddenly I found myself in a combat zone. Larkin wanted pictures of SAMS, HIND helicopter gunships, MIGS; in other words, hardware for war. It struck me immediately that there was something about him that wasn't just about journalism or getting the news or even a scoop. It was the way he seemed to throw himself at the subject. No, that wasn't quite it. It was the way he seemed to throw himself into the telephone, as if he was calling down an air strike. You could hear it in his voice. See it in his eyes. See it in the way his whole body coiled around that old black telephone like a spring about to snap. And that was when I saw the pain. Peter Larkin put the receiver down on the cradle, closed his eyes and slowly pulled himself back from the desk.

"Are you all right?" I asked.

"Vietnam," he said quietly, bending his head forward and stretching painfully as if trying to lift some great weight off his back. "I caught some shrapnel in Vietnam … have to swim every day at the Y. It helps the pain."

Larkin's personal revelation had caught me off guard. Five minutes into the meeting and he'd drawn me into the jungle with him, waiting for an F4 Phantom to drop its bomb-load of napalm on the Vietcong. For an instant I saw myself there crouched beside him as he called for another magazine for his camera, or maybe even a spare clip for his M-16. It was personal, visceral and filled with pain. It was war. His war.

"If you'd gone with somebody else you'd be on your own," he said as he pulled himself back from the edge of his personal abyss. "You go with us, we protect you."

Protect me? In the rush to negotiate the deal and get to Kabul, I'd forgotten there might be consequences. There might be people who wouldn't want me to go to Kabul and would be willing to do something about it. I tried not to sound concerned.

"Protect me? Why do I need protection?" I asked.

"Let's just say we have friends who'll keep an eye on you when you're over there. And when you come home, they won't ask any questions."

Oh, yes. Those kinds of friends. Friends in the government, friends in the CIA, friends who were desperate to see what was going on inside Soviet occupied Afghanistan and were willing to hand out a free pass just to get a peek.

At that moment Larkin's focus shifted unconsciously to the phone on his desk. "The only thing is," he said, "we're really not sure that you won't go native."

I have to admit at that point I almost laughed. I suddenly saw myself in *Apocalypse Now* as Martin Sheen upriver, facing Marlin Brando and gangs of machete wielding Montagnards beckoning for me to join with them in some kind of ritual bloodbath.

"Native? What exactly do you mean by native?" I asked, struggling to suppress the urge to make an inappropriate comment.

Larkin hemmed, hawed and then looked away, trying, I thought, to hide his embarrassment.

"Um, you know, sympathize with the Afghans. We're afraid you might go over to their side."

That time I did laugh as I repeated the phrase out of astonishment. "Go over to their side? Peter, I'm a registered Democrat. I just worked for Pat Robertson for three years and my wife is six months pregnant. If my plan was to go over to their side I wouldn't be sitting here talking to you."

Jesus, it was hopeless. How could you report on Afghans in Afghanistan if you didn't go there to find out what they were thinking? And then it dawned on me. The people Peter worked for didn't want to know what the *natives* were thinking. They just wanted to get the pictures of the 75,000 Soviets and their war machines and evidence to back up what was now the Reagan narrative.

Larkin then proceeded to make it clear that if I was going to work for CBS News he expected the story to conform to what Dan Rather had reported the year before – the Soviets were using Afghanistan as the springboard for a Middle East conquest and that America had better wake up!

It wasn't until the phone rang a few minutes later that I realized, even at that late hour, my trip was still hanging in the balance. I'd given CBS no guarantees that I was going to give them what they wanted and Larkin was just buying time until the front office finally signed off on their approval.

"All right, it's a go," he said, hanging up the receiver and looking me square in the eye. "But I swear," he said, glowering, "if you are doing this to get Dan I'll get you."

"Dan" was of course, Dan Rather. And in case you'd forgotten, Dan had snuck in over the border from Pakistan a year before in a much-ridiculed premier as Walter Cronkite's replacement as editor and chief anchor for the *CBS Evening News*.

It actually hadn't crossed my mind that someone would think I'd go to all this trouble just to sabotage Dan Rather's credibility. He seemed to be doing a pretty good job of that himself, posing as an Afghan "freedom fighter." But the intensity of Larkin's threat stayed with me as I grabbed a cab to the airport to meet up with the crew. Peter Larkin wanted drunken Russians bayonetting babies, tearing down mosques, defiling Muslim women. Peter Larkin wanted Vietnam – Russia's Vietnam – and he'd made no secret of it. If I'd wanted to join the army I wouldn't have gone to CBS, but there I was in Peter Larkin's army of retribution.

He reminded me of a modern Inspector Javert from Victor Hugo's *Les Misérables*, who, with all his resources would hunt down anyone preventing him from bringing the Soviets to justice for what he believed they did to him in Vietnam.

I tried not to think about it as I boarded the flight to Delhi and the first leg of my trip. But as I crossed deeper and deeper into the mirror image of Peter Larkin's nightmare in Vietnam, I found myself looking over my shoulder, and it wasn't long before I saw something I didn't expect to see.

CHAPTER 10

A s I struggled to sleep, my head spun from the remnants of the flu and a half a dozen inoculations, and now I was approaching the eye of the storm. It had taken me five months to cross the Atlantic, much of Eurasia and the Indian subcontinent to get to this moment.

The next day the sun was out and the connecting flight from Delhi to Kabul was packed full with Afghan bureaucrats in suits and ties buying cigarettes and bottles of Scotch before they got off the plane and headed for home. From my limited knowledge of Islam, Muslims weren't supposed to drink, but these guys would have been right at home at an Irish wake. From up in the air the war against the Afghan "freedom fighters" was a million miles away. The mood seemed almost jovial as passengers exchanged stories and joked with their friends. Only when the plane approached the outskirts of Kabul did a peculiar quiet settle in.

The old 727 creaked and groaned as we descended through the snow-capped mountain passes to the MIG-lined runway. The Soviets were anticipating company and had surrounded the place with surface-to-air missile batteries. Added to that were rows of the dreaded Hind Mi-24 gunships. My cameraman Bob was nearly giddy at the sight.

As we left the airplane and crossed the tarmac I quietly impressed upon him the need to remain calm and keep a low profile. "The Afghans are going to be watching every move we make," I told him. "Don't think they aren't watching us from the tower with binoculars right now. So go easy. Don't try to sneak any photographs. We've got to gain their trust." He nodded in agreement. Then, I turned around and saw a tall blond man in tennis whites sticking his hand out to greet us.

"Hi, George Griffin. I'm the American consul," he said, smiling.

My back stiffened. Here I was about to ask my cameraman to steer clear of the American embassy and all of a sudden we were getting blown out of the water before we'd even gotten into the terminal building.

"We don't get too many Americans in these parts these days. Who're you working for?"

"CBS News," I responded as quietly as possible.

Griffin guffawed. "Gunga Dan? He sure got a lot of mileage out of that trip over the mountains, didn't he? Where are you staying?"

"Kabul Hotel," I answered.

"The Kabul Hotel is a dump," he responded with a grimace. "You want to stay at the Intercontinental. It's a little ways out of town but it's much nicer. I'd move myself up there if I were you."

I weighed whether Griffin was making a recommendation or delivering a not-so-veiled demand.

"I thought it might be better to be downtown and sample the local color," I responded, trying to eke out a smile. "You know, walk around the bazaar, check out the mood?"

I could hear the gears grinding as Mr. Griffin sized me up. He paused for an emotionless, untrusting second, then pulled out a card and shoved it into my hand.

"Well, drop by the embassy on your way into town and I'll give you the lowdown on this godforsaken place," he said with a half-grin before nodding a quick goodbye and marching back out through a break in the chain link fence.

"This godforsaken place." I followed Griffin with my eyes, looking to see if anybody stopped him and asked for credentials but nobody laid a hand on him as he vanished into the parking lot. What arrogance. I looked at the card. George Garret Byers Griffin, American consul, Embassy of the United States, Kabul, Afghanistan. Well, consul was his title.

I knew that stopping off at the U.S. embassy would slam doors before we even got started and I had to assume George Griffin knew it, too. By even showing up he was threatening to compromise my position.

It turned out the hotel wasn't quite the "dump" that Griffin implied. It reminded me a lot of Rick's Café from the movie *Casablanca*: A World War II movie set with old fans spinning from a high ceiling, a smallish lobby with a broad, winding staircase beside which stood life size cutouts of smiling Aeroflot and Afghan Airline stewardesses.

The lodgings were not world class but were far from inadequate. My room overlooked the courtyard and garden with a grand view of the old bazaar, and on the dry, rugged hill beyond, the ancient Bala Hissar fortress. From this vantage Kabul looked like a mountain oasis; not much different than it must have appeared to the British before they burned it down in 1842.

I pulled out a notepad and began to log my first impressions while they were still fresh.

Friday, May 15, 1981:

The first clue to how seriously the Afghan government was taking my visit came when I went downstairs to the lobby. An official from the foreign ministry named Rafat waited by the front desk, accompanied by a two-man security detail. And with that, we were off to a running start.

After ten days roaming the countryside I learned the first rule a journalist must know when covering a war. You *cannot* ever know what you're being told is true – even when you're in the middle of it. I found what I observed on the streets, villages and Kabul University campus to be strikingly different from the U.S. narrative. The Afghan government was claiming the Arab states were clearing out their jails and sending their criminals to kill Russians and Afghans. Reagan's "Freedom Fighters" were blowing up power lines, burning schools and throwing acid in women's faces. Rebel victories were fabricated to make the Russians look hapless and the Afghans unwilling to fight. Whether true or not, the whole operation had an immense propaganda value. It got a stalled Cold War up and running again, the Russians had been maneuvered into backing a regime they didn't want and didn't like, and Washington loved it.

Despite a massive security effort attached to the trip, cars fore and aft, the establishment of perimeters and even helicopters and the ongoing problems with translations, Soviet occupied Afghanistan had revealed itself in many ways. The two cities I visited seemed almost normal. Merchants and vendors traded, bartered and conducted business as usual. Locals flooded the marketplace, unconcerned for danger. Women, in modern dress, attended the university and walked side by side with men. Thousands were being taught to read for the first time.

The Soviet presence was obvious at the airports and near their installations. You could hear them at night and see them only when they come out to direct traffic to reposition equipment during the day. Afghanistan was – in the words of one of my Afghan guides – a third world country not only because it was under-developed, but because it had been kept underdeveloped by hostile British interests. The civil war was a struggle to bring Afghanistan into the 20th century. That much was clear. Why the U.S. should oppose that was not clear, and I couldn't see how any of this would end well.

***

Monday Afternoon, May 25, 1981 – Day 11:

At 1:30 P.M. the blue and white Afghan Ariana 727 shot down the runway at Kabul airport, past the rows of MIG fighters and SAM missile batteries and I was gone. I prayed that I hadn't committed a fool's errand.

It was the wrap to a frantic ten days that now seemed more like a sprint than a marathon, and by the time we landed in London early the next morning I could feel the desire to get home setting in.

Long delays on the flights out of Delhi and Frankfurt gave me ample time to collect my thoughts. After landing in London I made a phone call to Liz to let her know I was on my way home and to ask her to call Peter Larkin in New York informing him of my imminent arrival.

By 5:30 P.M. Eastern, I was back in New York and enjoying a joyous reunion with my beautiful and very relieved wife who informed me we didn't need to be at CBS until the morning. To my surprise the customs official was completely uninterested in the contents of the video tapes or even where we'd been and wanted nothing more than to check the serial numbers on the equipment to make sure we weren't trying to smuggle in a $75,000 Ikegami camera.

On the car ride back, again to my surprise, I find Liz to be torn between curiosity and envy.

"So what was it really like?" she asked.

"Incredible. The American consul was waiting for me when I got off the plane in Kabul."

"What?"

"CBS must have told them I was coming. He invited us back to the embassy."

"You didn't go, did you?"

"Of course not. But the pressure was unreal. I feel like I've been at war for two weeks."

"I wish I could have been there," Liz said as her true feelings began to emerge.

"If only you could."

"I'm still annoyed that I didn't get to go, you know. I have to admit I'm jealous."

"Have you been stewing about this for the last two weeks?" I asked.

"No. Just the last ten days. You get to go to the most important place in the world while I'm stuck here waiting for you to come back! It's not fair."

I shook my head and muttered, "Do you realize how difficult it would have been? Soldiers had to sweep for mines wherever we walked. We drove on roads where people had been killed only days before. The plane from Jalalabad nearly crashed."

"But it didn't." Liz gave me a long and lonely look and squeezed my arm. "I know I shouldn't have gone this time," she said, gazing down at her basketball-sized belly, swaddled in her stylish green Sanyo overcoat. "But even if I'm pregnant, I'm going the next time."

Sitting in the back seat of her parents' car I suddenly felt unsure. I hadn't considered her feelings when I'd thought up the trip. I didn't think I'd had to. But now that my wife had introduced a new and sensitive issue into the equation, I felt fear for the first time. Not the fear of getting killed. That was far too abstract a possibility. It was the fear about what would happen next and where we would go from here. It was all so simple at the beginning, the windup, the pitch and the homerun. Now the next act was not so clear but it would begin tomorrow morning at CBS News and I had to be ready to face it without any doubts.

CHAPTER 11

Wednesday May 28, 1981 – 9 A.M.

Liz and I arrived at the reception desk at CBS News on West 57th with my six cases of video tapes and were greeted by a young woman named Kathy Moore who introduced herself as "your producer."

For the next two days I sat and reviewed the tapes with her and a man from the special events unit as Liz went upstairs and sorted out the finances of the trip with the CBS lawyer. We made steady progress but after the first day it became obvious they didn't like what they were seeing.

At the end of the second day I was called out of the editing room to Peter Larkin's office at the rear of the newsroom. Peter was much calmer this time but had a curious look on his face.

"So, you did it," he said.

"I told you I had it under control," I replied.

"Well there's not much there."

I assumed this was Peter's way of saying *you didn't bring me pictures of SAM missile batteries and Russian soldiers bayoneting babies.*

"I gave you an interview with the President of Afghanistan installed by the Soviets."

Larkin said nothing.

"He said his country is in an undeclared war with the United States and that the Russians will go home when that war stops. That sounds like news to me."

"That's not what I read in the *New York Times.*"

I was annoyed. "Because the *New York Times* hasn't been to Kabul," I said. "And it hasn't talked to Babrak Karmal."

Larkin shrugged. It was obvious any further discussion would be pointless. The phone on the desk rang. He picked it up immediately, listened, and said, "Just a minute," then put his hand over the mouthpiece and turned his attention back to me. "I'll catch up with you on the phone. Make sure Kathy has your numbers. We'll need to interview you about the trip for the piece. Actually, Dan might want to do it. He's pretty hot on this issue."

As Larkin got back to work I headed back towards the editing room, thinking for a few seconds that all might in the end be well. Then I heard the senior news producer shriek from her office. "I told you we shouldn't be doing this story. It's a trap." Seconds later Kathy emerged with an embarrassed grin.

"We've been headlining a feature story all week about murder in America but by noon today nobody's been murdered."

She had to be kidding. "Tough break," I told her, trying not to wince.

We exchanged telephone numbers before Liz and I headed off for the weekend, but after two full days with the CBS staff it was clear there was just something not right about this. A week later we found out what – when we arrived back and discovered my interview had been downgraded to Dan Rather's fellow Texan Bob Schieffer, the *CBS Evening News* Saturday edition anchor.

Kathy Moore showed me to an upstairs office where Schieffer waited with a cameraman. After a nod and a handshake he asked, "You ready?" and I began a thirty minute struggle not to turn my story on Afghanistan into another episode of the "Gunga Dan Rather Show."

"Could you go over what's happening in Afghanistan today, what's the first impression that you brought back?" Schieffer asked.

I tried to stay calm and just told him what I saw.

"The Soviet presence is obvious at the airport the minute you land in Kabul," I said to him as the camera rolled. "Based on what I'd heard I expected it to be Saigon 1965, but when you get inside the city it's not like that at all. Jalalabad, the other city that we saw, was the same. Helicopters and jets at the airport, but the city appears under Afghan control."

Schieffer shifted uncomfortably in his chair. He paused to give me a kind of bemused stare then recovered and asked his second question.

"Well… tell us about how – how you got there and what were the rules that you worked under while you were there."

"Strict rules. They'd kicked the western media out because they didn't trust them and we were the first Americans to come back so I had to get permission."

"And you – you got permission fairly quickly after you applied," Schieffer said.

"No, it took six months," I pointed out. "It was a six month process that began back in December."

"So, how did you operate after you got there? Were you allowed to go wherever you liked?"

"No. I had to fight to get what I wanted. Sometimes I won, sometimes I lost."

"Well tell us about that. What did you ask to see?"

"I've been clipping newspaper articles since the Soviet invasion so I wanted to see some of these places and compare notes. But they explained how dangerous the situation was and we needed protection."

"But you don't really believe it was just your safety they cared about?" Schieffer said, feigning shock.

"Of course not. But, the danger *was* real. We saw it outside the cities. Places had to be swept for mines. Soldiers in armored personnel carriers would show up. But they also wanted to put their best face forward."

Schieffer lunged. "Well, why didn't you take any pictures of Russians!"

I was swimming with the sharks.

"We did take pictures of Russians. Lots of them. At the airports in Kabul and Jalalabad."

"But you were not allowed to take any pictures in the cities."

"The Russians weren't in the cities," I insisted.

"But when they told you, you couldn't shoot pictures of armored vehicles, what – what excuse did they give you?" he asked.

"They told me I had to get permission. So I went and asked from this army General named Gul Aqa. I thought it might help getting it straight from the top but he flat out refused. 'We don't want you shooting military hardware' he said. The Afghans were a little fuzzy about it till then, but after that they really clamped down."

Schieffer gasped in exasperation. "Well, you only went to areas that had been *sanitized* for you."

"We went to areas that had been cleared because they didn't want us to get shot. We also met with counterrevolutionaries who had been captured. Don't you want to hear about that?"

Schieffer's tone was incredulous – frustrated. "Well, in some of the interviews the people seemed just delighted with the situation, almost. You must have had some doubts about that!"

Now *I* was getting exasperated. "It was a captive audience." Schieffer took a beat then retrenched to the footage taken covertly at the Soviet airbase in Jalalabad.

"How many helicopters did you see? There – there must be just hundreds of them," he said.

So Schieffer *had seen* the footage of the Russians. He was annoyed at me because they weren't where he wanted them and wanted to call it a wrap.

"Okay, thank you," he said with a cynical laugh. Kathy ignored him and started shouting out more topics and asking for descriptions.

"Russians at the hotel, captured weapons museum, Babrak Karmal…" she said.

The name Karmal seemed to wake him up.

"You had that interview with Karmal. What – what did you think of him? Every indication is that his regime is totally supported by the Soviet Union…" Schieffer said finally.

"Karmal said the Russians are helping them. Afghanistan is a poor country and a lot of the city people work for the government. The rebels are up in the mountains. They come down and blow things up. Who would you support?"

I'd scored a point and Schieffer backed off. "Well, I suppose in Kabul the population supports the government, which might explain the relative calmness there. But did you get the impression nobody is really in control of the outlying areas?"

"There's a lot of activity just outside Kabul," I told him. "But we visited the chief military hospital and it wasn't overflowing with casualties."

Schieffer persisted. "But you weren't able to make any judgment about how the people that you talked to felt about having the Soviets there?"

"The feeling I got was that the Afghans really want to establish relations with America. When I asked them about the Russians they told me the Russians built the roads, the bread factory and the hospitals and gave them a hundred city buses."

"Looking at your film one gets the impression that this is a country that's been at peace for a hundred years."

What an exaggeration. I kept trying to give Schieffer an explanation for what I saw and he just wanted Kabul to look like Saigon in 1968. I got the feeling he was struggling to blame me for the Red Army not being there so I tried to put it on the level.

"I wouldn't go so far to say the country's at peace. But it is a lot different from the way it's been presented here in the U.S. It is not as active and as volatile as we expected it to be. Perhaps we hit it on ten good days. Perhaps the reason why they granted us the permission when they did was the feeling that they had reached a level of security where they could allow an American team back in. I'm only free to speculate on the possibilities of this, and that speculation could go anywhere."

Schieffer looked pained but that was all he was going to get and we finally wrapped. After travelling seven thousand miles and back that one hour at West 57th had been the most difficult part of the trip but at least I knew for sure how CBS News was working the Afghanistan story.

Washington created the myth. The *New York Times* embellished it and CBS News went out and got the pictures. The story had already been written from the top down and there simply wasn't anything but my own moral outrage to oppose it.

CHAPTER 12

As we negotiated the West Side Highway out of New York and back to Boston, the fog of war lifted for the moment and I began to sort out my place in the whole crazy fiasco. Afghanistan had performed flawlessly as a catalyst for the new Cold War and I had put myself squarely in the middle of it. I'd joined the rumble as a consequence of Pat Robertson's Holy War and experienced Dan Rather's determination to turn the country into Russia's Vietnam. Now I was seeing something emerge I hadn't expected and I didn't know what to make of it.

"So what did you think of Schieffer?" Liz asked.

"You remember J.Y. Henderson, the Circus Doctor?"

"Of course. Ringling Brothers. He was your father's best friend," Liz responded.

"Veterinarian – horse doctor. Doc Henderson they called him. Last of a breed. Chief veterinarian at the King Ranch. The army drafted him but they had no horses by 1944 so they made him a meat inspector. He wound up in the same medical unit as my father in France."

"What's that got to do with Bob Schieffer?"

"Texas. Schieffer's from Texas. So is Rather."

"You're saying Schieffer reminds you of J.Y?"

"No. I'm saying Schieffer reminds me of what J.Y. said about *"horse sense."* I always thought it meant you had good sense. He said it meant you were stubborn to the point of being stupid. A horse with a broken leg will kick off a cast. They'd rather bring on their own death than wait for it to heal."

Liz laughed out loud. "So Schieffer's a horse now?"

"No. He's a horse's ass. His buddy Dan Rather sent him to stop me from interfering in their holy war."

"How do you know they're buddies?"

"You remember that night we met Al Lowenstein in New Hampshire?" I asked as we escaped the New York suburbs and broke free onto the highway north.

"Who could forget that?" she said with a frown. "Since you are family?"

"Well, Dan Rather made his reputation covering the JFK assassination that day in Dallas in 1963 and so – did – Schieffer."

"He did?"

"The Texas twins – I kind of remember reading that Schieffer worked for a newspaper in Fort Worth. Oswald's mother calls the newspaper looking for a ride to Dallas and Schieffer winds up driving her to the police station. He spent the day with her and Oswald's wife Marina getting their personal story."

"Oh no," Liz said.

"And … Rather was hand-picked to view the Zapruder film and report on it for that evening's broadcast. He was the only reporter to see it. But instead of reporting that Kennedy's head jerks back and to the left at the grassy knoll, he misreports the direction as forward, in keeping with the lone gunman story."

"So both played a major role in framing the mythology that Al Lowenstein was about to unravel – until someone killed him, too."

"Odd, don't you think? Another coincidence linked to JFK."

***

For the next weeks we did little else but pitch the Afghan story. For us there was only one place to go: Boston's influential PBS station, WGBH. Six o'clock evening news with Christopher Lydon. National news director – former CBS News Producer Bob Ferrante. Hands on, independent journalism?

No. Hands off. Ferrante apologized for not being available to talk but explained that all his resources were in London covering the royal wedding of Princess Diana and Prince Charles. Why a Boston PBS station should so devote itself to the British royal family they'd exclude the greatest threat to peace since World War II was puzzling.

A visit to WGBH two weeks later resulted in a meeting with the station's documentary producer who admitted that since I was trusted by the Afghans, he obviously couldn't trust me. Another meeting with the six o'clock news producer revealed the widely held belief at PBS that any effort to present both sides of the Afghan conflict would be viewed as pro-Soviet and therefore not doable. Public Television? Local insiders joke: The PBS should stand for the Petroleum Broadcasting Service. Nobody at politically correct WGBH wanted to take on the board of governors or Mobil Oil.

Public Broadcasting ran "Freedom Fighter" documentaries in prime time paid for by CIA-connected Scaife foundation. And they were worried about my connections? I had the only footage inside Soviet controlled Afghanistan, "greatest threat to peace since World War II" and Public Broadcasting was afraid to touch it. Freedom of the press, American style.

Ferrante returned. Ferrante managed Dan Rather that day in Dallas in 1963. The circle was complete. This *was* getting interesting. He suggested that Channel 2's sister station WGBY in faraway Springfield might be interested. On June 10th we got a call from the station manager, Mark Erstling who wanted to see the material as soon as possible. I explained that ownership of the material returned to us after sixty days. He explained that, "Money is available from PBS to tell the story but having CBS do a piece on the evening news would help a lot."

And so we waited impatiently for another two weeks. But a call to CBS News confirmed things were not going well.

"I wish I had never heard the word Afghanistan," Kathy said as she exploded in anger over the phone. "This story has been a problem every step of the way. Every vice president in the front office has had a crack at it and I have to answer to all of them. I'm fed up."

"What about Schieffer?" I asked.

"Schieffer's not doing the piece. Everybody's terrified of how the White House will react. I've lost two correspondents already and I'm ready to bag it myself."

"So when will you know?" I asked politely.

There was a long pause. "They know they have an exclusive so there's no pressure. Call me back tomorrow. If anything's going to happen it'll be by the end of the week, but I'm not hopeful."

I hung up the phone and told Liz.

"It's obvious they'll do anything *not* to tell it the way you saw it," Liz said. "They've got too much of an investment in the narrative."

"Well at least we don't have long to wait."

Friday June 26: 10 A.M.

I called Kathy back the next morning and I found a woman possessed by a deadline.

"I don't have time to talk," she said. "We're crashing for tonight. Somebody upstairs got word that ABC was doing a piece tonight and so we're running with it."

"Is that good or bad?" I asked.

"As they want it, you won't like it," she replied. "They've mixed your footage with action footage from two other sources. The Soviets released a film about life in Afghanistan that looks really similar to your stuff. Look, I've got to go. If I don't call you back, call me around 5:00. I'll know by then."

The call back confirmed the story was on for that night.

***

Friday June 26: 7 P.M.

The *CBS Evening News* theme started up. "This is the *CBS Evening News* with Dan Rather," the announcer said. And we waited and waited until about twenty minutes into the broadcast when a map of Afghanistan popped up behind Dan Rather at the anchor desk.

"In Afghanistan rebel attacks on Soviet-led local military forces appear to have increased in the past several weeks. This at least is what several diplomatic sources in India and Pakistan and refugees have told CBS News. For the first time in months there are new reports of the Soviets using gas against the rebels. What kind of gas is unclear. The Russians vehemently deny they have ever used gas. Now shortly before these reports, the Soviet supported Afghan government authorized an independent American film team to visit the country. CBS News correspondent Steve Young, recently returned from Moscow, put the American film together with Soviet propaganda film for this report."

I could hardly believe my ears. "They put our film together with Soviet film they're calling propaganda? Jesus Christ."

The first footage available of life inside Soviet occupied Afghanistan from an American, and they couldn't accept it. This wasn't news, it was theatre. Theatre of the absurd.

"This film, made by Soviets for Soviets, did not show the Afghan guerillas resisting the Soviet installed regime in their country, but the film did provide one the few glimpses of life in Afghanistan's cities since the Soviet invasion until an American TV crew was allowed in, the first American journalists to be officially welcomed in sixteen months," said narrator Steve Young.

I soon watched myself describing the scene in Kabul and realized the editors had used the very last part of my interview with Bob Schieffer where I had carefully bracketed my words with the caveat that it was all just speculation.

"It is not as active and as volatile as we expected it to be. Perhaps we hit it on ten good days. Perhaps the reason why they granted us the permission to come when they did was the feeling that they had reached a level of security where they could allow an American team in."

Kathy was right. I didn't like it but I was sure the White House was pleased. They omitted Babrak Karmal's accusation of the ongoing secret war conducted by Washington. Nothing was said about the U.S. *wanting* the Soviets to stay in Afghanistan and they ignored Karmal's statement that they would leave if the U.S. backed off. They made no mention of the rebel attacks on the fragile infrastructure; the suffering caused by the Mujahideen holy warriors; and never mentioned how schools for women were especially targeted. It was not even a story about Afghanistan. It was a story about the Russians I hadn't seen.

I expected a flurry of inquiries about my experience from the local Boston media, but there was nothing. My next door neighbor shouted out to me, "Hey, you're a big deal," as he came home from work a few nights later, but I got the feeling that nobody except those directly involved in my trip had any idea what Afghanistan was being used for.

"So this is how the mythology-creation machine works," Liz said as Dan Rather signed off with a smirk. "The Texas twins Rather and Schieffer established the official mythology for the JFK assassination and now they've done it for Afghanistan."

CBS News special events and documentary units had no further use for the tapes or my experience. Kathy Moore called a few weeks later asking me to make an "executive decision" on how I wanted them returned. I suggested they place them on the New York to Boston shuttle with a CBS intern but she told me she had a better idea. Three hours later Liz and I greeted the CBS News helicopter at the Leverett Circle helipad and were delivered six yellow CBS News onion-skinned bags containing my tapes. I had now successfully completed phase I of my adventure. Phase II and the long, lonely process of making some kind of sense out of phase I was about to begin.

CHAPTER 13

C BS News was a double edged sword. They missed my story by a mile but they had aired it. WGBY offered no budget, but in-kind services and an air date in 1982. Six o'clock on a Sunday night in August when everybody would be at the beach. Beggars couldn't be choosers. We agreed to take it.

I made a call to Zarif at the UN about the CBS report. As I'd guessed, he was not at all surprised by the way they'd handled the material and not particularly disturbed by it either.

"It was not at all as bad as I expected it to be," he said, laughing. "They treated our President with respect and showed that life on the streets is quite calm as it should be, so there is no problem."

I tried not to read too much into it, but I thought I might have succeeded in laying the foundation for a future trip and maybe a shot at getting a less official and more personal story the next time around. I explained that I was in the process of preparing the documentary and he invited Liz and me to dinner with him and his wife the next time we were in New York.

And that was when George Griffin re-entered the scene.

> **Moscow (AP)** *The U.S. government protested Soviet charges of CIA involvement in an alleged plot on the life of Indian Prime Minister Indira Gandhi. The charges, which appeared Wednesday in the Communist daily Pravda, said the CIA was behind a conspiracy by Afghan rebels to sabotage a plane on which Mrs. Gandhi was scheduled to fly. The article named George Griffin as a CIA agent who allegedly directed the activities. Griffin is the U.S. charge d'affaires in Kabul, the Afghan capital.*
> Friday May 1, 1981

It was probably a good thing that I'd missed the May 1st news story implicating George Griffin in a plot to assassinate Indira Gandhi before going to Kabul. I wouldn't have known what to do with it. But it didn't take long to find out about him once I'd got back to Boston. I'd sensed that day at the airport in Kabul that there was something about Mr. Griffin that was definitely more than just diplomacy. Perhaps it was the rough arrogance, the self-assuredness that betrayed him the most. Whether there was any substance to the charges, the fact that they'd been leveled by another government made them an international issue. Mr. Griffin was on a mission to give the Afghans and their allies a hard time and avoiding him most likely saved the trip. The Soviets probably had him followed and the Indian government certainly had it in for him. But their naming him as a CIA agent put him at the center of the Reagan administration's escalating war against what seemed a growing list of countries.

"The United States is not on the best of terms with the Soviet Union for any number of reasons," Liz said, reading an editorial about Griffin from another newspaper. "But George Griffin seems to be at the top of the list."

Hearing about Griffin again set me off. "And the Reagan administration is waging a secret war in Afghanistan. So how do we tell Americans *that* story?"

Liz and I spent the rest of the summer transcribing video tapes, plotting out the edit for the documentary and just recovering from the ordeal. Everything was calm but I knew I had permanently stepped away from my old life and I would never be able to return to it. The baby was due soon and was demanding all the energy Liz could muster. She was well though, and we settled down to pulling the experience together for a documentary.

And that was when George Griffin again stepped back into the story.

Wednesday, September 2, 1981:
Liz picked a copy of the *Boston Globe* off the kitchen table and began to read. "The *New York Times* reported today that the government of India has refused to accept senior American diplomat George G.B. Griffin as political counselor, the third ranking post in the U.S. embassy in New Delhi, touching off a dispute with the Reagan administration. The article goes on to say that the action by India is 'unprecedented' and that the United States has retaliated by barring a senior Indian diplomat."

I took the paper and began to read from it myself. "India ostensibly objects to his performance at his previous post in Afghanistan, where he displeased the occupying power. The Soviets accused him of spreading false information about conditions in the country and having a CIA connection. Jesus, George Griffin must have his own line item in the defense budget."

"I did some background on Griffin after the Gandhi incident and found some interesting details left out of the news report," Liz said as she scrambled to find her notes. "Born in Istanbul in 1934 to an American who'd spent forty years in Turkey in the tobacco business, he entered the Foreign Service in 1959. And this is where that coincidence thing with JFK we keep stumbling on gets really freaky. He's sent to watch over deported mafia drug kingpin Lucky Luciano in Naples from 1959-61, liaises with Kennedy Secret Service agents Clint Hill and Paul Landis, who later wind up in the Kennedy motorcade in Dallas, while hanging out with Jacqueline Kennedy and her sister Lee Radziwill at her villa in Ravello in 1962. Goes to work at the State Department Operations center and manages Intelligence community operations in Vietnam during the height of the escalation from 1965-66, posted to India during the India-Pakistan War from 1969-72, Pakistan from 1972-79 and then back to Washington and the Bureau of Intelligence and Research – South Asia Division at the State Department. And that's where he meets Adolph Dubs, the future ambassador to Afghanistan who is killed in a shootout at the Kabul Hotel on St. Valentine's day 1979."

"Another St. Valentine's day massacre." A light went on. "Mr. Griffin's an important man to be posted to a fourth rate country," I added. "He'd broken off a game of tennis just to come out and greet me at the Kabul airport."

At that moment as the adrenaline receded in the quiet of my suburban home and I looked to the future with Liz and the fast approaching birth of our child, I found myself stifling a scream. I was caught in some kind of loop. From the JFK assassination to Al Lowenstein's assassination to the National Student Association and Afghanistan, to George Griffin and back to the JFK assassination. And then to Adolph Dubs, the assassination that led to the Soviet invasion nine months later. Three assassinations. Three connections. And I hadn't seen them until now. Pattern recognition. What else was I missing? The same crowd of Washington insiders had used their fake prophecies on Eisenhower to escalate tensions with Russia in the 1950s, then on JFK in the 1960s and then on Jimmy Carter with Team B the year he was elected. They hadn't wanted good relations with the Soviet Union; they wanted bad relations and they always got them, by hook or by crook. The Cold War was now back on. The murder of U.S. Ambassador Dubs had made it inevitable. I'd seen the photograph of his grieving widow flanked by Jimmy Carter and Secretary of State Cyrus Vance the day that his casket arrived in Washington – I couldn't believe it.

Who would kill an ambassador? Not a rival superpower trying to get the American Congress to sign a nuclear arms deal they'd desperately needed. And certainly not a third-world backwater desperate for U.S. aid and recognition. Only someone trying to provoke retribution. And who would want that retribution? Zbigniew Brzezinski. Brzezinski blamed the Russians, but then Brzezinski always blamed the Russians. He was a red flag that went unnoticed in the Carter administration. Old European politics. Kill the Germans for business and the Russians for pleasure. Brzezinski had it in for the Russians because he was of minor Polish nobility and anybody who knew the way Polish nobility behaved, knew it. What was a known Russia-hater doing in the Carter administration in the first place and why had the "Peace President" elevated his role to cabinet level? Something was wrong about it from the beginning.

CHAPTER 14

December 13, 1981:

The morning after the Parker House Preview I was feeling victorious. But then WGBY TV producer Mark Erstling phoned to tell me his car had had acid thrown at it at the hotel and he wanted the Dunfeys to pay to have it repainted.

"Was it an accident or on purpose?"

"Don't know. Dropped it with the valet and it came back like that. Pretty careless if you ask me."

Careless, or intentional? "The Dunfeys didn't build a successful hotel chain by being careless or spilling acid on their guest's cars," I told him. "That's what religious extremists do to get attention." The news soured the Parker House victory and put Theodore Eliot's attack in perspective. The other shoe had dropped.

Was my producer being warned? Was he being used to undermine my hosts? Was I being paranoid? Or were these classic dirty tricks – unsettling, destabilizing, but ultimately not traceable to anyone. British spies had perfected it on Americans suspected of being pro-German before World War II. They'd written the manual on it – flattened tires, anonymous phone calls in the middle of the night, missing pets, a dead rat in your water tank. But acid was a special calling card from the Middle East. America's favorite "Freedom Fighters" in Afghanistan used it to scar their enemies, usually women. Who would be next?

The Canadian Consul-General Jean-Marie Gaétan Déry called and asked for a meeting. Over lunch the elegant lady told me Theodore Eliot's behavior was no surprise to her.

"That's how the Americans always treat us," she said. "It's surprising to have them acting that way towards another American. It's revealing."

I was more than intrigued. "If you don't mind my asking, what does it reveal?"

She smiled. "What you did clearly hit a nerve. Eliot is a very influential man. He's a director at the Asia Foundation, Inspector General at the Department of State, of course Dean of the Fletcher School as well as having been the ambassador to Afghanistan for six years."

There had been something bothering me about that, I confessed. "Afghanistan and Theodore Eliot don't seem to go together. If he's so powerful I'd have thought maybe London or Paris, but Kabul? The State Department rates it at the lowest priority."

"Maybe it's more important than you think. After all he is also the Secretary General for the United States to the Bilderberg Meetings, too. Maybe it fits into *their* plans."

Was that a slip? "Bilderberg?"

"I'm sorry. It's a conference of world business and political leaders. It was founded after World War II by Prince Bernhard of the Netherlands to maintain better relations between Europe and the United States. Some say the real intent is to forge a supranational governing body."

"Supranational? Like the European Union?"

"Exactly. Only this would include the U.S."

I couldn't help but suggest, "A one-world government."

Jean-Marie only smiled. Revelations, it would seem, were just beginning. So the Russians had crashed a party in Afghanistan that was in the making. A very big party. That would explain a lot. I thanked the nice lady for lunch and made my way across the common through the Christmas shoppers. I hoped that Santa would be good this year. Give peace a chance. Some publicity for the documentary would help. But with Reagan in office and the new arms race kicking in, I knew I was rowing against the tide. Boston was the high tech hub of the northeast. Avco, Raytheon, MITRE, MIT, Harvard and all the rest would get their share. Everybody wanted a piece of the action and Afghanistan was the engine making it work.

Days and weeks went by. Invitations for interviews evaporated. My cameraman asked me to remove his interview from the documentary. "I've got a kid and I can't afford to be blacklisted," he said.

Blacklisted? Jesus. We *were* back thirty years – before Vietnam, Watergate and the Church Committee. Demonizing works. Only Roger Fisher hung on, offering to film an introduction. Liz worked with me to reorder the scenes to reflect feedback from the preview. A couple of months of editing and we had a clearer narrative.

By the summer of 1982 Zbigniew Brzezinski had left the stage – but his influence remained. Right wing Bill Casey at the CIA wanted to keep him on. Ronald Reagan settled for the other Polish national – Richard Pipes. Two wild and crazy guys at the radioactive core of American foreign policy. Team B leader and Russia-hater now elevated to Director of East European and Soviet Affairs at the National Security Council. SALT negotiator Paul Warnke told us the U.S. now operated an "ethnic foreign policy."

The "New Right" began to de-legitimize the Soviet Union immediately. Socialism became a slur.

Headline: NBC News' Marvin Kalb blames the Kremlin for Pope John Paul's assassination attempt in May of 1981 based on claims by known British and American psychological warfare agents Claire Sterling, Michael Ledeen and *The Spike's* Arnaud de Borchgrave and Robert Moss.

Headline: June, Ronald Reagan appears at the United Nations. Asserts U.S. has "conclusive evidence" Soviets use chemical and toxic weapons in Afghanistan, Laos and Cambodia.

Headline: July, *Boston Globe's* William Beecher alleges Vietnam used Soviet-supplied chemical warfare agents against Chinese during their invasion of Vietnam in 1979. Cites unnamed "well-placed sources," unnamed "American chemical warfare specialists," unnamed "Western, mostly American officials based on hearsay evidence," and unnamed "Vietnamese military defectors [who] told US intelligence."

Despite Roger's involvement no sponsor came forward to help. We used our own money to complete *Afghanistan Between Three Worlds.* The station was a two hour drive on the Mass Pike, staffed by volunteers and equipment older than the Christian Broadcasting Network. A 6:00 P.M. Sunday release in the first week of August meant that almost no one would see it. In conclusion, we were all doomed.

Sunday August 6, 1982:

Six o'clock rolled around. It had now been three years and counting. The melodious tone of the channel 2 announcer startled me. "Next up; *Afghanistan Between Three Worlds with Paul Fitzgerald.*"

It was a hot, muggy night in August. I opened the doors and windows of the house so everybody in my conservative, middle-class suburban neighborhood could hear the TV.

"You are about to see a documentary, *Afghanistan Between Three Worlds,*" Roger Fisher said from behind his desk at Harvard Law School. "Behind the fighting in Afghanistan lies the fact that all Afghans of different points of view want to play a role in their future. Paul Fitzgerald has performed a remarkable diplomatic and journalistic task in bringing us this inside view of a piece of the puzzle that is Afghanistan. It is not the whole picture but is a key piece to understanding Afghanistan today."

Roger's introduction added authority. But if ideology was now king then Washington didn't care about diplomacy or journalism. In the summer of 1979 facts mattered. Or at least I'd thought facts mattered.

Afghanistan hadn't done it; it'd just let it out of the box. Thanks to Brzezinski, ethnic grudges had been institutionalized. Ancient hatreds had been seeded into the center of the American government and encouraged to grow. I was afraid the middle ground that Roger represented may not be there anymore. The center had not held and God only knew where the storm would take us.

The doorbell rang, and we were visited by two French doctors from Aide Médicale Internationale. They'd called earlier after reading an article about me in the *Boston Herald* and wanted to watch the documentary with me. They were in town raising money for the Mujahideen "Freedom Fighters" and were unwaveringly hostile to the "communist" regime in Kabul.

I tried to explain that the "communist" government wasn't very communist – that they didn't like the Soviets and the Soviets didn't like them and wanted them to share power with other political parties. They wouldn't listen. They became agitated as they watched, and it's not surprising they didn't like what they were seeing. I wasn't sure who was more uncomfortable, them or me. After an hour they left for the train in a huff, muttering vaguely hostile sentiments. Their visit was an unpleasant surprise but left me wondering. What was Aide Médicale Internationale and who was behind them? I had myself a new mystery to unravel.

CHAPTER 15

Searching for background on Aide Médicale led me back to Harvard Square. The place used to be fun but the unique little boutiques and shops I knew from the 1960s had been replaced by trendy chain stores that reeked of corporate cool.

I'd read in the *Los Angeles Times* that Colin Gray, author of *Victory Is Possible,* was helping Reagan make Carter's "Plan for N-war" operational and that "twenty million U.S. fatalities would present a level 'compatible with Western values.'"

This was utterly insane. By going into Afghanistan the Russians had given these people every excuse they needed to stage Armageddon. Now they were legitimizing the concept of nuclear annihilation and further destroying the prospects for peace.

Those two French doctors weren't interested in peace either. They just wanted a place to give the Soviets what they deserved, and heal the wounded who were giving it to them.

I pulled a copy of *Microcomputing* magazine off the shelf. Some strange American guy dressed like an Afghan had brought a "personal computer" the size of a coffee table into the Hindu Kush to aid the "Freedom Fighters" and written a story about it. I could just see him bobbing and weaving on a mountain trail as a Soviet MI-24 gunship bore down on him. Go tech.

A young woman in coveralls saw me reading an article in *Soldier of Fortune* and glared her disapproval. Tsk, tsk, tsk. "*Soldier of Fortune* indeed," she snorted, shook her head in mock ridicule and stormed out of the shop. God love her. What use would it have been to explain it to her.

The magazine was filled with gun ads, paramilitary rantings and come-ons for all kinds of mischief. "Mercenaries needed in Biafra. Must know automatic weapons." How did one get to *know* an automatic weapon?

Unfortunately, it was only one of the few magazines reporting on Afghanistan, although completely jaundiced. Another magazine that *was* doing some good reporting was called *Counter-Spy*. It had detailed articles about CIA covert action in Afghanistan. It also published the names of known agents which would probably get it into big trouble someday. It also had a very interesting article about the use of humanitarian "Non-Governmental Organizations" (NGOs) as a weapon in the war on communism. I rummaged around some more and found a U.N. catalogue.

Ah, there it was. Aide Médicale Internationale (AMI).

"AMI is one of three Paris-based organizations that are well connected to the pool of anti-communist international aid money. AMI wants to go where others don't go and do what others don't do, refusing to testify on what it does and sees."

And so it did. Cambodia 1980; Laos 1981; Afghanistan, since 1980. Crossed the Pakistan border illegally and implemented medical programs on the Mujahideen side only. "AMI doctor arrested and accused of spying by the Red Army."

AMI received money through the International Rescue Committee (IRC) and the Afghanistan Relief Committee, the ARC.

Ahh. And so the tumblers fell into place.

IRC went back to World War II, Leo Cherne and his business partner William Casey – Reagan's CIA director. Cherne created a propaganda bureau with ex-communists and Trotskyists to attack the Nazis, then after the war turned them into the main lobby for war in Vietnam. After Vietnam Cherne convinced CIA Director George H.W. Bush to let Team B have access to classified CIA files and the neocon takeover of the intelligence community was complete.

The Afghanistan Relief Committee, the ARC, was founded by top level American officials, including Theodore Eliot, and operated out of the law offices of John Train.

John Train. I shuffled around the bookstore some more and found that Train was a psychological warfare specialist with a long history of creating sophisticated CIA-backed front operations.

He showed up early – co-founder and managing editor of the magazine *Paris Review*. *Paris Review* was the drive wheel in the CIA's culture war in Europe known as the Congress for Cultural Freedom.

The CIA paying for well-known writers and artists was a huge scandal when *Ramparts* magazine revealed it in the 1960s; Hemingway, Truman Capote, T.S. Eliot. All edited by co-founder George Plimpton.

Wait. George Plimpton? We'd hired the N.Y. law firm Debevoise and Plimpton to negotiate the deal with CBS. It couldn't be the same Plimpton. I searched a little deeper. It *was* the same. We'd hired a CIA law firm and hadn't known it. Jesus, it was all there. You just had to know what to look for.

Train managed old money, very old. Returned from Paris in the early 1950s. Created a boutique Wall Street investment firm and became a devotee of the radical British economist Cyril Northcote Parkinson. Parkinson believed modern nation states should be broken up into mini-states and ruled by a restored monarchy. A monarchy? I'd thought the whole idea of the Cold War was to establish "democracy" like we had in the U.S.

Parkinson gave an interview and revealed that Hitler's plan for a post war Nazi-ruled Europe mirrored his own.

I found myself staring out the window at my beloved Harvard Square. John Train had opened a window into a powerful clique of Anglo-Americans which had been quietly moving the United States towards fascism since the Cold War began. In fact, they'd actually created the Cold War.

Could I have been imagining this? Or was I just understanding it for the first time, like the Latin logo over the gates into Harvard Yard. *Truth – Veritas*. The esteemed Harvard law school and its emblem with its three sheaves of wheat. How many knew that it was the emblem of an 18th century Boston slave trader named Isaac Royall? Who could have imagined that the oldest and most distinguished law school chair in America – bought, paid for and named after the richest Yankee in the colonies – had been endowed from a fortune made by trafficking in slaves. It began to seem that the noble truth about the West's values was not what I'd believed. Theodore Eliot should have been hysterical. Afghanistan connected him to a *very* bad crowd. And as the documentary made its way through the PBS system, a deeply disturbing long-term political agenda began to reveal itself.

CHAPTER 16

A *fghanistan Between Three Worlds* hit the system like a cluster bomb. Syracuse; San Bernardino; the Maryland Network – five stations. The Nebraska Network then L.A.; Washington; Pittsburgh; and San Francisco. But never New York City.

The local response was immediate. The foreign editor for the *Christian Science Monitor* called and informed me I was to be guided by the Swiss reporter Edward Girardet's style or else.

"Or else what?"

"Or else I'll have the *Christian Science Monitor* TV critic denounce you." Too late for that.

I called the WGBH program director who told me not to worry. My documentary was one of the best pieces of straightforward journalistic reportage he'd ever seen, he said. But would he be so bold as to say that in public? I doubted it.

Christian Science Monitor did nothing. They may not have wanted to call attention to their part in the Reagan administration's "major propaganda offensive" surrounding chemical weapons.

My suspicions were confirmed the next day. *The Monitor* made new "eyewitness" charges of Soviet chemical warfare – only the charges weren't new and weren't eye witness. The report merely repeated U.S. government statements nearly word for word as published in the *Los AngelesTimes* three months earlier. Wasn't anybody watching this but me? *They* were making stuff up and were angry at *me* for not playing by the coveted "standards" of American journalism?

New claims of chemical warfare appeared weekly thereafter.

Without providing proof, on March 8th Deputy Secretary of State Walter J. Stoessel testified the Soviets had killed 3042 persons with such weapons between 1979 and the summer of 1981. Then without explanation two weeks later on March 22 the figure rose to10,000.

Despite the ongoing propaganda war, viewer comments on the documentary were positive. But the highlight of the week arrived from Afghan expert Selig Harrison who wanted to include our work in his research. Having his recognition of our work was a shot in the arm. We flew down to Washington to meet him and he shocked us with the briefing he received from U.S. Ambassador Adolph Dubs on his last trip there in 1978.

"Dubs arrived with a mission," he told us. "Bring the Afghan leader Hafizullah Amin closer to the American side and keep the Russians out. It's really a shame we lost him. He was uniquely qualified – one of the few Americans with a nuanced view of the Soviets."

"How so?" I asked.

"He'd spent years at the U.S. embassy in Moscow developing relationships with his Soviet counterparts. He wanted everybody to know destabilization would induce an invasion and was adamantly against Brzezinski's anti-Soviet plots."

"But how did that go over with the neocons?"

"Not well," he said. "Brzezinski thought it was all nonsense. He saw the Soviet invasion as a great vindication of his point of view."

"So in a sense Brzezinski wanted to provoke the Soviets to invade."

"I don't want to go on the record as saying that, but that's what I believe. Brzezinski and Dubs were working at cross-purposes during late 1978 and early 1979. Dubs tried to play it safe by ordering a research paper on the possibility of provoking a Soviet invasion before he left. But no one took him seriously."

Harrison was giving us a clear view of the power struggle inside the White House and how the struggle with Brzezinski endangered Dubs' objectives.

"I met him out there that summer. He was alone and I had a long evening with him. He came out with a very sophisticated conception of what he was going to do, which was to try to make Amin into a kind of Tito, in other words, detach him. Dubs knew how subtle an operation it had to be. He had no illusions it could be done quickly. He would still be pretty close to the Russians, but he'd have more freedom of action and it would be enough to make it safe from our point of view. He met with Amin fourteen times and quickly understood that he was not a loyal Communist. He even bragged that the Soviets needed him more than he needed them. But the trick would be to keep a back door open to American influence while not triggering Soviet countermeasures."

"How did that work with the Soviets?" I asked.

"They were greatly alarmed because they thought Amin might be a CIA agent. And Brzezinski was actively promoting an aggressive covert anti-Soviet Afghan policy without the State Department's knowing much about it. So it was extremely dangerous," Harrison added.

Harrison's analysis confirmed our suspicion. The issue with Afghanistan didn't originate in Moscow; it originated in Washington and was likely triggered by Brzezinski.

We visited others we'd interviewed back in 1979 before the Soviet invasion and all admitted nobody saw Afghanistan coming.

Tom Halsted from Arms Control and Disarmament told us, "It's a changing of the guard. People are leaving that have been here since Roosevelt came in 1934. The New Deal is over."

The old New Deal *was* over. The *New* New Deal was Reagan's massive World War II-size military buildup and it was all going to the Military Industrial Complex. Reagan was pushing Brzezinski's agenda on Afghanistan, and as reaction to our documentary trickled in we found ourselves under attack.

Letter: "[h]ow doubly tragic to have your distorted picture appear on national educational television. I would have liked to have seen your 'interpretations' after the Gestapo 'guided' you through Buchenwald."

Now *that* was a nice touch. By going to Afghanistan I'd apparently become a Nazi apologist. Conflating Soviets with Nazis sure did ring a bell. It was always 1939 to a neoconservative but now Nazi had been transformed to Soviet. This was the Team B mishmash Richard Pipes had presented on *MacNeil Lehrer*. Once you accused somebody of being a Nazi, magically they became one.

I thought I'd heard it all until I received a phone call in late October from the Committee for a Free Afghanistan's (CFA) Karen McKay. Ms. McKay got right to the point. "Your documentary is the most explicit piece of Soviet propaganda I've ever seen on American television," she said. "I was called by a community of refugees in Texas who wanted to voice their complaint. They think you're a KGB agent."

The pattern of 1950s McCarthy smears was holding. I'd graduated from being a conduit for Soviet propaganda into being a Soviet agent. I tried to suppress a laugh. "Do you really think I work for the KGB?"

Silence. "No," she admitted. "But I do think you were duped."

Duped? Wow. I was talking to Joe McCarthy's ghost. "The American people don't know anything about Afghanistan, Ms. McKay. I'm just giving them a chance to make up their own minds."

McKay began to get edgy. "There is nothing to make up," she insisted. "The Afghan Freedom Fighters are liberating their country from Communist oppression."

"Then why do they burn down schools and target women?"

"They don't," she said confidently. "That was staged by the Communists for your benefit."

This was getting absurd. "C'mon, Karen. You know these guys hate women. They throw acid in their faces."

Silence. I could hear the gears clicking. Then McKay retaliated.

"Then what about yellow rain? You didn't mention anything in your documentary about the Soviets' use of chemical or biological weapons."

"That hasn't been proved," I said.

"The *New York Times* and the *Washington Post* have accepted my evidence that mycotoxins have been used by the Russians in Afghanistan. What makes you so special?" she said, trying to move me off the subject.

McKay was a seasoned propagandist. I didn't expect to change her mind. "Look, if the Soviets are using germ warfare they should be condemned. But everything I've seen so far comes from second- or third-hand sources or based on hearsay evidence. Don't you think you could make a much better case if you had some *hard* evidence? I mean if it's as widespread as you say then why is it so hard to prove?"

McKay wound up for the denouement. "When it comes to the Russians we don't need proof," she spat out with a new harshness in her voice. "We know they're guilty."

Ah. There it was. *We know they're guilty!* I was shocked but relieved. Karen McKay had just summed up everything I'd been hearing long before the invasion of Afghanistan. It was the same self-fulfilling prophecy Richard Pipes and Team B used to justify their claims. But the clincher came a few weeks later when Karen McKay wrote me a letter telling me about the negative impact I was having on her campaign, and "in the pursuit of truth and justice," offering to hook me up with some of her friends in Pakistan so I could sneak over the mountains into Afghanistan and get the "real" story.

I took McKay at her word and wrote to tell her that in the pursuit of truth and justice I would be very open to going to Pakistan if the money could be raised. But I never heard from her again.

I was not surprised. When I looked into the Committee for a Free Afghanistan's brief history I discovered that CFA's backers were not in the business of truth and justice. And that was when the pieces really began to fall into place.

CHAPTER 17

Autumn was turning to winter. The days were getting shorter and I began wondering if I'd made the right decision. Not on Afghanistan, but on life. Maybe I should have taken that football scholarship and accepted my fate. Downhill racer going for the gold. I thought about driving a Porsche and skiing in St. Moritz knowing it would never happen.

I'd done a bunch of different things after finishing school and a decade later I found myself right back where I'd started. I'd gone to war, but not over Vietnam; over Russia's Vietnam. The dining room in our drafty old New England home had long been turned into what? The command center? I needed all the help I could get and so I called on a reliable old friend in D.C.

Ron was a cross between Enrico Fermi and Lieutenant Columbo – a schlumpy introvert whose appearance forced you to underestimate him only to later have him floor you with his genius and intuition. I'd met him just after he'd worked for USAID in Saigon. At that time he worked for the GAO investigating Pentagon fraud and I'd asked him to do some digging.

The old black rotary phone in the dining room was my link to the outside world and it was ringing.

I took a deep breath and tentatively picked up the receiver.

"Are you sure you know what you're getting into?" Ron asked before I could even say hello, his voice crackling and hissing out the other end. There was no way this phone was not being tapped.

"I've already gotten into it. I'm just trying to figure out how deep this goes."

It hadn't taken him too many calls to discover what I'd suspected.

"Karen McKay is actually *Major* Karen McKay of the U.S. Army Reserve and a former Delta Force commando," he said. "The Major studied unconventional warfare in the 1960s. She preaches that 19th century Brzezinski/Pipes bullshit stuff about the Czar and his obsession with gaining a warm-water port."

"That's why they invaded land-locked Afghanistan and left Iran alone," I added.

"McKay claims the Russians are using every kind of modern weapon except nuclear bombs. Chemical warfare is being used as well as 'scatter bombs' disguised as toys to maim children."

"I've heard that. Who's behind her?"

"According to one account her organization was founded by Lord Nicholas Bethell, a British conservative, which would make her a liaison with British intelligence. He was part of Thatcher's entourage when they visited Reagan last year. Bethell supports Russia's internal protest movement, Samizdat. He runs an organization called Radio Free Kabul with Soviet dissident Vladimir Bukovsky out of London."

"London?"

"London shows up a lot. It's all twisted together with some MI6, CIA and NATO stuff. Convoluted. Bethell himself was accused of being a KGB stooge by Prime Minister Edward Heath in the early 1970s. They dismissed him from Parliament for being a security risk. Another account says McKay's group is a CIA front, which it is, while a third has it funded as a program of the ASC, the American Security Council."

That rang a bell. *The SALT Syndrome.* "The American Security Council? Their documentary is the reason I got into this mess. Tell me more about them."

"The ASC is the mother of all anti-labor, anti-communist organizations dating back to 1938. Again, very Anglo/American right-wing. And get this ... one of its founding members was Jay Lovestone."

"Should I know who that is?"

"Born Jacob Liebstein in Russia. Executive Secretary of the Communist Party USA from 1927 to 1929. Gets kicked out in Stalin's purges, becomes an American union organizer and eventually goes to work for the CIA."

"So which is it?" I asked. "Which group is behind the Committee for a Free Afghanistan?"

"All of them," Ron said. "Take a look at the fine print under McKay's letterhead. They're all ringers for the New Right."

I picked up the letter and squinted as I read down the list. "Arnaud de Borchgrave?"

"Got fired from *Newsweek* when he compared the Soviet invasion of Afghanistan to Nazi Germany's march into Czechoslovakia in 1939."

"1939 is a propaganda theme with these guys," I said. "They're trying to confuse the Soviet Union with Nazi Germany in people's minds."

"His senior editor thought so too and spiked his dispatch from Kabul. De Borchgrave goes over his head to the company president and they canned him."

"De Borchgrave jumped the gun, probably accused his boss of being a KGB agent."

"That's what I heard. His credibility was already stretched thin so he teams up with this right wing MI6 British guy named Robert Moss."

"I didn't know intelligence agents are allowed to be political?"

"When it comes to Russia they are. Moss is a special unit guy. Politicized intelligence, disinformation and sabotage. The two co-authored a novel called *The Spike* – a thinly veiled attack on Seymour Hersh's revelations about the My Lai massacre in Vietnam."

"Oh yeah. I remember them. They're the ones who blamed the Kremlin for Pope John Paul's assassination attempt in May of 1981."

"De Borchgrave insists *The Spike* isn't really fiction. He claims the Soviets have turned western correspondents into their agents to tell lies about us."

The logic stumped me. "But My Lai happened. The Army convicted Lieutenant Calley for it."

"Calley was just the fall guy," Ron grunted dismissively.

"Yeah, I figured that. But they can't say it's a lie if the army admitted it happened."

"Get serious. They do whatever they want. They used to call it *Red baiting*. You report a story that makes them look bad and they label you a Communist. No one will talk to you. Reagan and Casey brought it all back with the help of the British and the French. De Borchgrave's cousin is Alexandre de Marenches. Ever heard of him?"

I was getting that creepy feeling. "Should I?"

"Heads the SDECE, the French CIA; de Marenches advises his cousin to be in Kabul the day the Soviets invade."

This was becoming theatre of the absurd. "So de Marenches wasn't surprised. He knew."

Ron grunted cynically. "He probably slipped the KGB some bad information, triggering the invasion, then sends his cousin in to fabricate some more sensational stories to back it up. It's standard procedure for a PSYOP, a psychological warfare operation. We used to do it all the time in Vietnam until the press caught on. Set the fire then blame the Communists for doing it."

"I heard about the press problem from the Afghans. The Western reporters were just making up stories so they threw them out. All of them." I glanced down the list. "Tell me about the others."

"All are right-wingers. Most are ex-military or CIA or both. Only a couple are Afghan. Louis Dupree is the CIA's anthropologist, studying the natives. Wrote the book on them – *Afghanistan*. Even admitted Hafizullah Amin, the guy the Soviets overthrew, took money from the CIA. Tom Gouttierre recruits Afghan talent for the CIA. Puts them in a program he runs at the University of Nebraska. General Danny Graham is Team B *and* American Security Council. You know all about that. But you may not know how he's connected to Singlaub."

The print was so small it was barely legible. "Singlaub? Yeah, here he is. Major General John K. Singlaub USA, retired."

"Retired because Jimmy Carter fired him," Ron said.

I could still see the stolid look on the general's face staring back from the headlines. "Insubordination, wasn't it?

"If you term calling for the assassination of a standing President insubordination."

I felt a sudden disorientation as the surreal descended on my dining room.

Ron continued, "Rumor is Carter found out Singlaub met with some of his old assassin friends and was plotting a palace coup. He has all the requisite credentials. OSS during World War II. William Casey was his case officer. Joined the CIA, deputy station chief in South Korea. Oversaw political assassination programs in Laos, Cambodia and Thailand during Vietnam. Headed a delegation sponsored by the American Security Council to Guatemala with General Danny Graham in 1979. Called for a 'sympathetic understanding of the death squads.' In 1980 joins WACL, the World Anti-Communist League, and becomes active in right-wing causes. WACL is where your Committee for a Free Afghanistan goes wide."

"Wide? How wide?"

"WACL is a big supporter of Karen McKay, but it's bigger than Afghanistan. Much bigger."

The longer I listened the more I realized how deep the Afghan story went and why Theodore Eliot would have been so desperate to shout me down. Ron promised to send me copies of what he'd found and within few days the whole ugly picture began to emerge with clarity.

CHAPTER 18

How in the world could a person live a normal life knowing these things? They couldn't. Liz took it all in stride, though. "It's all going on whether we know it or not. I'd rather know it," she said.

I couldn't shake the feeling I'd been through all this before. The surrealism engulfed me. I was *in* an episode of *The Twilight Zone*. Had I returned from a past life to finish something I started so I could get on with my cosmic life?

We packed up the old station wagon for a visit with Liz's family before the meeting with Farid at the UN on Sunday. Travelling with a one year old required packing for an army. But it was *our* army. We were doing this for the future, right? I kept telling myself that, but it was getting harder to believe there would be a future I wanted to live in.

For me the five hour drive was a welcome break from the routine in our creaky bunker. At least it provided a different view, a chance at fresh air and fresh scenery.

I had shared the contents of Ron's package with Liz. My "hunch" that had brought me to Afghanistan had turned out to be beyond anything I'd once imagined. I had travelled to the inner sanctum of a struggle between the forces of light and darkness, between a fascist global criminal empire selling itself as the answer to the "other" global empire, communism, and we were in the middle of it.

We entered the toll booth in Weston and headed straight out the Mass Pike towards Sturbridge. Then down through western Connecticut and New York State. A once beautiful landscape of rustic farms and rolling hills, getting bulldozed into subdivisions, Burger Kings, J.C. Pennys and Toys R Us's. How could that possibly end well?

Ron's research dossier was way better than radio.

Liz's hands spanned the pages as she read. "WACL was formed in 1966 as an international, anticommunist mercenary group in support of right-wing governments around the world to assist in carrying out 'extra-legal' activities. WACL brings together three principal groups: Asian gangsters backed by former Axis Japanese fascists, former West German Nazis and their East European collaborators, and elements of Western intelligence keen to reorganize Hitler's anti-Communist crusade. At least three of its European chapters are controlled by former SS officers."

She grimaced in disbelief. "How can Americans not do something about this?"

"Would it make any difference?" I asked.

Liz gave me one of those looks and continued. "WACL played a major role in the CIA's drug-funded covert wars in Vietnam and now in Latin America. It has affiliations with over a hundred other right wing organizations including Young Americans for Freedom, College Republicans, Students for America, Freedom's Friends, the Conservative Caucus, Alpha 66 and the American Coalition for Traditional Values. I didn't realize we shared traditional values with Nazis."

I try to keep my eyes on the road. "Ron said WACL was where the Committee for a Free Afghanistan went wide. Who is wide?"

"It looks like everybody. Your old boss Pat Robertson from Christian Broadcasting and the WACL supports it. The American Security Council is behind it. Geoffrey Stewart-Smith, who ran the British affiliate of WACL, stated in 1974 that 'The World Anti-Communist League is largely a collection of Nazis, Fascists, anti-Semites, sellers of forgeries, vicious racialists, and corrupt self-seekers.'"

"And that's from an insider?" I commented.

Liz gazed down the long list. "They all seem to share interlocking boards of directors and organizations. The chairman of the Committee for a Free Afghanistan, Karen McKay's group, is Major General J. Milnor Roberts who is also on the board of the U.S. Council for World Freedom, the USCWF, which was also founded by Singlaub in 1981 as a parent foundation for WACL in the U.S. Lieutenant General Daniel Graham is also on the board of USCWF *and* the American Security Council, Team B and is an advisor to the Committee for a Free Afghanistan. Roger Pearson, WACL chairman from 1978 to 1980, was ousted from WACL in 1980 for his Nazi affiliations in Europe. Pearson is a proponent of eugenics and spent a lot of time in Pakistan where he adopted the Aryan racial theories popular to Hitler's inner circle. Lev Dobriansky was on the WACL board before Singlaub in the 1970s while he was chairman of the National Captive Nations Committee."

Liz shuffled around for more on Dobriansky. "Lev E. Dobriansky, author of the Captive Nations Week Resolution, 1959. Celebrated annually by Congress ever since. OSS during World War II, Pro-Nazi Ukrainian nationalist. Early neoconservative. So, WACL ties Karen McKay's Committee for a Free Afghanistan to former SS officers, the American Security Council and now the Captive Nations Committee. Theodore Eliot connects Afghanistan to the Asia Foundation, Tufts Fletcher School, Raytheon and the Bilderberg group."

I could see the picture as clear as the roadway ahead. "And the Bilderberg group oversees them all. The objectives of the American far right and Europe's World War II Nazis are the same thing. I thought Afghanistan was about getting back at the Soviet Union for Vietnam. It's not only Vietnam, is it?" I asked.

Liz shuddered, shut the folder and turned her attention to our daughter in the back seat. "It looks like the Reagan administration could care less about Vietnam. They want to finish what the Germans started in 1933 and everybody seems to be going along with it."

"And all because of Afghanistan."

We cruised into the winding hills of Milburn Township after dark. Neat streets, stately homes, large lawns bordering tree-lined avenues. Even at night it was beautiful, the outlines relaxing and reassuring to the eye. Made me feel at home, if only an illusion.

***

Sunday morning came fast. Being the first to break the blackout on news from Afghanistan had brought out the unexpected. No one from the so called "left" had rallied to our side. I'd come to appreciate James Burnham's contempt for Liberals but we couldn't stop there.

I'd come upon an internal RAND "Trip Report" written by Francis Fukuyama from 1980. It gave the strongest impression yet the Soviets had no intention of staying for the long haul. Fukuyama also suggested they wanted to get out as quickly as possible. Rumors had circulated for years that Brezhnev defied the Soviet politburo and the KGB. *If* Brezhnev had made the decision to invade on his own, then it hadn't been the politburo. *And if* it wasn't the politburo then it wasn't Soviet policy.

Nobody was putting two and two together – or appeared to want to. Aside from demonstrating a fatal weakness in Soviet leadership, Brezhnev's fiasco threw Brzezinski and Pipes' theories about Soviet intentions out the window. *Time* magazine's November 22nd issue reported that KGB defector Vladimir Kuzichkin maintained "Brezhnev himself overruled repeated advice from Andropov's KGB *not* to turn Afghanistan into a Soviet satellite." Kuzichkin also revealed the KGB considered Hafizullah Amin,

THE VALEDICTION: THREE NIGHTS OF DESMOND

the man they overthrew, to be a "cultivated Oriental charmer" who proved "to be a smooth-talking fascist who was secretly pro-Western ... had links to the Americans ... and the CIA."

The ice was beginning to melt.

Reports had been filtering out of the Soviet Union since Brezhnev's death on November 10th that the new Kremlin leader Yuri Andropov was eager to quit Afghanistan. It was hard to know what to believe. But it wasn't hard to see how Reagan was doing a rope-a-dope on the Russians. First he demanded they pull out. Then he dismissed their efforts to pull out as propaganda. And nobody called him on it. The peace process was in perpetual quagmire because the crazies wanted to keep the Soviets pinned down in Afghanistan.

The mainstream media rags were filled with articles downplaying any talk of a Soviet withdrawal. But, if they *did* want to leave and we could prove it, Carter's "greatest threat to peace since the second World War" would cease to exist. This was a huge leap that would require going back to Afghanistan to get the proof. But as fate would have it we were in exactly the right position to do just that.

CHAPTER 19

The drive to New York City was a chance to clear my head. I'd tried drafting a plan for a second Afghan trip but there were too many unknowns. I'd known nothing about the place until the Soviets crossed the border, but now I'd been flooded with facts, half-truths and wish fulfillment. I'd scheduled a meeting with the Afghan ambassador to the U.N., Farid Zarif. I hoped he was ready to move the game forward.

The ambassador was Oxford educated and well connected to Kabul's old guard upper class, trained in decorum and protocol. His background was as unlike mine as any person I'd ever met. Yet I felt as if I'd known him all my life. How strange it was, that feeling of familiarity. I'd kept Zarif up to date on our progress. Roger Fisher was on board for a trip to Kabul. "I suppose it's a long shot, but put me in for a visa and we'll see what happens," he'd said. Roger's book *Getting to Yes* had full page ads in *The New York Times*. A high profile visit to Kabul by a world-famous negotiator to clear the air on Soviet intentions would be a game changer. But even without the Soviets, sorting things out politically in Afghanistan would require all of Roger's talents.

Afghanistan's ruling "Marxist" party, the People's Democratic Party of Afghanistan (PDPA), was split into two factions – each of whom violently disagree. The PDPA shared a long tradition of progressive reforms with the royals going back centuries. But that's where the comparison stops.

My original take on his attitude toward Moscow had been right on the money. The Kremlin and the Afghans didn't get along either. Kabul's internal political problems had worsened. The feud between the Khalq and the Parcham factions was eating away at Soviet resolve. The irony was sublime. The U.S. wanted to overthrow a Communist government that the Kremlin viewed as a middle class bourgeois disaster with no support from the population. And the Kremlin was right.

Communism couldn't exist without a working class, and Afghanistan simply did not have one. But that trivial detail didn't matter to Washington.

Zarif and his family occupied a pleasant second floor apartment in Queens in a quiet neighborhood, replete with hibachi on the back porch for grilling kabobs. It was an old-style New York neighborhood, unlike the barren glass and steel death star of Manhattan. I parked down the street and around the corner in case somebody was watching. I had to assume they were. Reagan had declared a state of emergency and Americans didn't even know it.

We made our way upstairs and were greeted warmly by Zarif. But the apartment was empty – uninhabited. "Alia and the boys are in California visiting family," he said, "but sit and I'll get some coffee."

Now I really was suspicious. Zarif represented a whole country at the UN. He always had people around him – staff, bodyguards. But that day, nobody. He wanted to talk to us alone.

"We've been getting feedback on the documentary," I offered as he returned with the coffee. "Most is good but some dismiss everything I saw as propaganda. I even had a call from Karen McKay from the Committee for a Free Afghanistan."

Zarif was visibly taken aback. "You mean Karen McKay from the CIA," he said, as he drew circles in the air with his finger. "What was that name? Rewind the tape!"

"Yes. We were just reading about her," Liz whispered.

Now I was the one taken aback. Zarif grinned and walked over to a nearby radio and switched it on to a local news broadcast.

"I have a variety of bugging detectors," he said as he pulled up a chair opposite us. "I haven't had time to sweep recently, so this will have to do."

"Do the Russians give you those?" I asked, trying to cover my general ignorance of such things.

Zarif grinned. "No, I bought them in Times Square. Whatever Moscow has it wouldn't be as good." We both laughed.

Of course it wouldn't. James Bond and SMERSH were fantasies cooked up to sell a gullible public bigger defense budgets. The reality was much simpler. America was a high tech paradise and Moscow was a long way away.

"Did you receive the tapes I sent you?"

Zarif was candid. "Yes. Your documentary was well received. They all agreed," he said. "It may be the first time."

"So when do we go back?" I asked, trying to anticipate his mood. "Roger has offered to return to Kabul with us."

I reached into my briefcase and pulled out the full page add in *The New York Times* for *Getting to Yes*.

Zarif was impressed as he read the ad. "Fisher is well known to us. He is respected in the Muslim world."

"He's also known to the Soviets and the Pakistanis," I added. "He worked the back channel for Washington for the hostage negotiations with Iran. He might be able to get through where others can't."

Zarif lost himself in thought. "The Americans are making it very hard for us," he said finally. "And that doesn't make sense. They were never against us, even after Daoud was killed. They were always friendly. But these people they're supporting want to destroy every-thing we've built in the last hundred years." He sat back in his chair and reflected thoughtfully. "Since I've been at the UN I have tried to figure out who is pulling the strings. But now I don't think it's the Americans."

Zarif reached over to his briefcase next to the sofa, withdrew a docu-ment, and handed it to me. "British commandos have been training rebels in Pakistan. SAS soldiers established a camp inside Afghanistan but they were caught in the act," he said.

"SAS?"

"Strategic Air Services. Their soldiers escaped but we retrieved their passports."

I scanned the document then passed it on to Liz. "I haven't seen any reports about this," I admitted.

"And you likely won't." Zarif moved over to the radio and turned up the volume.

"The British were given control of the media. William Casey has in-vited two of their top people in to, as you say, run the show. Karen McK-ay's Committee for Afghanistan is a subgroup under the control of Lord Nicholas Bethell's Radio Free Kabul. Bethell is a lord-in-waiting to Queen Elizabeth."

"A lord-in-waiting?"

"He holds the rank of the Sovereign. He's one of the Queen's stand-ins when she's not available. It's the highest possible rank in the British government next to the queen herself. He is also a career MI6 official, specializing in Iranian and Arab affairs."

The true depth of our involvement was sinking in fast. "And who's the other?"

"The other is Afghan Aid UK. It was founded by Viscount Cranbourne, Lord Privy Seal and Leader of the House of Lords. But it's run by the wife of a British journalist working undercover for MI-6, John Fullerton."

To say I was shocked would have been an understatement. "House of Lords? Nicholas Bethell? Viscount Cranbourne?"

"Cranbourne is a member of the Cecil Family. One of his ancestors was Lord Privy Seal and Treasurer to Queen Elizabeth I."

It was a good thing I was sitting down. Here I'd thought I had Afghanistan to myself and I was finding out I'd been sharing it with two British Lords and two Queens of England, both named Elizabeth. That made three.

I'd wished Zarif was kidding but I'd known he wasn't. Everything about this project had my home address written all over it. From the moment I'd met him to the time I'd set foot in Kabul to the confrontation with Theodore Eliot, there was an overwhelming sense of Déjà vu, as if I had fought this fight before. Over the years I'd discovered the name Fitzgerald came with a legacy of some fictional Camelot.

I knew our family had descended on England with William the Conqueror and then on to Ireland with a Norman Baron named Strongbow. I'd never given it much thought but the family history was filled with soldiers, priests and a heavy dose of mysticism. There were also ghosts, phantom armies and fantastic legends. But what if the real legacy wasn't a fiction, but a metaphor for something else. The more I looked into it, the more the real legacy began to make sense. Medieval ruins all over my grandfather's Irish village shot through with cannonballs told the true story. They'd been on the good side, and the bad side of the royal family for centuries. That was until they came up against Elizabeth I and things turned very bad. Elizabeth brought the full weight of the emerging British Empire – Reformation, war, famine and theft. And here she was looming out of the past because of Afghanistan. Was it coincidence or something more?

God knew Theodore Eliot carried his ancestors' Puritan legacy in his back pocket and went overboard to pick a fight. Was there a feud still on? I'd begun to feel as though a voice of the dead was calling out to me. Sitting there in that second floor flat in Queens, I realized that voice was speaking with a British accent – and it was telling me in no uncertain terms to get on with it.

CHAPTER 20

The American government was acting as if it was under remote control and it looked like that control was coming from London. Reagan's CIA director William Casey had been station chief in London during World War II and picked up the empire's holy mission while there. Together with his buddy Leo Cherne they'd basically invented America's military industrial complex. The direction behind that complex appeared to be the old British Empire, but it hadn't been obvious to me until then. Was I missing something, and if so, what? Washington acted as if America was calling the shots, but America had absolutely no history with Afghanistan. I had no connection to Afghanistan either, yet I felt instinctively drawn to the place. So where was that coming from?

Zarif believed Roger's long shot at an invitation wasn't all that long. If we could do this trip, we might be able to change a lot of peoples' thinking and maybe influence the course of history, but getting the story out was becoming increasingly difficult.

It was no secret the Reagan administration was doing everything in its power to build support for its anti-Soviet agenda in Afghanistan. What *was* a secret was their plan to use the Public Broadcasting System to bathe the American people in fascist propaganda by using private money to cover their tracks.

This well-crafted script that had started with Theodore Eliot and Richard Pipes on *MacNeil Lehrer* within days of the Soviet invasion had warped into a full-blown disinformation campaign out of the Reagan White House. Right wing philanthropies were now underwriting a fascist agenda on Afghanistan and nobody in the PBS system had any interest in confronting them.

WGBY's Mark Erstling had passed along one of the new privately funded offerings titled *Afghanistan: Caught In the Struggle* which made it pretty clear what Liz and I were up against.

"DESCRIPTION: IS AFGHANISTAN THE SOVIETS' VIETNAM? THIS DOCUMENTARY EXPLORES THE STRATEGIC SIGNIFICANCE OF RUSSIAN TROOPS IN AFGHANISTAN AND THE

TRAGIC EFFECT THIS HAS ON THE AFGHAN PEOPLE. AR-
NAUD DEBORCHGRAVE, AUTHOR AND FORMER SENIOR EDI-
TOR OF *NEWSWEEK* SERVES AS HOST AND NARRATOR."

Sponsored by: The Shelby Cullom Davis Foundation, Sarah Scaife
Foundation, Pittsburgh-Des Moines Corporation and the Afghanistan
Relief Committee.

When hanging out in Harvard Square, I often went to the Brattle Theatre to see black and white film classics. It even had a bar attached to it
named the Blue Parrot in honor of the film Casablanca. That was where
the Harvard frat boys could practice being Humphrey Bogart almost any
night of the week.

So I recognized the outpouring of concern for the "tragic effect" of
Soviet troops on the Afghan people as the stock Hollywood come-on it
was. Cue Bogart from the scene at the Blue Parrot. *What time is it in New
York? I'll bet they're asleep in New York. They're asleep all over America.* Dan
Rather had even used it in his coast-to-coast broadcast from the Afghan
border: Wake up America. The bad guys are coming for you.

The CIA's psychological warfare project Mockingbird exposed by the
Church Committee had done its job on the American mind. Fascists
calling Communists "Fascists." Unbelievable. Belgian Prince Arnaud de
Borchgrave, author of *The Spike* and cousin of the director of French intelligence, Count Alexander de Marenches, was the voice of the old European aristocracy. Shelby Cullom Davis: Wall Street banker and one
of the 400 richest men in America with a lineage that traced back to the
Mayflower. The Sarah Scaife Foundation: Named after Richard Scaife's
deceased mother. Richard Scaife was also one of the 400 richest men in
America and the most generous donor to fascist causes in American history. The Pittsburgh-Des Moines Corporation was the steel company that
fabricated the exterior façade of the World Trade Towers which was home
to CIA headquarters in New York. And of course the Afghanistan Relief
Committee was the quasi-official U.S. government operation run by investment banker John Train who wanted Europe's deposed aristocracy
returned to power.

Another package arrived from Ron in Washington. The search nar-
rowed. Scaife was the lynchpin between Washington and London. He
tied the American fascists to the CIA and the British Intelligence Service,
MI6. Scaife had been secretly funding a British agent named Brian Crozier and one of his propaganda organizations, the Institute for the Study of
Conflict (ISC), since at least 1973. Crozier operated other secret groups

with interlocking directorates that kept their identities and activities hidden. With Scaife's help, Crozier, his protégé Robert Moss and Arnaud de Borchgrave had been actively engaged in a plot to undermine democracies in Europe, South America and even North America.

Ron included a recent *Der Spiegel* article naming one of Crozier's secret groups as the "Pinay Circle" or "le Cercle." It documented claims that the Circle had been slowly setting the stage for a fascist rollover of Western Democracies since the 1950s. With the election of Ronald Reagan to the White House, they had realized their goal.

I doubted that most Americans had any idea how PBS was being controlled by people with an openly fascist agenda. The Committee for a Free Afghanistan's Board of Directors and advisors were an encyclopedia of the farthest right you could get with direct links to Hitler and the Axis powers of the 1930s.

I was finding it unbelievable that this could be happening here in the U.S. The depth and breadth were almost too much to absorb, but I had to focus on the objective: Find a network to underwrite another trip to Kabul with Roger Fisher, Director of the Harvard Negotiation Project. The headline was *Getting the Soviets out of Afghanistan: What are the chances of unwinding President Jimmy Carter's "Greatest threat to peace since the Second World War."*

***

We arranged to meet Roger for lunch at a popular eatery in the middle of Harvard Square known as the Wursthaus. I actually liked German cooking – bratwurst, sauerkraut, beer. Always beer. But the Wursthaus would have been better named the Worst House. That time of day the place was packed with grumpy grey-haired men in Harris Tweeds and wingtips. Some were probably famous in their own right, but you wouldn't have known it from their gruff manner and lack of personality. I'd never gotten used to the old Yankee culture and its deathlike embrace of that grim, bleached-out Puritan existence. My mother used to say the Yankees put their money in the bank and not on their backs. If she'd gotten a load of that place she'd see they didn't put it into their stomachs either.

Roger joined us and got right down to business. "I was in Moscow in October and an old Soviet friend spent several days trying to get a hold of me. When he did he said, 'How do we get out of Afghanistan?' I told him that was the last question I expected him to ask."

There. We had it. "So they *do* want to get out."

"He said by *we* I mean Americans as well as Russians."

I wondered what Roger knew of the U.S. involvement. "And you told him what?"

"I said it's a lot easier for us to get out than you."

Liz perked up. "And how would that work?"

"Well, that depends on what they're willing to give up. We don't know that yet. We have to assume their military has *some* strategic objective, or maybe just tactical objectives."

"And that's where you come in."

Roger smiled. The situation was clear. "Exactly."

Roger was a Harvard lawyer who wrote the book on getting to yes. You could see his passion and enthusiasm for making negotiation theory work in any situation. He'd dedicated his life to it. But Afghanistan wasn't that clear. I knew from my first trip and my talks with Zarif that the official story pushed out by Ted Eliot and Richard Pipes was utter bullshit. Afghanistan was the opposite of the stark black and white they painted it. But they were too deeply invested in it to ever back out. The Afghan "communists" were unhappy with the Soviets and the Soviets were unhappy with the Afghan "communists" who weren't really communists at all, according to the Soviets. The Soviets had been tricked into going in and then wanted to get out as quickly as possible, but the U.S. was keeping them tied down. Revenge for Vietnam was clearly a motive. But it went deeper than that. An enormous public relations campaign was underway to make Afghanistan Russia's Vietnam in everyone's mind. It was a Hollywood movie in the making and it was being scripted by a gang of Nazis, posing as brave freedom fighters. Reality had been flipped inside out.

And where was the American left in all this? Where were the liberals and the moderates who were so incensed by the Nixon administration's extension of the Vietnam War and its domestic covert abuses just a few years ago? Overwhelmed with a multitude of causes both at home and in Central and South America, the "left" were nowhere to be found and wanted nothing to do with Afghanistan. And so we were left to do it on our own.

CHAPTER 21

"A re you sure you want to continue with this?" Ron asked.

"You already asked me that."

"No, I asked you if you wanted to get into it. I thought by now you might be having second thoughts."

I tried to ignore his concerns. "What have you got?"

There was a brief silence. "This guy Crozier. I don't understand it."

"Don't be cryptic. Don't understand what?"

"I never heard of the guy before now, but he's been moving around inside the system for decades. He shouldn't be there. I mean he shouldn't be here. He's British, writes for *The Economist*. But then he runs Forum World Features for the CIA. Fabricates stories and delivers them to hundreds of newspapers around the world. When his cover was blown he went private and created the Institute for the Study of Conflict, the ISC."

"Remind me about the ISC?"

"ISC is the privatized version of Britain's World War II propaganda office. Puts out phony 'studies' to emphasize the Soviet threat. In 1973 Crozier and his protégé Robert Moss wrote the instruction manual for overthrowing the Chilean government. Claimed the KGB infiltrated the British election of 1974. Recommended to the British military they stage a coup of their own government to prevent a Soviet takeover based on information he's fabricated. He's exposed in the press as a British agent working for the CIA but it doesn't stop him. Then in 1975, despite a ban on the CIA backing propaganda inside the U.S and even as Congress investigates his covert activities for the CIA, he sets up a Washington branch of ISC called WISC. And get this. Who does he get to help him set it up? Two of the biggest movers and shakers in Washington; George Ball and Zbigniew Brzezinski. He brings in Kermit Roosevelt who'd staged the 1953 coup in Iran, Robert Komer, architect of the Phoenix program in Vietnam, and none other than Richard Pipes. Pipes is picked the next year to head the B Team experiment which uses Crozier's methodology of fabricated threats and misinformation and the rest is history."

I am mystified. "So Crozier brings Brzezinski together with Richard Pipes at WISC which formulates the creation of Team B. Team B then fabricates a distorted picture of the Soviet threat and Brzezinski goes in as National Security Advisor under Carter to implement it."

"It's worse than that," Ron said.

"How could it be worse than that?"

"Carter elevated the National Security Advisor to cabinet level and asked Brzezinski to devise a new chain of command. Brzezinski gives himself control of all the important stuff before they even step into the White House while everybody else is left to blow hot air."

"And what about the Secretary of State?"

"All Vance can do is react."

"So Brzezinski staged a silent coup and nobody even knew it."

"Except Carter. But it didn't end there," Ron said as he filled in the blanks.

"Less than a month after he takes over, Brzezinski introduced a new approach to the SALT talks that neither Vance nor the Soviets are prepared for. He even rigged the delivery of the instructions to arrive at the last minute so Vance had to meet the Soviets unprepared. When negotiations fail as expected, he then expanded nuclear targeting options from 25,000 to 40,000 which the Soviets view as a huge provocation."

***

"I'm not surprised," Liz said when she hears what Brzezinski did. "Carter was one of Hyman Rickover's boys. The guy who fathered the nuclear navy?"

"Carter claimed that after his parents Rickover was the greatest influence on his life. Brzezinski must have been third. Carter was Brzezinski's protégé as well. It's the opposite of what people think. Brzezinski picked Carter as a presidential candidate for David Rockefeller."

"I thought a totally unknown Georgia governor got to be President because God wanted it," I said, trying to lighten the subject but Liz was on the case.

"Carter was supposed to advance détente and SALT, not start a new Cold War. Pundits joke he's so innocent and pure he can't find his way to the bathroom but he brings a known Russophobe into the White House? Then he gives him the power to make every top level decision and nobody notices?" Liz leaned forward in her chair. "That's Machiavellian."

"But even Machiavelli needs a sacrifice to make the plot work – and that's where Afghanistan comes in," I added.

Liz thought for a moment before a flash of brilliance struck. "They needed a sacrifice. But they needed someone to set the trap for it – and that's where Adolph Dubs fits in."

***

I couldn't deny the logic. From the outside, the events surrounding the February 1979 death of Ambassador Adolph Dubs made no sense. The Soviets desperately needed better relations with the U.S. and so did the Afghans, but his brutal murder at the hands of the Afghan police ended any hope. Brzezinski used the event to turn the tide, claiming the Soviets wanted Dubs dead to fulfill their evil plan to conquer the Persian Gulf. But if you looked at it from within the context of Brzezinski's strategic plan, it was Brzezinski who benefitted from Dubs' death, not the Soviets. Just before Dubs was appointed, Afghanistan had been lowered to the bottom of the State Department's priority list. It had long ago been passed over as an ally. Its main source of economic and military aid was the Soviet Union and it offered them nothing in return.

"Afghanistan wasn't really important to anybody," Liz said. "So why all the fuss?

"Because it's a perfect trap," I told her. "It's off everybody's radar."

"Except Brzezinski's?" she said before I dive in.

"There are three critical events that are tied together: The April 1978 Marxist coup that brought Hafizullah Amin to power, the kidnapping and death of Ambassador Dubs in February 1979, and the Soviet invasion ten months later that took Amin out. We know Brzezinski initiated covert action inside Soviet territory from the minute he got into the White House in 1977," I said.

"And that covert action meshes perfectly with Brzezinski's operation to enflame ethnic tensions with his Nationalities Working Group," Liz said, following up.

"Exactly. And a key operative of that group is the Kabul CIA station Chief Graham Fuller. Fuller is on board with Brzezinski's objective to stir up Muslim hatred but that backfires and brings down both Mohammed Daoud and the Shah."

"Which may have been the intent," Liz countered.

"The April, 1978 Marxist coup against Daoud does play perfectly into Brzezinski's 'predictions' of a Soviet master plan. Cyrus Vance dismissed Brzezinski's claim as just another Cold War fantasy. The State Department's intelligence unit found no evidence of Soviet complicity. But

Brzezinski uses it anyway to enlist the Chinese to train the Afghan warlord Gulbuddin Hekmatyar's rebels in Xinxiang province."

"Why would Brzezinski undermine Daoud?" Liz asked.

"Daoud had been detested by the CIA since the early 1950s. He played the U.S. off against the Soviets, courted the leftists, and threatened Pakistan. Nobody in Washington was sad to see him go and the so-called Marxist PDPA was greeted with enthusiasm by U.S. Ambassador Theodore Eliot. The CIA had been messing with Daoud through Pakistan and Iran from at least 1973. They set the stage for the 1978 Marxist coup. The coup caught both the Soviets and the State Department by surprise and the Soviets only supported it after it became a fait accompli. The coup plotters fought bitterly and the coup leader, Hafizullah Amin, raised doubts on both sides as an agent provocateur."

"And that's where Al Lowenstein's student organization comes in," Liz said, recalling her research. "The CIA used the NSA as a recruitment tool for future Third World leaders, and Amin had become one of those leaders."

"And Adolph Dubs intended to reel him in," I said. "But there's something missing from the picture."

Both Liz and I sensed it.

"Selig Harrison told us Dubs met with Amin fourteen times and that the meetings were often impromptu," I said, trying to make sense of the scraps of evidence we'd pulled together.

"The people at the embassy reported he did no such thing," Liz replied.

"Dubs is responsible for coordinating with eight competing U.S. agencies assigned to the embassy – 150 official Americans – DEA, USIA, DOD, AID, Peace Corp, CIA. The conflict with Washington had to reach inside the embassy. He knew Brzezinski didn't approve so he kept his meetings off the record."

"So Dubs met with Amin secretly so Brzezinski can't find out. What's the big deal?"

"Brzezinski has been running a covert operation to undermine the Afghan government since January of 1977. He *wants* religious fanatics running the government not Afghan nationalists, and Dubs is screwing it up."

I reached down to a growing pile of papers and pulled one out. "I found the Post-Profile job description issued by the State Department just before the coup back in April 1978. 'A succession struggle, when aging President Daoud passes from the scene, could well lead to unpredictable – possibly violent – political developments affecting the stability of the region,' it says."

It was Liz's turn to be shocked. "So the State Department expected a coup."

"And Brzezinski's covert op made sure it happened. Everybody on the ground I talked to in Kabul said Amin was behind the whole thing – assassinating his rivals, murdering the Royal family and wrecking his own political party, the PDPA. He had Daoud's police in his pocket the night of the coup. They arrested everybody else but him."

Liz thought it over. "So all this happens just before Dubs arrives and a year after Brzezinski started destabilizing."

"Dubs' assignment was to establish a 'close personal relationship' with Amin and detach him. That was the word Harrison used – detach. He has to 'implement a complex AID program and coordinate an intensive multinational and UN effort to control narcotics production and trafficking.'"

Liz's interest was piqued. "It says that?"

I pulled the sheaf of papers off my desk and handed it over. She reads, "'Afghanistan is a major source of opium and cannabis production, and we are working *closely* with the Afghan Government and international agencies to control narcotics cultivation and trafficking.' Remember what that whistle blower who said she got a look at the classified folder told us?"

"Who? The crazy one?"

"She said the Dubs' murder wasn't about politics. It was about a drug deal gone wrong."

"Then maybe she wasn't so crazy."

Liz flipped through the pages. "The U.S. was already working closely with the Afghan government on narcotics trafficking when Dubs arrived. 'Closely,' it says. It was part of the ambassador's job."

"Yeah. But Brzezinski keeps up the destabilization. Dubs complains to Washington but Brzezinski blocks Vance from doing anything. The situation on the ground gets worse and worse. Brzezinski sends his guy, Thomas P. Thornton from the NSC in January of 1979 to tell him to knock it off. But he doesn't. But Dubs is having a problem with Amin, too. The CIA has sheep dipped him."

"What does that mean?" Liz asked.

"It means the CIA *wanted* the Russians to think Amin was on their payroll. He's compromised but too bullheaded to realize it. He disses the Soviets. The KGB is convinced he's CIA. Dubs goes to his station chief and demands to know if he is CIA. He's told no, but no matter what Dubs does to assure the Russians, Amin keeps raising Russian suspicions he's plotting something."

"So now Dubs is caught between the Russians, Amin and Brzezinski."

Liz took one more look at the Post Profile. "It says here that Afghanistan is 'a remote and unhealthy environment.'"

I tried to fit it into the task at hand. "It certainly was for Adolph Dubs and Hafizullah Amin. Let's hope it's not for us."

CHAPTER 22

The year came to a close with a propaganda barrage declaring the Soviets had too much to lose to quit Afghanistan. By the end of March Yuri Andropov had gone public with his support for the UN peace talks. But Reuters still insisted "there are no signs of a breakthrough and the Soviet leadership has given no indication of a willingness to withdraw." It was becoming clear the U.S. didn't want the Soviet Union out of Afghanistan and the press was just parroting the Reagan administration's line.

Getting back to Afghanistan in 1983 would not be like the spring of 1981. Since the last trip the story had settled into a no-man's-land of fabricated unrealities created by the CIA and British intelligence. It would be harder than ever to tell what was real.

Reagan had brought some old 1950s Cold Warriors back to Washington who behaved as if the 1960s and 70s never happened. The warring parties were divided into two camps – neoconservative ideologues and realists, and the ideologues were clearly winning. Their spell hung over the town like a drug. No one even considered the Soviets might have actually wanted to leave Afghanistan because nobody wanted the spell to end.

After some initial questioning over Soviet motives I got the feeling the media was running scared. The wisdom of supplying weapons to radical, drug-dealing Islamic terrorists to kill Russians was never questioned – only whether the weapons supplied were doing the job.

The *Columbia Journalism Review* noted the strangeness in an early 1981 issue and put Dan Rather at the epicenter of the media problem.

"By April 6, 1980 Tad Szulc in the *New York Times Magazine* was discussing the CIA's supply operation in considerable detail. That same day, *60 Minutes* broadcast *Inside Afghanistan*, a report on Dan Rather's journey across the Pakistani border. By relying almost entirely on the statements of Afghan rebels and a Pakistani information officer, Rather managed to consolidate popular misconceptions about the war into one high-impact, coast-to-coast broadcast."

Misconceptions, falsehoods, fraud and outright lies. According to the *Review*, Rather's broadcast represented a "watershed" event that swayed the *Times,* the *Post, Newsweek,* and *U.S. News & World Report,* away from exposing the CIA's operation to either denying its existence or dismissing its importance.

"Today, many hard questions are not being asked," it said. "Among them is whether, in fact, the U.S. wants the Soviets out of Afghanistan, or prefers to make the country Russia's Vietnam." Dan Rather – how could one report, by one reporter have carried such weight? Rather was chosen to chronicle the Zapruder film of the JFK assassination and he misreported the critical moment of Kennedy's death that would have shown the Warren Commission was a lie. Rather was an inside joke. People had laughed at him when he showed up in Pakistan dressed like an Afghan "freedom fighter." Gunga Dan – George Byers Griffin had snickered in Kabul when I told him I was working for CBS News. He would have been more accurate calling him *Flashman* – George MacDonald Fraser's cowardly Victorian adventurer who gets drawn into the Indian Empire's conquest of Afghanistan and winds up a hero. I remembered reading it back in the early 1970s. Absurd comic book-fiction, Saturday matinee cliffhanger – How to get away with bullshit in the Hindu Kush and come out smelling like a rose. That was Dan Rather and it explained why he didn't like my Afghanistan. I wasn't following the *Flashman* script. But what was the script? Hell, what was American policy? What did American policymakers even know about Afghanistan? Afghanistan was a British thing – the Great Game they called it. The record showed the U.S. had no experience there. None. The idea got me thinking. Who was the first American to go to Afghanistan?

Liz agreed. There was a huge gap in our understanding of Afghanistan. She dug around at the local library, and what do you think she found?

"*The Memoirs of Colonel Alexander Gardner,*" she said proudly. "*Soldier and Traveler.*"

I read the cover out loud. "*Colonel of Artillery In The Service Of Maharaja Ranjit Singh.* Sounds pretty British. William Blackwood and sons, Edinburgh and London MDCCCXCVIII?"

"1898. Yes it does and it is," Liz said before adding to the colorful picture. "Educated in Ireland. Some say he was of Scottish descent, some say Irish. But he's an American. The first."

Gardner's unusual picture caught my eye. He was holding a sword while posing in a Tartan plaid suit of his own design with matching turban; he practically leapt off the page.

"Look at this guy," I said in amazement.

Liz was ecstatic. "He'd bloodied that sword soldiering through Central Asia in the 1820s. Signed on as a mercenary with the rebel prince Habibullah Khan to challenge his uncle, the Afghan King, Dost Mohammed, then went native," Liz said, winking. "Married an Afghan princess, fathered a son by her and then lost them both to murder when Habibullah was defeated by his uncle. He fled to Kafiristan high in the Hindu Kush and then wandered on to the Punjab where he served as a colonel in the army of Maharaja Ranjit Singh and become a legend in the Great Game. He is the role model for both Fraser's *Flashman* and Kipling's *The Man Who Would Be King*. But he's real."

"Two British icons who were in the end one American," I said. "How strange."

Liz was ecstatic. "Gardner's exploits were so fantastic Royal geographers back in London thought they were invented."

I wasn't surprised. "That's because he wasn't one of *them*. If he'd been from a noble family you can bet they'd have knighted him."

"But they couldn't deny he'd singlehandedly saved the City of Lahore," she continued. "After his fellow soldiers deserted him he fired off the canons and killed 300 attackers as they charged the gates."

"Wow, 300 attackers?" I was glad to find a fellow American I could empathize with over Afghanistan but even Alexander Gardner would have blanched at the fictions that continued to pour out of CBS News. A letter from my producer Mark Erstling read:

> *Dear Paul,*
>
> *This article appeared in the April 6 edition of* Variety *about CBS News. Thought you'd find it most interesting, especially some of the claims that CBS and the independents involved are making. You might find it to your best advantage to respond in some form.*
>
> Sincerely,
> Mark

Gunga Dan and Peter Larkin had outdone themselves this time. Not content with the footage I'd brought back two years ago they'd finally found someone to get them what they wanted and they couldn't stop bragging about it.

> *In a real journalistic coup, CBS News this week had begun airing videotapes of Soviet troop movements in and around Kabul, the Afghanistan capital. It may have been the first time a Western country had smuggled*

> *uncensored videotapes out of the Soviet-held sector of the country in the*
> *past two years, and it was certainly a first for any U.S. news organiza-*
> *tion. "When the Russians see this they'll go bonkers," said Peter Larkin,*
> *foreign editor for CBS News. "This shows the world what's happening.*
> *It doesn't show shooting or villages burning, but it does show Russians*
> *there in large numbers."*

It just kept getting better. It had taken Peter Larkin another two years to get Dan Rather what he wanted, but denying our story had ever happened went too far for me.

The *Columbia Journalism Review* had warned its readers about Dan Rather's original effort to "consolidate popular misconceptions about the war." I'd been called by Major Karen McKay to get my misconceptions in line. But this was ridiculous.

"'Just think of it,' said an obviously jubilant Larkin," I read, my eyes burning a hole in the text. "After looking over some five or six full video-cassettes of uncensored news, 'when the Vietnam war was going on we saw it – for ten years. But the Russians are in Afghanistan with 100,000 troops rewriting the manual about how to conduct a military operation, and they've managed to do it for two years and no one's ever managed to see a thing.'"

The story ended by saying that the image of Soviet forces "is almost certain to stir up renewed international furor over the Soviet military presence in Afghanistan," which was exactly what Peter Larkin and Dan Rather wanted to do. It was now clear. CBS wasn't reporting news. They were making it up. This couldn't go on. We had been told by Farid Zarif that Roger would be invited to accompany us on another trip to Kabul. CBS was probably the only network that would have the budget to cover something like that. So I used *Variety* as my chance to re-connect with Peter Larkin and offer him the chance to repent his Kabul extravaganza.

CHAPTER 23

"I saw your footage of Kabul," I told Peter on the phone.
He was not jubilant to hear from me. "Yeah, wasn't that something? The Russians are all over the place. It's just like Saigon."
"I read your interview about it in *Variety*," I said as I quoted his words. "The first uncensored videotapes out of the Soviet held sector? A view from the other side of the battle? A point of view seldom heard before in the West since the Soviet invasion? Wasn't that exactly what I gave you two years ago?"
"That was two years ago."
"But you claimed this guy Eric Durschmied was the first one to do it."
The phone went silent again.
"We're going back to Kabul. Are you interested?"
"I'm always interested," he said in that cold, border-guard tone I'd first encountered two years ago.
"And we're bringing Roger Fisher from the Harvard Negotiation Project this time," I added.
Now it was Larkin's turn to be mystified. "Why?" he asked after a long pause.
"To find out what the chances are for a Soviet pullout."
Peter Larkin's curiosity was miraculously renewed. "Everything we hear indicates they're staying for the long haul. You saw the videotapes. They're bringing in thousands of reinforcements."
"Andropov has been making overtures," I replied.
"Andropov? Overtures? He's a KGB guy."
Larkin was stalling so I asked again, "Are you interested or not?
"You can come in and we'll talk about it."
"Liz and I will be in New York on Monday."
Larkin was cold and abrupt. "Monday's all right. Mid-morning," and that's all he said.
We drove down to New Jersey the next day and spent the weekend with Liz's family. Now that we had the permission, the pressure was on to find a sponsor for the trip. There were only three games in town; ABC,

CBS and NBC, but so far nobody was biting. Somebody must want this. We started the next day by visiting NBC News foreign editor Jerry Lamprecht. NBC was known for taking risks and they weren't as ideological as CBS.

"I watched your documentary. It's good. Afghanistan's a tough assignment. It was never easy to move around there, even before the Russians," Lamprecht said.

We presented a detailed background on the UN negotiations and what we'd like to cover and we were momentarily encouraged. "So can you back the trip?" I asked.

"I'd be interested in a right of first refusal," he countered. "Just to look at your material to see if we could use it, but that's as far as I can go."

We called over to West 57th for a meeting with Peter Larkin but found my definition and his definition of mid-morning to be two different things.

Peter was in a sour mood. "I'm already too busy. Come by this afternoon after two. Things might be quieter then but I can't guarantee it."

"Don't get your hopes up over CBS," I told Liz. She tried to reach a possible contact at ABC but had no luck. We traveled over to the East side for a meeting with our lawyer at Debevoise & Plimpton before heading over to West 57th.

"I don't understand why you're having such a hard time," he said. "I was sure that story would make you a star. You got CBS a world-wide exclusive. And now they're claiming it never happened? Very strange."

***

Strange indeed. Events were moving very quickly over Afghanistan but the American media didn't seem to care. The Arnaud de Borchgrave/Robert Moss system – tarring everyone that doesn't agree with them as a KGB dupe – seemed to rule the media. Afghanistan was owned by the right-wing and most news people just didn't want to touch it. We arrived at West 57th and found Peter Larkin to be at his most uncomfortable, which is to say, very uncomfortable.

"They won't let you shoot any military," he said. "The Russians censor everything now."

"You're sure it's Russians?" I asked.

"Yeah, it's Russians."

"So how did your guy Durschmied get his footage out?"

Peter looked down despondently at his desk. "If I don't tell you then you won't have to lie," he said, avoiding eye contact.

"I have been to Afghan TV. I've met their people. They have the latest Sony 3/4" machines. What makes you think the tapes are censored by Russians?"

The question annoyed Peter. "Because the Afghans are too stupid to know how."

"Oh," I said, backpedaling. "Have you thought over what I told you on the phone?"

"What's to think over? Kabul is crawling with Russian soldiers. They're beefing up their forces. They're not going anywhere."

"That not what I read in the *New York Times*," I said as snidely as I could. "The Soviets have been making it clear for months that they want to withdraw their forces. There's even talk of bringing the king back from exile to form a coalition government."

"Well I don't know what you've read, but those things take time. Besides, they never tell you what's really going on."

"Roger Fisher's been talking to people behind the scenes. He says they're ready to go, now."

"And who is Roger?"

"*Getting to Yes*? Harvard Law School? Did a documentary series for PBS called *Arabs and Israelis*?"

Larkin seemed distracted. "I'll have to talk to Dan." He checked his watch. "And what does he want from us?"

"You'll have to talk to him."

"Then we'll do it on a conference call. I have to go."

***

Having failed to raise any direct interest from anybody, a conference call was better than nothing. We got back to Boston, briefed Roger on our history with CBS and his secretary set up the call. By the end of the week we were in his office at Harvard Law School and on the phone but Larkin is glum.

"We don't think there's much credence to the Soviets getting out of Afghanistan," he said.

"Look," Roger replied, "I've been in contact with Soviet sources as well as Diego Cordovez at the UN. Cordovez has an agreement on a comprehensive settlement at Geneva. Differences can be overcome. Moscow wants a withdrawal over eighteen months. Pakistan wants it done in six. Moscow will slowly phase out the Karmal government and give the rural tribes more autonomy if Pakistan agrees to stop supporting the insurgency."

"So what do you want us to do about it?" Larkin asked.

"I want to go to Kabul and meet with Afghan officials," Roger replied. "I then want a live interview on the evening news– "

Larkin interrupted. "Dan doesn't do dead interviews."

Roger glanced at me and smiled. "You know what I mean. I don't want to be edited."

"Live interviews aren't part of the format. We'll interview you when you get back, but I can't guarantee you won't be edited."

The conference call ended without a commitment or even encouragement. I called Peter Larkin the next day and he confirmed that Dan Rather has no interest in the story.

"It's just not the kind of thing we want to do right now," he said.

That was just great. I'd convinced Roger Fisher and the Afghan government to let us go to Kabul and find out what it would take to get the Soviets to withdraw their forces, and the American media could care less. So what did I do next? Time was now of the essence. We had to find a network sponsor while the window to Kabul was still open. Roger agreed to intervene directly and a meeting was arranged with Bill Lord, head man at ABC's *Nightline*.

Back in New York the entire event was short, low profile and all business. Lord would back the trip. He left me with the distinct impression he thought I was somebody's secret agent, but not sure whose. I got that a lot. Actually there were moments when I felt I *was* being driven by some secret code. I just wished I knew where it came from.

I wangled a few boxes of blank video cassettes and considered myself lucky to get them. I would fly to Delhi alone at midnight and arrive in Kabul on Wednesday the 4th of May. Liz would stay behind to finish the contract then fly to Prague on Saturday with Roger, his wife Carrie, the crew and the equipment and arrive on Monday the 9th.

It was to be a sprint and I was on the back stretch. I'd already lost fifteen pounds to anxiety over the last month and the strain had caught in my throat. My years as a professional singer had left me with damaged vocal cords that made speaking and sometimes breathing difficult. Combined with all the pressure, it was an added nuisance I didn't need.

CHAPTER 24

T he flight to Delhi from New York was a welcome breather. I buckled my seat belt and closed my eyes. I'd done this run before, so I was on autopilot. I had accepted my fate. I knew who and what to ask for, how to deal with the Afghan government, and what to expect from the American media. I had found myself helping to engineer a backdoor deal to resolve an international crisis. There was no telling where this would go.

I was returning to Afghanistan to assess the chances of a Soviet withdrawal and gain an uncensored view of life. I was continuing in the enterprise because I found myself siding with the Afghans. It wasn't altruism or ideology. The Afghans had a story to tell and I'd found myself in the position – enviable or not – of being able to tell it. They'd been trying to build a nation for five hundred years. The British held them back for a century, and they thought the U.S. would help them. But the U.S. was trying to throw them back a thousand years. Why? What had the Afghans done to deserve this? Like that American character Alexander Gardner, I'd come to appreciate their independence, but they also possessed something else very human. In fact, I think they may have been the first *real* human beings I'd ever met.

Having been warned by Peter Larkin, I would make sure that my tapes were not erased either by the state censor or the Russians. I was coming in at a somewhat official level so I was almost certain they wouldn't be. I hoped.

The real problem was you never knew what to believe until you got there. And even then you couldn't be sure. The Western reports were nearly useless as a gauge to what was really going on. But they were a picture of what the *CIA* wanted you to think was going on. I'd brought along a research piece by the German-American reporter Konrad Ege for *Counter-Spy* magazine. Outside Selig Harrison, Ege had been the only objective source asking valid questions. He cited from nearly three dozen examples showing how the mainstream press ill informed, misinformed, or just plain fabricated Afghan stories in support of Washington's policy.

He then explained the underlying flaw. "Given the faulty understanding most Western journalists have of Islam, it is no surprise that most of them conclude that the conflict in Afghanistan is a religiously motivated war. However, careful analysis of available facts about the rebel groups and Afghan government strategy suggests that religion is more of a tool than a source of the conflict. As a rule the Western media has not done that analysis. Instead, the conflict is reduced to a simple Islam versus Marxism."

Maintaining an ignorance of Afghanistan's history played directly into Washington's game plan. The U.S. had people who knew that history but wouldn't listen to them. U.S. Ambassador Leon Poullada even stated for the record that the British saw a modernizing of Afghanistan as a threat to their rule in India so they kept it suppressed. But the American empire didn't want Afghanistan emulated for its moderate Islam either. Afghan politics were complicated by a dozen post-colonial dysfunctions. But the Western press was focused on religion because that was what got the "Freedom Fighters" the headlines and the financial support. The Afghan government was supporting Islam but Saudi Arabia wanted to spread *radical* Islam into Central Asia. They also wanted to control future oil pipeline routes. Pakistan wanted to legitimize its occupation of Afghan lands stolen by the British Empire in the 19th century and control events in Kabul. Communist China wished to curry favor with the United States and expand its control over its Muslim Xinxiang province. And the U.S.? The U.S. wanted to fuck the Soviet Union for Vietnam and roll back the Bolshevik revolution of 1917 once and for all.

***

After a brief refueling in London, the 747 was back in the air and for the next eight and half hours we stole into the Indian sub-continent. A hundred years ago the same trip would have taken months, if possible at all. Each province of India posed insurmountable problems – different languages, different customs, different peoples. Negotiations could drag on for months before passage was granted. It took the British East India Company nearly two hundred and fifty years to work their way from Surat in the Arabian Sea up to the Afghan border. Bloody wars were fought. The Russians dominated the Afghans from the north. The British answered with invasions from the south. The Afghans fought them to a standstill and a temporary peace. India's governor, Lord Curzon, admired the Russians – even envied their "civilizing" influence in the northern regions. From 1919 until 1978 and the Marxist Coup, Afghanistan was poor, but self-sufficient in food, and politically neutral. They fielded a national army, gave women the right to vote in 1923, and expanded education a thousand fold. And then the Cold War closed in and destroyed it all.

The darkness outside the plane was too big to contemplate. Beneath the window thousands of feet below an enormous lightning storm was spreading out for miles. I saw it as symbolic of the region's onrushing role in history and it was bigger than geopolitics. Something was coming to its fulfillment over this place as had been prophesied.

Henry Wallace, Franklin Roosevelt's Vice President was on to it back in the early 1930s. He and the Russian mystic Nicholas Roerich. I remembered reading about it years ago. It was 1934 and they wanted to establish a settlement in the Himalayas. "The Plan," they'd called it – just, the plan. It began in the late 19th century as Helena Blavatsky's "Shambhala Project" but this was bigger.

Wallace loved the mysticism. He wanted Roosevelt to get the U.S. government behind his secret mission to find the hidden city of Shambhala. "The political situation in this part of the world is always rendered especially intriguing by the effect on it of ancient prophecies, traditions and the like," he'd written. Wallace believed the prophecies were coming due. The Nazis were all over the place looking for it and he wanted to find it first.

A hidden city, invisible to human eyes, that Tibetan Buddhists said would be revealed at the end of time. Was it real? When the press got wind of it, there was a scandal. But there were others who claimed an actual Shambhala was hidden somewhere in Northeastern Afghanistan.

This was the Shambhala Wallace really wanted. The one that concealed the lost wisdom, the secrets of immortality and the purest beginnings of the human race. Of course the Russians already knew all about it.

The 19th century Russian Futurist and Orthodox Christian philosopher Nikolai Fyodorov considered the whole region from the Himalayas to the Pamirs to be the most important geographical location on the planet – the original site of Eden. Fyodorov believed this was the place of humanity's resurrection – a place of spiritual geography so severe it served as the model for what was needed to heal humanity's broken soul. He even proposed a joint Anglo/Russian expedition "as a first step in restoring the wasteland to a garden..."

Fyodorov was pleased that the region was finally gaining the world's attention so that the spiritual plan for the human race could proceed and the resurrection of the dead begin. But then came the carnage of World Wars I and II, the Cold War and the present…

I fell asleep thinking of Fyodorov's prophecy and dreamed of my dead father, lying in a hospital bed smiling back at me. He had never made it to a hospital bed. He'd died where he'd fallen when his heart broke. In the spring of 1968 my father's death was the unimaginable. He and I never quarreled but we had the night before he died. It never occurred to me that we'd never speak again. It never occurred to me that such a thing was possible. It never occurred to me how powerful words could be and how dangerous they could become when used in anger. Now, for the first time I could see it as it might have been – as he might have been, alive and recovering. Was this how Fyodorov's resurrection worked? Was I helping to restore my father's life by trying to do the impossible?

The dream shook me awake just as the 747 began its descent into Delhi, but the vision of my father's smiling face stayed with me. It was a good omen. The first leg of the trip was over. The next part would not be so easy.

***

Delhi's international airlines transit lounge was a small, dingy room on the ground floor with a tacky bar, worn asphalt tile floor, and bay window. It could easily be mistaken for a rest stop on the Jersey Turnpike were it not for the Hindi Coca Cola signs and the two Indian fighter pilots accompanied by two French Air Force officers who'd just walked through the metal door next to the bar.

The place was empty but for one other passenger – a man about my age, dressed in a white shirt, khaki pants and scuffed desert boots reading an old newspaper.

"Was that a sales meeting?" I asked.

"No, an appetizer," he said, stifling a very British snicker. "The French are handing out lollies and the Indians are lapping them up."

He put down the week-old *London Telegraph* and turned towards me. "French planes are more suited to India anyway. So are Soviet – less expensive, more reliable."

"More reliable than American, you mean."

The idea amused him. "The American stuff is very high tech. You need spare parts, technicians, rare metals. India's a poor country. The U.S. sold the Shah all those F-16s and they can't keep them in the air."

"I guess I didn't expect to see the arms race up close the minute I got off a plane from New York."

"You get to see a lot of things here you don't expect," he said, smiling for the first time. "Where are you headed?"

"Kabul. I was there two years ago. I'm going back for a TV program."

Mentioning Kabul always got a rise. "You're a journalist."

"And you?" I asked.

"I run an NGO up north. I'm on my way back."

"What's that like?"

"Well, it's hard. Conditions are primitive. There's never enough money," the man said wearily. "It's worth it though. The way of life is so simple."

Now I was really intrigued. "How'd you wind up doing that?"

"I was on my way to Delhi to finish my PhD and thought I'd stop off in Kabul on the way."

I thought I'd heard this story before. "This must have been the 60s."

"Early 70s actually. Things were beautiful then. They called Kabul the Paris of Asia. Very welcoming. And moderate Islam. Sufi Islam. Not this extreme stuff coming out of the Middle East these days. Lots of whirling dervishes and cheap hash. Intellectual discussions in every tea house. So I befriended this holy man Abdul Yassin and he sort of became a guru."

"And you stayed."

"For a year. Eventually I got my degree and moved back to London. But I missed the place. Then I had a dream."

"A dream?"

"It was after the Marxist coup in '78. Things got violent. Abdul Yassin appeared to me and told me I needed to come back. Things were being thrown off balance. So here I am doing what I can."

I knew the power of the holy men here. I'd met some of them on my first trip to Kabul and I knew what they had *was* real. I'd gone to Catholic school for years and was bathed in its priestly rituals. I'd sung the so called sacred music as a soloist and chanted the sacred chants but I'd never felt any connection to the divine. Not a hint. But these men were different. They used a kind of mystical network to communicate. You could feel it. They'd send you a summons over it, and if you were spiritually ready, you'd come.

"I can see by your face that God has sent you to tell Afghanistan's story," a mullah named Dr. Afghani had told me. I'd nearly forgotten about it but here I was going back to do just that. And here I realized it, just because I'd been stuck in the transit lounge talking to a stranger. God did work in mysterious way.

CHAPTER 25

Wednesday May 4, 11:00 A.M.

It wasn't until the beat up Air India 727 banked and twisted into its descent over the Hindu Kush that the full memory of my last trip came back, and I was telling myself *I'm supposed to do this*. Kabul's solitary runway was a thin black ribbon stretched out inside the bottom of a narrow ravine five miles ahead and 10,000 feet below. A thirty-knot wind constantly threatened to heave the plane against the jagged cliffs that got nearer as we descended. The passengers grew quiet as the pilot struggled to keep the plane on course. Oil had leaked from the engine under my window the entire way from Delhi. The leaking was bad but if it stopped it was worse. The overheated engine would catch fire and seize, causing the plane to jerk to the left and plow right into the cliff. The closeness to death was fascinating, but I wasn't ready to die. And just like that it was over.

The wheels hit the runway and we were down. We were lucky as we'd arrived only minutes after an intense rain storm which made the place look older and grimmer than I remember. I was relieved just to be taxiing down the runway, but the real fun was about start. The last time I'd gotten off a plane here I was greeted by George Beyers Griffin. Would I be pressured to come to the U.S. embassy again? This time I was ready for an encounter but no one showed up. Bill Lord had not called any friends at the CIA and told them to meet me at the airport. I was a freelance secret agent on my own, working the back channels so Roger Fisher could make some kind of deal.

As I reached customs, my audio and video tapes were confiscated for "censoring" by the Ministry of Information and Culture. It was made clear that this trip would be unlike the last.

"How do you plan to censor blank tapes?" I asked the uniformed official but received only a shrug in reply. I was getting the benefits of Peter Larkin's latest Russia's Vietnam scoop before I even got out of the airport.

At first glance the Soviet presence appeared diminished from two years prior. Not at all like the CBS News story. The half dozen military helicopters had Afghan markings not Soviet. The Soviet encampment at the end of the runway was gone. So were the SAM missile batteries Larkin made such a big deal about two years ago. So where were the Russians? This was strange.

Outside in the small terminal lobby, I was flagged down by a government guide named Massoud. He struck me as being in his late 20s but mature beyond his years. He was better dressed than most Afghans I'd met and seemed well educated.

"I'll be staying at the Kabul Hotel," I said. We proceeded immediately by car to the foreign ministry and a meeting with the ministry's press officer, a Mr. Roshanrowan.

"Roshan means 'the enlightened one,'" he told me. "One of Afghanistan's great poets who fought for independence was known as Pir Roshan and I have followed in his footsteps."

There was a calm clarity to Roshanrowan that I'd only glimpsed in other Afghans. I presented my wish list and he observed that there should be plenty of time to accommodate my schedule. It was a pleasant exchange.

"I think you'll find things more in order than two years ago when you were here," he said. "The back of the counter-revolution has been broken. We have less need of Soviet troops but they are still helping us combat small bands of counter-revolutionary 'bandits' in the countryside."

I saw my opportunity which brought me to the issue of censorship. Roshanrowan listened carefully. "My tapes were taken at the airport. I was told that you now have a policy of censoring everything before it leaves the country. I hope you realize that I don't expect to be censored."

My demand took Roshanrowan by surprise. "That's up to the state censor," he said, mystified.

"But you realize that the success of Roger Fisher's involvement depends on an uncensored view of what's happening here," I responded.

"I have no control over it," he insisted. "But you might bring it up with the Foreign Minister Shah Mohammed Dost when you interview him."

It was a deal. We parted amicably and I walked the few blocks back to the hotel with Massoud. Radio Kabul played popular music laced with political messages from loudspeakers set on poles along the streets. It was your constant companion wherever you went. The smell of roasting kabobs filled the air. Security was stricter and more pervasive than last time, particularly as it applied to people like me. Government guides were mandatory for the duration. All recorded or unrecorded tapes had to be submitted to the president of foreign publications, Sahir Hushbein, for review and censoring. I warned Massoud that I hadn't come all that way to have my tapes erased.

On the street, controls were tighter. Afghan soldiers or youth paramilitary with Kalashnikovs guarded every building downtown. There wasn't a Russian soldier in sight. Two years ago only government buildings had received that kind of protection. Groups of eight to ten Afghan soldiers hung out on street corners. They checked identity cards of draft-age men and flagged cars at random. We were stopped twice and Massoud was asked for identification and frisked. I was stared at suspiciously as he explained who I was.

Wednesday, 10:00 P.M.

May 4th – the longest day of my life was over. From New York to London to Delhi and on to Kabul, dozing in upright airplane seats. I'd been breathing geopolitics for months. I was on overload. Jet lag was on me. The climb to the second floor of the Kabul Hotel was like dragging dead weight. The foyer at the top of the stairwell sat in a dark corner with a window overlooking the street. The corridor beyond was a hazy, uncertain vacuum which drew me in, and then suddenly I was face to face with it – room number 117. I'd been so preoccupied I'd nearly forgotten about the room where the American ambassador was killed. And I was standing in front of it.

I tried to imagine it, the event that started it all, and built a picture in my mind. But the pieces of the puzzle didn't fit and neither did the published reports.

Cold, clear Kabul. February 14, 1979. Valentine's Day, 8:45 A.M. A kidnapper posing as a police officer stopped the ambassador's car. The chauffeur opened the door and the policeman pulled a gun. Three more kidnappers jumped into the ambassador's black Chevrolet. Or was it a beige Oldsmobile? Nobody knew who they were. *Newsweek* reported them as radical Shiite Islamists protesting a godless communist regime. But the U.S. embassy reported they were separatist Tajik Maoists. Reports said the Afghan driver Gul Mohammed rolled down the window. But the windows didn't roll down. Or had Dubs unlocked the door himself? The ambassador had political immunity. The car was bulletproof and bombproof. It had run-flat tires and a siren. He could have escaped, but he chose to stay? Either way the kidnappers were in. They brought the ambassador to the Kabul Hotel where the chauffeur was released and drove to the embassy. And the Cold War between the U.S. and the Soviet Union was back on.

My second floor room overlooked the courtyard and garden. I could hear the sound of barking dogs and the distant thumping of machine gun fire through the open window. The Afghan boys I'd seen this morning must be out roaming the streets, blasting away with their Kalashnikovs at America's "Freedom Fighters." Thanks to Saudi Arabia and the United States, Kabul was no longer the Paris of Central Asia and I was living out Graham Greene's *Quiet American* in Russia's Vietnam. How bizarre. Ambassador Dubs was now a very quiet American and it didn't make sense. Back at my desk I pored through my notebook and the details of his death.

The kidnappers were nameless and faceless. They only made demands of the Kabul government and never talked to the Americans. If they'd wanted something from the Soviet client regime why hadn't they kidnapped the Soviet ambassador? They had absolutely no leverage unless … unless the abduction of Adolph Dubs wasn't meant to be a kidnapping. That would explain why he hadn't driven away. Or why he might have unlocked the door. I marked it down as issue number 1.

Back at the hotel he was led into the lobby, then taken upstairs to second floor room 117 by three of the kidnappers. Afghan witnesses claimed the kidnappers didn't speak the Afghan language very well. One Western reporter overheard the police say the kidnappers were Czechoslovakian. But the fourth kidnapper disappeared and was never heard from again. Nobody in the lobby saw him or described what he looked like. The driver of the limousine would certainly have gotten a look at him, but he was never questioned about it.

Upstairs the kidnappers realized the door was locked and sent the third kidnapper back to the lobby for the key. Why would they have assumed the room would be available without a key? Were they expecting someone to be waiting for them? A Soviet security officer asked the Afghan police whether the terrorists had registered for the room they were occupying. Why would they have bothered to do that? So they could order from room service? And why would he have asked unless he suspected something else was going on? Something was missing from the whole story. Brzezinski had it in for the Russians, and Dubs was literally battling Brzezinski. Dubs needed the embassy's official protection. But if he was doing it all on his own, he had to take risks. He met with the Afghan Prime Minister Hafizullah Amin fourteen times, often unannounced. How unannounced? The embassy had denied he'd met with Amin so many times because they hadn't known what he was doing. Would one of Amin's policemen have stopped and searched his car beforehand? Of course he would have. Is that why the chauffeur hadn't raised an alarm? Is that why the whole event remained a mystery? Because Dubs had something going with Amin that nobody wanted to talk about? Something was missing. And I was determined to find out what it was.

CHAPTER 26

Thursday May 5, mid-morning:

I returned with Massoud to the foreign ministry to formally present my requests and my program for the rest of the stay. On our way through the city we were again stopped twice by young Kalashnikov-toting Afghan soldiers. Massoud was already getting annoyed with the procedure and on the second stop, shook his head in frustration and treated it as some kind of joke.

On climbing the white marble steps to Roshanrowan's second floor office, I encountered one of my government minders from the first trip, Naim Uqouq. Of all the people it had to be Naim – paranoid, suspicious and often drunk. In a totally Muslim country that was an amazing achievement. Naim had come close to wrecking my first trip and I prayed meeting up with him again was just an accident.

"Naim. What a pleasant surprise," I said. "It's good to see you."

"It's good to see you, too," he said in that unique squirrely-nasal tone of his.

"And what are you up to?" I asked, hoping to God he hadn't been tasked to me.

"I've been promoted by the foreign ministry."

A relieved sigh. "Congratulations," I offered.

"I've been assigned to our embassy in Prague."

"Nice going," I said. "Prague's a beautiful city."

"I have seen your documentary of your trip. It's very good," he said.

"Thank you, Naim." There was an awkward silence before I said, "Naim, I have an appointment."

"I must go, too," he said.

I shook his hand. "Good luck on your new assignment."

I breathed a second sigh of relief and continued on my way toward Roshanrowan's office. I turned and watched Naim disappear down the stairs and out the front doors of the foreign ministry. Naim had to be the one person I hadn't necessarily wanted to see. Accident, coincidence or just plain dumb luck? I felt as if I'd just been nicked by a bullet until I entered

Roshanrowan's office and met a man struggling to contain his anger. I had expected to get right down to business but Roshanrowan had a different idea.

"Have you seen this article in the *New York Times*?" he asked suspiciously as he handed me a transcript.

"I've been in transit since Monday. I haven't read anything," I said as I take the paper.

U.S. SAID TO INCREASE ARMS AID FOR AFGHAN REBELS

By LESLIE H. GELB, Special to the New York Times

WASHINGTON, May 3—The United States has stepped up the quantity and quality of covert military support for Afghan insurgents fighting Soviet forces and the Soviet-backed Government in Kabul, according to Administration officials.

The officials said President Reagan made the decision last fall with the purpose of forcing Moscow to pay a higher price for its more than three-year-old effort to assert control over Afghanistan.

I didn't need to read any more than the first two paragraphs to understand why my host was angry. Leslie Gelb was a heavy hitter for the U.S. establishment; Assistant Secretary of State for President Carter, Senior Fellow at Brookings. He'd been director of the Pentagon Papers project on the Vietnam War for Lyndon Johnson. The same Pentagon Papers that Daniel Ellsberg had exposed, revealing the true deception and nihilism of the U.S. war. If anyone knew what Washington had planned for Afghanistan it was Leslie Gelb, and Roshanrowan didn't like it.

I took a deep breath and put the paper down as I realized that whatever my status as an independent freelance journalist, Roshanrowan was holding me personally responsible.

"Who is this Leslie Gelb to write about such things?" Roshanrowan said in a demanding tone.

"He was a very high level official in the Carter administration," I explained.

"And why is your government doing this to us?" He picked up the paper and read from it. "'Officials spoke of an internal debate between what they call the 'bleeders,' or those who wanted to draw more and more Soviet troops into Afghanistan and those who sought a more cautious approach.' The American government wants to draw more and more troops into Afghanistan to bleed them?" he said while shaking his head. "Your government claimed they didn't want the Soviet Union to invade Afghanistan and now they don't want them to leave?"

I managed to mumble, "It would appear so."

He continued to quote from the article. "'The Soviet-backed government of Babrak Karmal remains hopelessly unpopular and that his army is of dwindling utility.' This is not true. How can he say such lies?"

I saw my opportunity. "That's why I'm here. It's very important that I get the full picture about what's going on. The press is filled with this kind of thing and it needs to be addressed. But I can't do it unless you help me."

I'd struck a chord. Roshanrowan bit his lip. At that moment he had nowhere else to turn but me and he knew I knew it. I handed him my typed pages of requests and waited while he sat down at his desk and reviewed them.

The *New York Times* article illustrated what I was up against; both the Afghans and the *New York Times*. It was nice to see the administration admitting to what I'd been suspecting all along, but what I'd been suspecting was nothing short of crazy. It was all a self-fulfilling prophecy. Andropov wanted to call it quits but wouldn't leave until the U.S. stopped supporting the insurgency. The administration wouldn't stop funding the insurgency until the Russians left, and so the deadlock continued. Reagan's policy was a major contradiction but absolutely no one was picking up on it. On the one hand he was publicly demanding the Soviets withdraw their forces and on the other he was covertly doing everything in his power to draw them further into the conflict and hold them down so they *couldn't* leave. That was dangerous for lots of reasons. First of all Washington was convincing the Soviets they actually wanted a war and if they pushed them hard enough and long enough somebody would start one. And secondly, everybody in Washington who should have known better was letting them get away with it.

My meeting with Roshanrowan was soon over. He agreed to help in every way he could. He suggested I return on Saturday for an update and I went on my way. Massoud was waiting in the courtyard of the foreign ministry and we walked to the Ministry of Information and Culture where I had to officially register as a visiting journalist and get my press pass.

Kabul was a bustling metropolis. Long blue and white Kabul busses passed by packed with commuters. Automobile traffic was heavy everywhere we went. Mercedes diesels, Peugeots and Russian Ladas clogged the streets. The Soviet presence had clearly diminished from two years ago; no tanks, only the occasional big green eight-wheeled armored personnel carrier parked outside a store where a Russian civilian was shopping. The picture here didn't match the CBS News report from just two weeks ago.

The young guys at Bakhtar were friendly and helpful. One of them asked if I can get him a visa to the U.S. He had a cousin in Milwaukee he wanted to visit. They snapped a dour, unsmiling color photo, stapled it through my forehead to a blue card and I was authorized as foreign journalist number 279. The back of the card read "The DRA committee of the Bakhtar Information Agency most respectfully requests all Party, Government and Security authorities to extend all possible help to the holder of this card." I assumed this made it safer for me to walk the streets of Kabul. But that remained to be seen.

On our walk back through the bazaar I stopped to browse a row of kiosks selling old books and bootleg Bollywood music tapes. I was tempted to grab a tape or two to use as background music but I was drawn to a cheaply printed paperback titled *The Nest of Spies*. Upon closer inspection, I realized the book was published next door in the Ayatollah's Iran and the "Nest" was a collection of shredded secret cables from the U.S. embassy in Tehran, pasted back together. And it was in Farsi and English. It was the jackpot and would make my next few days' reading a lot more interesting.

An afternoon drive to the outskirts of town was worth the price of the ticket. The place was growing on me. It was alive, unpredictable. Women in Western dress – some in mini-skirts – walked the streets. Young boys were everywhere. Some played at kicking an old soccer ball. Others worked, hauling carts of firewood or old rags destined to be spun into fiber for carpets. Nothing in that ancient place was wasted.

To the Afghan government officials we met, the Soviets appeared invisible. As Massoud pointed out various sites in the city, we passed the gates to the Soviet's Bala Hissar headquarters. A few military trucks were parked and Soviet soldiers guarded the gates. Massoud avoided eye contact, his monologue paused, and he looked straight ahead and smiled. It was obvious he didn't like the Soviets being there, or worse – that his government needed the Soviets to be there and couldn't admit it. As we passed by he resumed talking as if nothing unusual had occurred.

"Do you have much personal contact with the Soviets?" I asked.

"Of course," he said, keeping his eyes on the road ahead.

"What about friends? Do you have many Soviet friends?

Massoud shrugged, smiling begrudgingly. "Yes," he said and the discussion ended.

The Kabul Hotel was an active intersection in sight of the bazaar. Clientele was mostly Warsaw Pact bureaucrats on holiday. Eastern Europeans who dressed like tractor salesmen from Iowa who'd come for the 5th anniversary celebration of the April 1978 "revolution" still hung around. In the dining room next to the patio, a Soviet musical troupe and a delegation of East German radio commentators stood out. The atmosphere was a must. It couldn't have looked any different in the 1940s. Rick's Casablanca Café in the flesh. I would do my best to find out what they thought of the Peoples' Democratic Party of Afghanistan and its chances of survival.

CHAPTER 27

Thursday-Night May 5:

L entil soup, beef shish kebab, Afghan naan and rice. The hotel's food was cheap and very good. The service was excellent. The economy was booming. A daily stream of brightly painted lorries ferried Japanese electronics over the mountains from Pakistan – TV sets, radios, tape recorders. A local band played popular Afghan music in the ballroom to a packed house. If it wasn't for the rumble of artillery shelling, you'd never have known there was a war on.

I finished typing up the day's notes after dinner. The lights were on at Soviet headquarters in the Emir's old fortress looming off in the distance – the one Massoud and I had passed by earlier in the day. The Bala Hissar they called it. The wall zigzagged up the mountain like the backbone of a dinosaur. It used to have gates as you entered the city but this place had been invaded so many times the gates were long gone.

I'd passed through there the night I took a walk with General Gul Aka two years ago. I could still hear the music blaring from the loudspeaker in the background. That was a great stunt. The General wanted to demonstrate it was safe for him to walk anywhere in the city. The driver of the General's Mercedes pulled out a Kalashnikov and put it in the passenger's seat beside him while the General cocked his Makarov automatic pistol and put it on the seat between us. Yeah. it was safe. When I got back to CBS News, people had asked me if I wasn't afraid. For some reason I hadn't been. It was strange I know, but I felt more alive at that moment than I'd ever felt in my life. It made me feel as if I'd come home from a very long journey. Home, to where I belonged. And yet I didn't belong there. How strange.

This city confronted you everywhere you went. The aroma of spices, the fresh baked naan, the smell of charcoal and kabobs was intoxicating. It evoked memories. Made you wonder whether you weren't fated to revisit where you'd left off in a previous life.

I dug back into my notebooks. The Dubs thing haunted me. My room was no more than a hundred feet from where the kidnappers held him after the chauffer dropped them off. The chauffeur drove back to the embassy and triggered the alarm, but someone was already on the phone with Police Superintendent Sayed Taroun. How had he gotten the word? Taroun was Deputy Prime Minister and Foreign Minister Hafizullah Amin's right hand man. Amin had been meeting with Dubs on a regular basis. It was February of 1979, and he'd only been there seven months.

"Dubs has been arrested by the government," the chauffeur told political counsel Bruce Flatin. Flatin gathered a crew and then returned to the Hotel in Dubs' armored Oldsmobile. Flatin noticed the U.S. flag had been removed from the car's right front fender and its American eagle top was missing. Was that a signal to someone? Like the umbrella man in Dealey Plaza? Or was it the chalk mark on the postbox to signal a meeting?

The hotel lobby was swarming with police and Afghan troops when they got there – Police Chief Mohammed Lal, Internal Affairs Superintendent Major Saifuddin and Yosuf Sahar, Chief of the Anti-Smuggling Unit. The Americans were told "terrorists" had seized the ambassador, but the police in charge were all Afghan drug police. Major Saifuddin introduced himself to Flatin. His ministry oversaw narcotics trafficking. What was that all about?

Saifuddin was a former air force officer. He sported a half-dollar size scar on his right cheek, was well dressed and appeared to be in charge of the operation. He disclaimed any Afghan government involvement in the ambassador's abduction.

Police held the third kidnapper as a prisoner in the lobby. It struck Flatin odd that if they were really kidnapers they wouldn't have chosen a busy hotel in the middle of town and then given away their whereabouts.

The pieces of the puzzle were getting harder to fit together. The Americans met with Afghan police and military and some Soviet embassy people. A high level Soviet security officer named Sergey Bakhturin assured the Americans of the strong Soviet interest in the ambassador's safety. They were also told the kidnappers were demanding the Afghan government release a rebel leader in return for Ambassador Dubs.

The people holding Dubs hadn't made any direct contact with the Americans. Everything they knew had come through the Afghan leadership and Bakhturin.

Back at the embassy the deputy U.S. chief of mission was told by the State Department to negotiate with the kidnappers and to not do anything to endanger the ambassador. He failed to reach Amin by phone. He then sent embassy officers all over the city to sniff him out, but Amin was nowhere to be found.

Hours passed. Rumors abounded. Numerous other members of the embassy staff trickled into the hotel. CIA officer Warren Marik and Drug Enforcement Agency attaché Harold "Doug" Wankel arrived around noon. Wankel observed three Afghan police officers with automatic rifles on the balcony of the bank building across the street.

Wankel had a close working relationship with Superintendent Taroun and Chief Sahar from an ongoing DEA-funded drug enforcement program. Wankel had just met with Sahar on January 17, to cosign a payment of 11,700 Afghanis to an Afghan drug informant. 1.17, 11,700 and room 117 all in three weeks. What a strange coincidence.

Superintendent Taroun's police were known to be corrupt and violent. They'd been accused by Afghans and foreigners of inflicting cruel and inhumane punishment. Taroun had been known to level a machine gun at someone he was interrogating.

Flatin met with a Russian security officer and told him he wanted to talk to the ambassador. "What languages does your ambassador know besides English?" he asked.

"Russian," Flatin tells him.

"Besides Russian."

"German."

Minutes later Flatin was approached by a plain clothes Afghan secret police official he knew and was asked to come upstairs. "We'd like to have you talk to your ambassador in German so that the people inside the room will not be able to understand what's being said."

Upstairs, Flatin knelt at the keyhole of room 117 and wondered what it would be like to swallow a mouthful of bullets. He spoke to Dubs in German but the kidnappers quickly caught on. "Stop this conversation! We won't stand for any tricks!" a kidnapper yelled through the door.

Dubs stopped talking. Then the policeman said, "Tell your ambassador that exactly ten minutes from now he is to fall to the floor."

Flatin freaked out and they retreated to the foyer at the top of the stairs where he saw Police Chief Lal preparing an assault team. Lal was known to be dangerous. Probably a psychopath, and he'd taken control of the operation.

"We've spent the whole morning telling you that we don't want any precipitous action here, and you're telling me to help you light a fuse that's going to go off in exactly ten minutes?" Flatin demanded.

Flatin wanted a further delay. Lal became very upset and backed off, but an hour and a half later Lal was again seen preparing his men to hit the room.

Flatin went to the Soviet advisor Bakhturin and for the first time learned that the Afghan police were working under a deadline imposed by the kidnappers. Bakhturin told him the Afghans were in charge and that he was powerless to stop it. The U.S. Security Officer transmitted over his radio that the Afghan police had decided to storm room 117 in eight to ten minutes. He transmitted that the Afghans had been told not to do that but they were acting under someone else's orders. But who might that be? Afghans, Soviets or some third party?

Wankel, Marik, and two other embassy staff carried a stretcher upstairs to the foyer. Events were happening in quick succession.

A man who was assumed to be Soviet KGB by DEA man Wankel but may have been a fair skinned Afghan provided a weapon to one member of the Afghan assault team in the corridor. Bakhturin and two other Soviet advisors headed off to the balcony presumably to position the Afghan snipers across the street.

Afghan commandos in flak jackets and AK-47s moved into position near the door. A picture of Adolph Dubs was passed around the foyer area and studied by Afghan police. Flatin overheard an Afghan policeman ask if that's the terrorist. He also observed there were no Soviets present or involved with the assault team. In a final ploy, a small, slender individual, the third kidnapper was roughly marched into the foyer. He shouted to the kidnappers behind the door. The kidnappers shouted back they want him released, but he was not allowed back into the room.

At 12:45 another man presumed to be a Soviet advisor went to the window of the foyer. He then signaled five minutes to the Afghan police snipers across the street on the bank balcony.

Then at exactly12:50 a gunshot rang out inside the room. The single gunshot was followed by heavy gunfire in the corridor, inside the room and from the balcony across the street. Everyone was shooting at everyone – both single shot and automatic bursts. Smoke and flying debris filled the hallway for what seemed to the Americans to be forty to fifty seconds until the Soviet advisor reappeared at the foyer window and waved his arms, signaling a cease fire. Flatin headed for the splintered door but was held back by Police Chief Lal who entered ahead of him. Four more loud bursts were heard by Flatin from inside the room. Then silence.

Wankel, Marik and the two embassy staffers rushed to the room with the stretcher as Flatin peered inside. He saw the ambassador slumped in a chair by the wall with multiple wounds to his head and body, his two kidnappers sprawled nearby. The floor was covered in water from radiators shot up in the barrage. Flatin observed that half of the ambassador's clothing was wet, as if he'd been lying on the floor and somebody propped him up in the chair. Either way the ambassador was dead. But had he been killed from the bank balcony across the street or by someone in the room, and if so, who?

CHAPTER 28

In addition to the kidnapping, the conflicting interpretations of how Adolph Dubs died revealed the growing divisions between the Team A and Team B split represented by the Carter administration. Flatin was a State Department diplomat tasked with maintaining American policy. Wankel and Marik were DEA/CIA policemen with a Team B agenda who wanted to pin the rap on the Soviets before the facts were even known.

The DEA/CIA connection itself was well known as a marriage forged in hell during the darkest days of the Nixon administration intended to provide cover for CIA covert action and political assassination under a veil of law enforcement. Wankel's DEA background included Detroit police street-thug narcotics – buying drugs from informants, dealers, pimps and prostitutes. Marik was covert operations – an agent provocateur specializing in propaganda and political subversion. Like Zbigniew Brzezinski, in their minds the KGB was behind everything and they saw KGB plotters surrounding room 117 at the Kabul Hotel.

Flatin stood outside the door as the two dead kidnappers were dropped at his feet while the third – who'd been in police custody the entire time – was wrestled down the stairs and out the door very much alive. Flatin never saw the fourth kidnapper until later that night when the police displayed four dead bodies and claimed he was one of them. Police exited the room with Dubs' sport coat and tie. Flatin asked to take it but the "tall senior Soviet police advisor" informed him it needed to be kept for examination.

As the ambassador's body was driven to the USAID complex, Wankel, Marik and a third embassy staffer returned to the scene of the crime and discovered a lone man in Afghan garb giving room 117 a cursory examination. They assumed he was a policeman, but no one really knew. The room had been stripped of evidence. Upon inspection, Wankel maintained that Dubs was killed immediately by Soviet directed gunfire from the bank balcony across street and died slumped in his chair. But Flatin's observation that "one-half of Dubs' body was wet as though he had been lying on the floor," contradicted it. Had somebody picked him up and put him in the chair after he was killed? Wankel's opinion implicated the Soviets; Flatin's implicated the Afghan police. Only thirty seconds had elapsed between the second shootout and when the Americans got into the room. And who'd done it? Police Chief Lal Mohammed? Why would he kill the U.S. ambassador?

A pattern emerged. Some unnamed Americans claimed the Soviets wanted Dubs out of the way so they could set up for their invasion. But the Soviets got along famously with Dubs because he wasn't an anti-Soviet Russophobe like Brzezinski. There was also plenty of evidence to show the Soviets didn't want to invade. They went on record with the U.S. embassy throughout the summer of 1979 trying everything to avoid it. And besides, the rules of the game made ambassadors virtually untouchable. There was no upside to killing one, and a big downside.

Others claimed the Soviets were afraid that Dubs would win Hafizullah Amin away from their control. But Hafizullah Amin was never under Soviet control. The idea that he was their puppet was a Team B fantasy pushed by Brzezinski. The Soviets reviled him and tried everything short of invasion to replace him. They'd even tried to get the exiled king back to form a new government.

And then there was the cable from Deputy U.S. Chief of Mission Bruce Amstutz denying that there had been a second shootout. Had he failed to listen to the dozens of eye witnesses who'd observed the second shootout by Afghan police? Or was he trying to divert responsibility from the Afghan police inside the room to the Soviet advisors on the balcony?

So the Americans were divided on exactly what had gone down. It was beginning to show the same slanted conflicts as the JFK assassination. Divert attention from the grassy knoll – the easy kill shot – to that book depository building off in the distance and then blame the Russians. Wankel's "eyewitness" assumption implied the Soviet advisors on the bank balcony had a hand in the killing, but it was only his assumption based on the fact Dubs was sitting in the chair. He then ignored the second shootout from inside the room which was led by the psychopath police chief, Lal Mohammed. He made no mention that Dubs' clothes were wet and never mentioned Lal Mohammed's name in his reports, but as the DEA's Special Agent in Charge he had to know who he was. So why was he ignoring him?

The American side was split between the ideologues that were out to blame the Russians and the career diplomat who suspected the Afghan police.

131

It was too much to handle in one sitting and I needed a break. I thumbed through my volume of *Nest of Spies* and decided to take it down to the patio for a closer look before curfew.

***

It was a clear cool night. I could see artillery flashes just over the Bala Hissar. There was a rumble going on just outside Kabul. I could feel it under my feet. I parked myself innocuously into a corner of the patio with my book tucked under my arm. I recognized a handful of other guests from dinner. They milled around at the edges, quietly talking small among themselves. Some smoke nervously. We all glanced at the flashes and waited for the vibrations to reach us. It bound us together, a shared moment of potential doom. I couldn't believe how much I liked this stuff. That primal twinge in the pit of the stomach. The urge to run knowing there was nowhere to go. You reached the truth, the absolute truth about yourself and your connection to death.

I couldn't take my eyes off the Bala Hissar – built in the 5th century A.D. on the Kuh-e-Sherdarwaze Mountain, the British had failed to occupy it when they came to Kabul in 1839 and soon found themselves easy targets down below. The Russians had not made that mistake and made it their command center.

I was so absorbed I didn't even notice that there was a man, older, gray beard, standing next to me, until he speaks.

"We're standing on the ground floor of a whole new estate," he said, in an oh-so-appropriate British accent, his bright blue eyes lighting up with the fireworks. "Himmler wanted to privatize the SS in 1944. Rudolph Speer wrote about it in his memoirs on page 372. He convinced Hitler to build up an economic empire from raw materials to manufacturing that would outlast the war and any future German government."

"And what's that got to do with Afghanistan?" I asked the stranger.

"You're looking at it. Privatized warfare beyond state control. And all financed by the opium trade. Just like the British and the East India Company."

"But Germany lost the war."

"Hitler's intelligence group for the Soviet Union was brought into the CIA lock, stock and barrel, and as you can see, they're still at it."

I turned and stared at the man. He was sixtyish, somewhere around at six feet tall, but youthful and very spooky. I almost expected him to say Bond, James Bond, but instead I took his lead. "I think we have something to talk about," I said, introducing myself.

"Desmond FitzMaurice," he responded.

Another Fitz, another coincidence. "Great name. We must be related," I joked.

FitzMaurice was glib. "I can see by that book under your arm, we share more than a name."

I handed him the book and watched silently as he thumbed through the pages, stopping here and there to read a passage. "Imagine. A five-thousand-year-old culture of weaving complex patterns into carpets and the CIA thought they could outsmart them with a mechanical shredder. How stupid. Tehran station was critical to what was happening here back in the 70s," he said, smirking. "Dick Helms set up the CIA to run out of there so Carter couldn't see what they were up to. And he got away with it," he added before handing it back. "I think you'll find it very intriguing."

Intriguing? Now that was funny. "That's what Henry Wallace called it," I said. "'The political situation in this part of the world is always rendered *especially* intriguing by the effect on it of ancient prophecies, traditions and the like.'"

FitzMaurice looked out thoughtfully toward the Bala Hissar. "Standing here right now, I'm inclined to believe him. The oldest civilization on the planet began here – the Harappan. Indus valley culture. Then there's the Greco-Buddhism, 4th century B.C. – Gandharan – arrived with Alexander," he said, sweeping an index finger down his nose. "The oldest Buddha's are Caucasian, not oriental."

I'd visited Hadda, the center of Gandharan Buddhism on my last trip. The Macedonians had established cities all over Central Asia. "Buddha, a Caucasian? That would be controversial."

"No more so than the Aryan origins of the Afghans," he added. "I'll wager you haven't read about that. The findings have never been published. Not outside Nazi Germany."

I'd touched on the Nazi racial theories with my friend Ron. But I'd thought they were crazy right wing fantasies. "So that's true?"

"The Afghan foreign minister met with Hitler in Berlin and gave him the story – the original Indo-Europeans. I understand his son is now in Pakistan working with the CIA," he said, directing his gaze toward me. "Looks like Wallace's prophecies are coming due."

"And are you working with the CIA?" I asked, seizing the opportunity.

Desmond FitzMaurice looked the consummate British expatriate or spy – a seasoned traveler. Casual, self-assured and experienced with a deceptively hardened core. He betrayed no emotion.

"Hardly. I'm in antiquities," he answered coldly. "Those rare objects you only find buried in the ruins of Central Asia. Are *you* with the CIA?"

His bounce-back momentarily knocked me off base. "I'm just trying to put the pieces of a puzzle together."

"And what would that be?"

"The death of Ambassador Adolph Dubs." Another burst of gunfire shook the patio beneath us.

"And how is that going?"

"It doesn't make sense. The pieces don't fit."

"If the pieces don't fit you don't have all the pieces," FitzMaurice said, staring back at the book in my hands. "Try looking at the cables pasted together by the students. I think you'll find some of the pieces you might not even know are missing."

Another explosion rumbled through the patio. The nearness of the flash caught everyone by surprise, and by the time I looked back FitzMaurice had gone. What a strange encounter.

CHAPTER 29

Back in my hotel room I did as FitzMaurice recommended and soon found a State Department cable dated August 1979. Just like the 1967 *Ramparts* article reported, the U.S. had informers all over the Afghan government and one of them – code named L/1 – had come for pilot training at Douglas Aircraft in Los Angeles.

"Summary Dubs assassination: Kabul Chief of Police and Air Force Colonel and two of his assistants came to L/1's home. Lal Mohammed departed with secretary, leaving his two subordinates who proceeded to become intoxicated. These men are the source of L/1's story. They were assigned to fire machine guns for approximately twenty seconds into the hotel room where Ambassador Dubs was being held before Lal Mohammed and some other police officers were to storm the room. L/1 was not sure how the timing of these events took place, but apparently everything went off on schedule. The two men opened fire on the room from the roof of the bank building across the street and as soon as they ceased firing the door was forced by the Lal Mohammed party. Ambassador Dubs was, according to these two men, sitting in a chair covered with blood and either already dead or very near death when the Lal Mohammed party entered the room. L/1 believes Lal Mohammed personally killed the ambassador but cannot give any reason or proof for this belief. The information provided by the two drunken police officers does not support L/1's views. L/1 says that Lal Mohammed personally told him that he had killed over 2000 Afghans. L/1 hates Lal Mohammed and believes him to be a butcher and capable of anything."

The cable added little to what I already knew. It told me Lal Mohammed had police stationed on the bank balcony *and* the roof. But I'd seen with my own eyes that the roof of the bank building was at too sharp an angle to see more than a few feet into room 117. The cable made clear the policemen's observations didn't support L/1's belief that Lal Mohammed killed Dubs. But at that angle and distance they couldn't possibly have even seen Dubs let alone ascertain his health or who might have killed him. So the cable was a bust except for L/1's statement about Lal Mohammed. Lal was put in charge of the assault and of writing the official report filed in April of '79. His account was so filled with outright lies, fabrications and omissions the State Department rejected it out of hand. And then the autopsy done at Walter Reed Hospital back in Washington determined that although Dubs had been hit by a number of slugs, he was killed by four bullets to the head from a small .22 caliber weapon fired at close range.

The Afghan government refused to turn over the weapons collected in the room but sent a diplomatic note listing the weapons found and none of them were .22. So L/1's accusation that Lal was a butcher and killed the ambassador would appear to be supported by the evidence, not by the two policemen. There was nobody else to blame. So why had the DEA's Wankel immediately assumed that Dubs was killed from the bank balcony and not even mention Lal's name in his report?

Friday Morning May 6, 8:00 A.M.
On the way downstairs to breakfast I passed the open door to room 117. I poked my head inside and saw four sets of bunk beds in the "living room" of the suite. There was no sign that anything of any importance had ever happened there.

Outside, Kabul reminded me of Castro's Havana – a city frozen in the past. A smattering of modern Soviet-style buildings like the Polytechnic Institute blended in with the old stucco and masonry. Because of U.S. boycotts and trade embargoes imposed after the invasion, older buildings like the Kabul Hotel lacked a whole generation of replacement parts and were patched together. Plumbing and electrical were just about used up and would require complete replacement when the war ended. The German telephone system built in the 1930s barely works. Afghans didn't like to talk about it, but the Nazis were Afghanistan's leading trading partner before the war. A German expedition moved in during World War I, looking to put pressure on British India, and stayed. Hitler had wanted to move through the Caucuses to Iran's oil fields but got stopped in Stalingrad. The rest was history.

A new and massive communications building was going up behind the hotel. It was a shocking contrast viewed against the backdrop of the medieval housing where most Afghans lived.

After breakfast I walked in the garden behind the hotel. The old Afghan caretaker sees me, drops his gardening tools and rushes inside. I didn't realize I looked that menacing. The first MIG I've seen this trip flies low overhead. It's quiet out here, and beautiful. I spent a few moments in contemplation of my strange life then walked back toward the hotel. When I got to the steps I was greeted by the machine-gun-armed soldier who'd been guarding the front door. He ignored me and pointed the gun out toward where I'd been walking. The caretaker must have taken me for a CIA guy and reported me. Papers please!

If I walked the city alone would I get arrested as a spy or maybe mistaken for a Russian and shot by a "Freedom Fighter?" I'd already been mistaken for one when I'd gone into a shop on Chicken Street. A young guy started talking to me in Russian as if I was his best comrade. The room phone had a telltale hum on it. Had it sounded that bad two years ago or was it bugged?

Observations: The Soviets looked and acted like Americans. If it weren't for the language you'd swear they were all tractor salesmen from Dubuque in for the convention; double knits, jeans, leather briefcases and cowboy boots. I saw them every morning when they came down to breakfast. They then proceeded to the garden to sun themselves while waiting for the Soviet embassy bus to take them to work. It made me wonder whether there were any Afghans who looked like Russians.

***

Friday was the Muslim Sabbath. I'd arranged for Massoud to take me to a Mullah I met on my first trip – Malawi Aziz Sadiq. His mosque, the Majnoon Shah, was a short drive out by the airport and I had lots of questions to ask him. Sadiq was a major figure in the Afghan government's campaign to prove the PDPA was not against Islam. He was actually a government official and had been to Mecca for the Hajj. His mosque was new, and he got a government salary.

I remembered him as a kind of gregarious guy with a white turban and long gray robes, and he laughed when he saw me.

"I never expected to see you again," he told me, grabbing my shoulders with his large hands.

"Same here," I replied. "The war has brought about strange things." He invited us in to his living quarters where his wife had prepared lunch and I began.

"You told me last time that you were close to Hafizullah Amin."

"I knew him well. I was one of his closest friends."

"In the U.S. it was claimed he was against Islam, that he tortured religious people and persecuted them."

Sadiq was immediately indignant.

"No. Those are lies," he said, resting his large forearms on the table. "He respected Islam. He wanted to work with us. He never once opposed anything we suggested."

"In the countryside? Amin's reforms were never accepted in the countryside."

"The religious men outside Kabul are ignorant of Afghan Islam. They have always fallen to the ways of foreigners. But the government of Babrak Karmal is working it out."

Negotiating the lines within Islam was tricky business. "Who do you mean by foreigners?"

"I mean the British and the French. They have always interfered. Gailani, Rabbani, Mojaddedi, Mohammedi all took money from the non-believers."

"And what about Gulbuddin?" I asked. "Hasn't Gulbuddin taken money from the non-believers?"

Malawi Sadiq was strangely silent, his eyes downcast. He was torn about Gulbuddin, so I backed off.

"I met someone from the BBC who was here the night the Soviets invaded. He told me when Amin heard the helicopters landing at the Palace, he said it was the Americans coming to rescue him."

Sadiq's sad eyes reflected the moment. "He might have wished they were the Americans," he said, shaking his head. "But he knew it was the Russians coming for him."

He'd known. He'd obviously known. "But how did he know?"

"Everybody knew there was a plot."

There it was. I had it. "A plot to overthrow Amin!"

"A plot to form a government with Gulbuddin Hekmatyar."

Now that was the shocker. "A what?"

Sadiq continued. "There was a meeting in Peshawar. It had all been arranged with Gulbuddin. He was coming to Kabul. The Russians found out about it. They told me not to go to the Palace to visit him that night. It wouldn't be safe."

"So Amin *was* going over to the Americans."

Sadiq's eyes flashed a burst of anger. "And the Americans could have saved him. Amin was now Prime Minister, Foreign Minister and President. He could appoint Gulbuddin to anything he wanted."

I was stunned. "Gulbuddin? Gulbuddin was an enemy of Mohammed Daoud. Wasn't he an enemy of the PDPA?"

"Gulbuddin had been a very early member of Amin's party and his friend. But Taraki was a Marxist. Taraki was trusted by the Soviets. He conspired with them to kill Amin so Amin had him killed."

I was trying to follow, but my head was reeling. "So Amin wasn't a Marxist?"

Sadiq smiled wryly. "Amin saw an opportunity. He and Gulbuddin were of the same tribe, the Ghilzai. They were related by blood and money."

Money? The idea hadn't struck me until that moment. "Money?"

"Gulbuddin had money. Lots of money. And lots of friends who were willing to help him spend it."

"Money from opium poppy?" I asked.

"I think you are seeing what happened to the April revolution," Malawi Aziz Sadiq said, finishing off with a sardonic smile.

CHAPTER 30

Malawi Sadiq had added missing pieces to the puzzle. If Amin was linked to Hekmatyar then Adolph Dubs' project to keep the Soviets out never had a chance. Amin's closeness to the U.S. was a major concern for the Soviets. They suspected he was a CIA agent and so did Dubs. Why had Dubs asked his CIA station chief flat out whether Amin was working for the agency? Was it because Amin was acting as a double agent and screwing up his delicate plans?

Gulbuddin Hekmatyar was the CIA's go-to guy for Afghanistan. He *had* been from 1973-on when Prince Mohammed Daoud drove him into Pakistan where he got the help of Pakistan's Inter-Services-Intelligence Directorate the ISI. The ISI wanted to overthrow Daoud as much as Gulbuddin so a marriage was made. But Gulbuddin's link to Amin would imply that Amin's "Marxist revolution" was only a cover. Daoud had overthrown the king in a bloodless coup in 1973. But Amin's takeover was one of the bloodiest in a century with many of the king's family executed and the rest fleeing for their lives.

The CIA hated nationalists as much as they hated Communists. Daoud's Afghan nationalism had been a thorn in their side for decades. His claims on Afghan land confiscated by the British and ceded to Pakistan made him dangerous. His political ties to the Communist Babrak Karmal made him anathema. Everyone knew Gulbuddin's operation was funded by drug dealing. To put Gulbuddin together with Amin made Amin a party to the CIA's agenda and the drug trade as well. And if Amin was in on the drug trade, then the Dubs' kidnapping took on a whole new meaning.

***

When I'd left NY I thought I knew what the story was. Now I was beginning to think there was another story – a bigger one where the Soviet role was simply in its shadow.

Afghanistan was considered a third-rate posting at the State Department when Theodore Eliot was there during the Daoud years from 1973 to 1978. Theodore Eliot was an important man; dean of the diplomatic corps – old line Boston Brahmin and a leading Bilderberg globalist. Yet he was posted there for five years and three U.S. administrations. How strange. Afghanistan had sunk to fourth-rate by the time Dubs replaced him and he was killed seven months later. Why? What had he been doing that Theodore Eliot hadn't? While Dubs was blocking Brzezinski's strategy to roll-back Soviet influence, absolutely nobody was paying attention to Afghanistan. Dubs thought he could still get along with the Soviets while detaching Amin from their influence. With the Shah next door in serious trouble he should have been getting major support from Washington. Instead, the resistance from Brzezinski got even worse. Brzezinski hadn't needed to harm him; he controlled the narrative in Washington. So why was he killed? *Cui bono* – who benefitted? Certainly not the kidnappers.

The Soviets? They'd lost détente and SALT and handed U.S. foreign policy to a right wing Russophobe. And Amin? He'd reached out secretly to Washington after Dubs' death, realizing he was out of his depth, but Brzezinski left him to twist in the wind. So all we were left with was Lal Mohammed, the psychopath in charge of the "rescue." Would a local police chief have taken it on himself to kill the American ambassador in cold blood? Not unless he'd had support from someone *much higher up.*

***

After a few days I was beginning to trust Massoud's judgement about things. I welcomed his suggestion to visit the Kabul Museum, so we drove out towards the Daruluman Palace in his black government-issued Lada so I could see some of "those rare objects you only find buried in the ruins of Central Asia."

I started the conversation. "You probably heard my chat with Malawi Sadiq."

Massoud smiled. He said nothing and kept his eyes on the road. I continued.

"He said Amin was in it with Hekmatyar. That's big news. No one back in the U.S. has ever suggested that."

"It's why the 1978 April coup was so bloody," Massoud said, nervously checking the rear view mirror for signs of a tail. "Amin wanted to wipe out the Durrani family line – the king's line. The Ghilzai and Durrani families have been at war for three hundred years. Amin and Hekmatyar are Ghilzai."

"Tell me more about Gulbuddin."

"He joined the PDPA in high school in the late 1960s," he said, his eyes carefully scanning the road ahead. "Attended military school in Kabul but he became involved with the extremists and joined the Muslim Youth. He went to Kabul University in the early 70s where he met Ahmad Shah Massoud, a Tajik. One day somebody thought they saw them holding hands, but they were holding a bottle of acid. They threw it at a woman dressed in Western clothes."

"That's the time when Gulbuddin murdered another student."

Massoud tensed. "From a Maoist faction of the PDPA. Some people said it was his lover. Anyway, he went to jail."

"So Gulbuddin is a murderer *and* a homosexual?"

"Gulbuddin is a very complicated man," Massoud said, smiling derisively. "After Mohammed Daoud overthrew the king, he freed Gulbuddin and he fled to Pakistan with Ahmad Shah Massoud."

I glanced toward the heavily guarded Soviet embassy as we passed by. "And that's where this all begins."

"Gulbuddin joined Ahmad Shah Massoud's Jamaat-i-Islami party. With the help of Pakistan's ISI they tried to stir an uprising against Daoud but Daoud shut them down. So Gulbuddin formed his own more radical party, the Hesb-i-Islami."

"Was that when he came to the attention of the CIA?" I asked.

"The path was clear. Afghanistan never wanted trouble but the real trouble came from Hafizullah Amin."

Amin sounded like a character out of a movie script – a kind of Pashtun Pancho Villa. Instead of being an Afghan or a Muslim or even a Marxist, he'd just been a clever opportunist who'd used anyone or anything to get what he wanted, and he wouldn't hesitate to kill if someone was in his way.

Massoud squinted, thinking about it. "At the time Gulbuddin was gaining power in Pakistan, Amin was tearing through the PDPA and ripping out his enemies. Daoud had come to power with the help of Babrak Karmal and his Parcham faction of the PDPA. But Amin's faction grew stronger and he had the military on his side. By the spring of 1978 he was ready to achieve Pakistan's objective and remove the last of the Durrani clan, but that was only his first move. Bringing Gulbuddin back to Afghanistan would have completed the circuit and put the Ghilzai in power for the first time in three hundred years, but the Soviets stopped it at the last minute."

***

Massoud wrapped up the saga as we pulled up the drive of the Kabul Museum. The world famous two story stone building resided comfortably in the lower garden of the Daruluman palace. On that late afternoon in May, it took me back to another era. The museum had been a favorite of European collectors in the 1930s and was considered one of the finest museums in the world. I could still see the women in print dresses, and Afghan royals and French aristocrats in their black tuxedos, drinking gin and tonics on the patio. The museum's treasures spanned a hundred thousand years of Afghan history. You could see the growth of civilization as it spread out across Asia merging East and West. And all paid for by the largest collection of Greek and Roman coins in the world. Mongols, Persians, Arabs. Everything there linked Asia to Europe to the Middle East from Neanderthal to the Vikings. Yes, even the Vikings. Made me wonder if that was why I was so comfortable there. All those Anglo/Norman Fitzgeralds and FitzMaurices trading on the Silk Road a thousand years ago – or maybe a hundred years ago… Hmm, FitzMaurices? Maybe my strange encounter the other night hadn't been as strange as I'd thought.

On the road back to Kabul we drove by the Soviet-built Macroyan housing project. Massoud told me a bomb killed one and wounded four there only a few days before. After spending thirty years competing peacefully with the Soviets, this was now America's contribution to Afghan culture – U.S. sponsored terrorism. Americans were told these atrocities were being committed by "Fiercely religious Freedom Fighters." What Americans didn't know was that the British used to sponsor this kind of thing long before the Soviets got here. Tories in London had been doing it since the 1840s, paying off tribal chiefs to cripple the Afghan government. The Forward Policy, they called it. After World War II, the creation of Pakistan kept the policy going but the king's cousin Mohammed Daoud threatened to turn it back on them and invade. And so entered the American-educated Hafizullah Amin and Afghanistan had never been the same.

Friday evening, May 6:
It was 8:00 P.M. and I was back at my typewriter. Today had left an impression of pervasive security – Afghan security, not Russian. Much more so than two years ago, the Afghan army was out in force. Massoud and I drove ten miles out and back from the city and the only Russians we saw were standing guard at their embassy, but the Afghan soldiers were everywhere. That CBS News report about Kabul crawling with Soviets still didn't add up. But a lot of other stuff was beginning to, bit by bit.

CHAPTER 31

The night was alive – dog fights – armored personnel carriers; the occasional shout and bursts of machine gun fire. It seemed a lot closer to the hotel than before. A few short bursts then silence. I was already getting used to it and fell off to sleep. I dream of Adolph Dubs on the floor of room 117 staring up at Lal Mohammed the drug policeman. Lal fires four shots into Dubs' head with an automatic pistol then grabs him roughly by the sport coat and hoists him into a nearby chair – the same sport coat the Soviet police advisor refused to hand over to Bruce Flatin in order to *"examine it for evidence."* What evidence had it revealed? Did the Soviet policeman suspect Lal? There is no mention of a "sport coat" in the official report.

The whole incident takes less than ten seconds. Lal Mohammed then signals for the American stretcher bearers to come. U.S. DEA drug policeman Doug Wankel is the first to enter the room. It's Wankel who pays out money to Afghan drug informers under the thumb of the Afghan drug policeman, Lal Mohammed. The circle closes.

Around midnight the call of the Muezzin woke me up in a cold sweat. Puzzle pieces were flying around in my head like slugs from a .22 caliber. Malawi Sadiq had said Gulbuddin had the money. The idea hadn't struck me until that moment. He'd said, "Gulbuddin had money. Lots of money. And lots of friends who were willing to help."

"I think you are seeing what happened to the April revolution," he'd said.

Amin was the revolution. But it hadn't been a revolution. It had been a coup organized by Amin and pulled off by his people in the military. Taraki was the useful figurehead for the PDPA – until he wasn't. Gulbuddin was now linked to Amin. Gulbuddin and drugs. Gulbuddin and money. The voice in my head whispered forget the politics and follow the money. Lal Mohammed worked for Amin. Lal Mohammed was a drug policeman. Lal knew who had the drugs. Lal knew who had the money. Doug Wankel was a drug policeman. Doug Wankel pointed the finger away from Lal and at the Soviets. Dubs was murdered for no obvious reason. Lal wrote the official Afghan police report. Lal lied. Lal refused to provide evidence. Lal was at the center of the murder of Adolph Dubs and nobody wanted to even name him except an unnamed CIA asset in a classified cable. Were drugs the missing reason?

That guy FitzMaurice last night said that this war was the beginning of a whole new estate. "Privatized warfare beyond state control. And all financed by the opium trade. Just like the British and the East India Company."

Maybe it was time to go back to the patio.

Getting past the desk unseen was the tricky part, but the rest was easy. Down the stairs and out through the glass doors to the ballroom. "I'm just ducking out for a smoke," I'd tell him if the soldier stopped me, but he was nowhere to be seen.

The patio was empty, the back gate locked. You would have thought a place like this would be a target for Muslim fanatics. The place rocked to the beat on weekends. Weddings were a big draw and everyone danced. But the place was quiet now, except for the rumbling of the guns and the flashes over the Bala Hissar fortress.

"How's your quest for truth and justice coming?" a voice from the shadows called. It was Desmond FitzMaurice, and I had questions about the night before.

"I was hoping you'd be here. That thing you said about a whole new estate?"

FitzMaurice stepped out of the shadows. "I should have said the New World Order."

"Is that what they call this?"

"That's what David Rockefeller and George Ball call it. I suppose Zbigniew Brzezinski as well. The Trilateralists, the Bilderbergers, the Pilgrim Society. And of course the *Priory of Sion.*

"*Novus Ordo Seclorum.* The New World Order is actually the Old World Order. Henry Wallace convinced Roosevelt to put it on the back of the dollar bill. At the end of World War II America was leaving its Republican phase and becoming an empire. He wanted the gods to favor that empire – *Annuit coeptis* – as a force for the good, for peace. A Pax Americana."

"It doesn't look very peaceful from here."

"Don't be fooled by the fireworks. Both sides want the same thing. They all start out wanting peace. The Roman poet Virgil called for *A New Order for the ages* to replace the chaos of the Republic. The Romans wound up with the most violent empire in the ancient world. If Henry Wallace were around today he'd be on the side of Team B."

"I don't believe it. Wallace wanted better relations with the Soviet Union."

"Didn't you ever wonder why the 'good guys' who want peace always lose? When the Cold War came he accepted it because he just wanted his side to win." FitzMaurice motioned toward the action in the night. "The KGB didn't want this war. They warned Brezhnev. But Soviet military intelligence, the GRU did. The CIA understands that. It's always a team effort. Team A and Team B. They need each other. You'll see."

I still couldn't believe it. "And you think Adolph Dubs knew that?"

"Accept that things are not as you've been told and you can begin to understand," FitzMaurice offered calmly.

Pieces of the puzzle rattled around in my head. "You mentioned opium last night. That it's financing this."

"During World War II the OSS got involved with the Chinese Green Gang in Shanghai and the Sicilian mafia. Lucky Luciano to be exact. The U.S. wanted to invade Sicily and asked Luciano to help out with his mafia contacts. That was the beginning of the drug relationship."

The tumblers clicked. George Beyers Griffin minded Luciano in Sicily for the U.S. government after the war. Adolph Dubs wanted Griffin to come to Kabul to be his DCM, Deputy Chief of Mission. Griffin knew the ins and outs of the narcotics trade but he hadn't been able to get there in time.

FitzMaurice continued. "Luciano had been dealing heroin since the 1920s and connected to the Green Gang crime networks of the Chinese Nationalists, the KMT, since the '30s. After the war the CIA picked up where the OSS left off and got heavily involved with the KMT in Southeast Asia. The French secret service had already worked out the supply lines with the Corsican mafia through Iran and Lebanon to Marseilles."

FitzMaurice was overwhelming me. "Slow down. How does that connect to here?"

"The communists were driving the drug traffickers out of business. They did it in China and then Vietnam. Since the end of the war in '75, the trade has been moving out of Southeast Asia. Nobody was even looking at it – except for the Deputy U.S. Assistant Secretary of State for Near Eastern and South Asian Affairs."

"I get it. Adolph Dubs."

"Dubs led a Study Mission on International Controls of Narcotics Trafficking and Production for the Senate Select Committee on Narcotics Abuse and Control six months before he came here as ambassador."

"So he knew this was where the drug trade was going."

"But he didn't know at the time that it was being privatized."

My mind was struggling to catch up. "What does that mean?"

"Bhutto was removed from office in Pakistan in July of '77. Daoud next door in Afghanistan in April of '78 and the Shah of Iran in February of '79. No state government interference. The drug trade was back to where it was in the 19ᵗʰ century; no controls, no regulations, no oversight. It meant the CIA could do what Himmler had wanted done with the SS in 1944. It could finance whatever it wanted to do, wherever and whenever it chose, and nobody would ever know."

I'd thought my head was about to lift off. "But how? You can't just privatize a government agency without somebody noticing. What about President Carter and Stanfield Turner at the CIA? What about Cyrus Vance at the State Department? What about the DEA?"

FitzMaurice looked amused. "What you mean is what about Alexandre de Marenches and the *Priory of Sion*? What about Alexandre de Marenches and the *Safari Club*? What about Alexandre de Marenches and the *October Surprise*?"

I was totally mystified. "I have no idea what you're talking about."

"And you won't until you start asking the right questions," FitzMaurice said as he turned toward the Bala Hissar.

I got the message and said nothing as he turned back toward me.

"Did you think Watergate and the Church Committee hearings were good things? They were – for the intelligence community. Exposing the CIA's dirty secrets triggered the opportunity for them to go underground. Jimmy Carter was a transition president. Zbigniew Brzezinski was brought in to manage that transition. France's chief of external intelligence Count Alexander de Marenches did the dirty work. He ran the operation to derail Carter's reelection and secure the Reagan/Bush presidency. The press labeled it the 'October Surprise.' All he had to do was delay the release of the American hostages, and with the Ayatollah's help, get Reagan elected."

"So how does de Marenches fit into the Dubs event?" I asked.

"The plan was always to rollback Soviet influence. It had been on a back burner for decades but Brzezinski brought it forward. Count de Marenches organized and managed it through an intelligence operation known as the *Safari Club*. They named it after a resort they used to hunt at in Africa. The "club" was exactly what the CIA was originally intended to be, an off-the-books covert-action force with roots in the old European nobility beyond the jurisdiction of Congressional oversight and answerable to no one."

The idea stunned. "European nobility?"

"A spinoff of the fascist cabal known as the Pinay Cercle – paranoid anti-Communist European nobility. The club had been active informally in the Middle East and Africa for years, destabilizing unfriendly governments and assassinating enemies. They'd been planning for years to take control of American foreign policy. But they found their opportunity when Watergate and the Church Committee hearings paralyzed the CIA's ability to act."

The door was opening wider. "And who is in this club?"

FitzMaurice continued, "At the time the Shah of Iran, King Hassan of Morocco, Anwar al-Sadat of Egypt, Kamal Adham, head of Saudi intelligence and eventually Iraqi strongman Saddam Hussein. But there were plenty of ex-CIA and freelance contractors to fill out the ranks."

I was beginning to see the light. This was the real meaning of privatization. "So the Safari Club wasn't just a *foreign* intelligence operation?"

"The whole idea was actually the brainchild of Clark Clifford, the Democratic Party's 'Wise Man' and CIA Director Richard Helms. Helms was appointed ambassador to Tehran to get him out of Washington so he could run the agency from there. CIA Director George Bush then outsourced covert operations to friendly foreign intelligence agencies. By 1976 the Safari Club had become *the real* CIA, covertly funded by Saudi Arabia through the Bank of Commerce and Credit International (BCCI) and run out of the U.S. embassy in Tehran. When Carter came in Stansfield Turner released over 800 veteran agents. Guess where they went?"

Under the glare of the distant firefight, FitzMaurice's tone had become darkly serious. "Now here's the point. Afghanistan offered the opportunity for BCCI to migrate the lucrative heroin business from Southeast Asia to the Pakistan/Afghan border under cover of the destabilization. President Carter supported Brzezinski's provocations into Soviet territory from the minute they got into the White House. He then sanctioned Brzezinski's plan to use Afghanistan to lure the Soviet Union into its own Vietnam and lied to the public about it when they fell into the trap on December 27, 1979."

It was a rude awakening. I'd swallowed the Watergate and the Church Committee hearings as victories over secrecy. Who hadn't? *All the President's Men* anyone? I'd seen Jimmy Carter as a weak but positive development in the post-Watergate corruption of American democracy. I had remembered Clark Clifford as an esteemed senior policy advisor for over fifty years, and law partner to SALT negotiator Paul Warnke. Here I was being told that it had all been a distraction.

"So why does French intelligence play such an important role? Why are the French at the center of rolling the Soviet Union back?" I asked.

"Because it was always about the French," FitzMaurice said in a near whisper. "The French behind the First Crusade. The French behind the American Revolution. The French who invaded Russia in 1812. The French behind Vietnam. The French behind the heroin trade and the French behind the Soviet invasion of Afghanistan."

"I recall de Marenches predicted it. He told his cousin Arnaud de Borchgrave to go to Kabul that December."

"Count de Marenches could predict it, because he'd provoked it. And he provoked it because it was part of a plan that's taken centuries to unfold – the Priory of Sion's plan. That makes the Priory the most important connection of *all* the French connections. And you've decided to put yourself in the middle of it. Have you ever asked yourself why?"

CHAPTER 32

Asked myself why? Why not, was more like it. I'd never given it a thought. Afghanistan was the biggest story out of the Cold War since the Cuban Missile Crisis. Everybody wanted it. If I'd asked myself anything it would've been why everything had fallen into place like clockwork; meeting Farid Zarif, gaining the exclusive visa, CBS News, George Beyers Griffin, PBS... even Theodore Eliot and Roger Fisher. Had my presence there been part of "the Priory's plan that had taken centuries to unfold?" That was ridiculous. What did I have in common with the Priory of Sion, if there even was such a thing? The Crusades? That had nothing to do with me. But there really had been something strange about Theodore Eliot and his behavior. I woke up the next morning not knowing whether last night on the patio was real, or if I had dreamed it. The story was out of control. Tri-lateralists, Bilderbergers, the Pilgrim Society... drugs, Nazis, and the CIA and now the Priory of Sion? The New World Order theme *had* been kicking around for two thousand years. Henry Wallace had invoked it. The Nazis called it the "Jewish/Masonic conspiracy" and were driven to stop it. I'd seen Henry Lincoln's 1970s BBC documentaries and read the popular book *Holy Blood and Holy Grail*. But did anyone really believe that the blood was the blood of Jesus of Nazareth and the Grail was the womb of his bride Mary Magdalene? Oh please. Even if it was, after all that time what gave their descendants the authority to take over the world now? Desmond FitzMaurice had been digging around in Central Asia for ancient relics and come up with a doozy. The Priory of Sion story did, however, add a motive to Count Alexandre de Marenches' involvement. The Priory was dedicated to restoring the House of David and the ancient Kingdom of Israel. French royals were connected to the American Christian right wing and they were both dedicated to advancing Israel's interests, so there *was* a match.

According to popular legend the Priory had backed the taking of Jerusalem in the First Crusade in 1096 and created the Knights of the Temple of King Solomon to help them hold it – the Templars. The Templars had created the first banking empire and put Europe's royalty in their debt by loaning them money for wars. All those wars had earned them vast treasures and they'd built fortified castles from Dublin to the Holy Land to protect it. The Catholic "Wild Bill" Donovan had referred to his OSS agents as the Knights Templar and if anyone was positioned to establish a new world order after World War II it was them. I'd always thought it strange that the leader of America's first elite spy force should identify his mission with a medieval military order of gnostic monks who'd been burned at the stake by Rome in the 14th century for engaging in heretical practices. But then I was beginning to see that the world didn't work the way that I'd been taught to believe.

Saturday morning May 7, 8:00 A.M.

I picked up the English language *Kabul New Times* newspaper and took it with me to breakfast. The lead story was about a U.S. embassy diplomat who had been ordered to leave the country for being "engaged in the sex and pornography business" after attempting to "pervert Afghan youth" by trying to buy a rug with a copy of *Playboy* magazine. The article went into great detail how the decadent Americans would use any trick to seduce innocent Afghans to their cause and were using similar anti-Islamic incentives to support the counter-revolutionary, drug-dealing bandits. I couldn't believe an American official could be so stupid, but I was learning.

My driver turned up at 8:45 in an old white Peugeot 404 I'd rented, with Massoud already onboard. We headed back over to the foreign ministry to reinforce my "program" and found Roshanrowan in a demonstrably better mood. I pressed him on my request to grant Roger Fisher an interview with Babrak Karmal and he assured me that it was being arranged, and that Roger would be offered only top Afghan officials. His reluctance to confirm my request was a telltale sign that something was up with Karmal.

We then drove to the airport to pick up my impounded tapes. We parked about thirty yards from the small terminal building and Massoud asked for money.

"The tapes will cost one hundred Afghanis a piece to retrieve."

"I won't pay it," I told him. I didn't think he was used to journalists haggling over official state policy.

"OK," he said, laughing. He got out of the car and proceeded inside. While I waited, I got the show of a lifetime as a flock of green camouflaged Mi-24 Hind (Rambo) helicopter gunships circled the airport and came in for a landing one by one. The Hind was the locomotive of helicopters;

short, stubby wings crammed with rocket pads. An enormous, armed alligator. Somebody had nicknamed it the flying crocodile. It was no exaggeration. Mi-24 gunships didn't fly like normal helicopters, either. Instead they followed one another onto the runway in slow motion like hungry velociraptors on a Macy's escalator, equally paced and distanced one after the next. The sight was an awesome display. Had I been on the receiving end out in the countryside, I'm sure I'd have been quite terrified.

I assumed a major operation was underway but I had no way of knowing what the target was. After a half hour a very disgusted Massoud returned bearing my boxes of Sony cassettes, muttering, "Stupid Khalqis," and we moved on.

I spent the rest of the afternoon getting the bureaucratic approvals demanded of foreign journalists. It was no wonder they got such bad press. First they wouldn't let anybody in, and when they finally did they wanted control over every detail of what you saw.

Next up was Abdullah Shadon, the young and innovative president of Afghan television I'd met two years before. Abdullah was dressed in a military uniform and was a lot more sure of himself than when we'd first met. He had a lot of opinions, and like most educated Afghans was mystified by the U.S. support for the Mujahideen.

"Why is the U.S. backing these medieval people when all the country wants is to become a modern nation?" he asked. He was particularly upset with the misinformation coming over the Voice of America.

"The broadcast reported the destruction of two buses on the way to the anniversary celebrations last week," he said, adding that, "The buses were said to be filled with Party officials." He then said, "There were some officials on board but the majority of people were innocent families who were not even politically affiliated, but were headed to Kabul for the festivities. They did not report that."

I asked if he had any documentation of who and what the rebels had been targeting and he said, "Lots."

And for the next forty minutes I watched raw footage of recent attacks around Kabul; bomb blasts, bus hijackings and mass murders by "freedom fighters." Brutal scenes showed a shot-up bus on a dirt road with bodies sprawled across a hillside blackening in the sun. The murderers had not discriminated. Men, women and children were equally represented in the video clips. Those murders were not intended to be political but they were because the U.S. had supplied the weapons and the ammunition.

The bomb blasts were even worse. Rescuers dug through rubble to uncover bloody faces crushed by the weight of falling concrete, their bodies flattened like paper dolls.

Abdullah Shadon offered me copies of the carnage and I accepted. If I'd spent the last six months there I could not have shot better footage.

"Do you want film from the anniversary parade?" he asked as he puts another cassette in the machine.

"Of course," I said, but as the tape rolled I realized someone was missing.

"Where is Babrak Karmal?" I asked.

He shrugged and shook his head. "I don't know, but he wasn't present at the anniversary parade."

I had footage from the same parade two years before and it had featured Babrak Karmal prominently at the podium of the reviewing stand. This time he was nowhere to be seen. The rumors were accurate. The Russians were making a deal, and removing Karmal was part of the bargain. Andropov had been saying it for months. The Soviets were pulling back and the Afghans were fighting more. All I had to do was convince them to let me do what I'd come for and maybe Liz, Paul and Roger could correct the phony narrative that surrounded the place.

***

The phony narrative. If it hadn't been for the Dubs murder the phony narrative would never have stuck. If it hadn't been for the Dubs murder there would never have been a Soviet invasion. Outside I found Massoud waiting with the old Peugeot, and I climbed into the back seat.

"Did you get what you wanted from Abdullah?" he asked as we started off for the hotel.

"I got some great footage," I replied.

"So you can go back and tell them in Washington that Afghanistan wants good relations."

"If Afghanistan wants good relations, Afghanistan must explain what happened to the American ambassador."

Massoud was unfazed. "All those people are dead."

"All what people?"

"The police chief, Lal Mohammed, Superintendent Sayed Taroun. Taroun was killed by Taraki. He was shot protecting Amin. Lal was killed in a gunfight outside Kabul. Amin was... Well, you know about him." Massoud smiled a cynical grin. "They were bad men. Amin put the wrong men in charge. And now they are dead."

"There must be something else," I suggested strongly.

Massoud shook his head. "What else do you need?"

"I need to know more about the kidnappers. The newspaper reports said they were from a Tajik Maoist group called the 'Setam I Melli.'"

"No, this is not so," Massoud said, surprised. "The government said they were from a smaller Maoist group called SAMA, from Badakhshan on the Soviet border. They demanded their leader Bahruddin Bahes be released from jail."

"That's a good start."

"But Bahes had already been executed by Amin."

"So Amin is just stalling?"

"Amin was hosting an official delegation from Iraq that day. They were staying at the hotel."

That was a shocker. "Saddam Hussein's delegation was staying at the hotel when the ambassador was kidnapped?"

"Yes. They had a security detail there, a large one. Some were still at the hotel and the rest were with Amin."

"Were the Iraqi security working with the Afghan police?"

"Of course. They were coordinating security together."

This was a significant breakthrough. "Amin was in a conference with the *Iraqis* the whole time?"

"Yes. The whole time."

Jesus Christ. "The State Department accused him of not making himself available."

"Amin was tied up in official business," Massoud said. "Saddam Hussein is important to Afghanistan. Amin couldn't just break it off. He personally escorted the Iraqi ambassador to the airport."

"Why was Saddam Hussein's ambassador more important than the American ambassador?" I asked.

"The Shah of Iran had promised to help Daoud, but it was only a trick to send his secret agents, SAVAK. SAVAK murdered a lot of PDPA people, but the Shah was overthrown two weeks before the kidnapping. Saddam was promising to give the aid the Shah promised but never gave. It was the worst possible day to kidnap the ambassador."

"So Amin was under pressure."

"Yes. And besides, no one was even sure the ambassador *was* being kidnapped."

"How do you mean?"

"The men who brought the ambassador to the hotel had been there with him the day before."

"Say what?"

"Soviet security followed the ambassador everywhere he went. They reported that he had met these same men in the same room at the hotel the day before."

CHAPTER 33

assoud had just taken the kidnapping of Ambassador Adolph Dubs, turned it upside down and cracked it *wide* open. Back in Washington, Brzezinski had been painting Amin as hopelessly pro-Soviet, but it was clear that Amin couldn't be pro-Soviet if he was working with Saddam Hussein. Saddam Hussein was working for the Safari Club and the Safari Club was working for the CIA – like Gulbuddin.

"The kidnapping doesn't make sense because it wasn't a kidnapping," I stammered. "You're absolutely sure about this meeting?"

Massoud stared back at me from the front seat. "The Soviet security man reported the ambassador carried a travel case into the room on the day before. He came and went of his own free will, alone. Why would he do that unless there was a meeting?"

My mind started reaching for an answer. "And what was in the travel case?"

Massoud sniffed as he gave me that cynical look. "Money? Drugs? The Soviet security man couldn't see inside the room."

The pieces were finally beginning to fit together. The DEA man Wankel paid out to Afghan informants. He bought their drugs. If Dubs had his own informants he'd pay them, too. That explained why he unlocked the door of the car. Dubs had a secret relationship with the supposed kidnappers that nobody from the embassy could talk about or may not have even known about.

"The kidnappers never made any demands of the U.S embassy," I told Massoud. "They never even contacted the embassy. Police superintendent Sayed Taroun did."

Massoud filled in the gaps. "Taroun was in charge of the operation. After they arrived at the room they found the door locked. One kidnapper came down for the key and was arrested. They must have thought someone would already be there, like the day before."

What hadn't made sense was now becoming clear. "Massoud, then they're trapped by Afghan security, by Lal Mohammed, and started making desperate demands. Amin can't fulfill the demands even if he wants to because he's trapped in a meeting he can't leave."

Massoud started thinking out loud. "It is possible. SAMA had lots of enemies. They fought against the PDPA, they fought against the Soviets and against Hekmatyar all at the same time. They assassinated party officials, recruited bandits and sometimes stole police uniforms. But there is something else."

I waited for the other shoe to drop. "What else?"

Massoud glanced over toward me and raised his eyebrows. "The man who came down for the key kept yelling at the policeman, 'Whose dog are you? Go tell your boss that I am under orders from Amin.'"

That couldn't have been. "He was bluffing."

Massoud wasn't so sure. "Seven days before the kidnapping, two men approached the manager of the hotel and asked to reserve a room. He took them upstairs and told them room 117 was available but it was very expensive. They said that was OK because they would have an important visitor with them."

Now it was my turn to think out loud. "And the important visitor was the American ambassador. Jesus. Dubs must have had a secret deal going with Amin until something happened."

Massoud raised an eyebrow. "So what happened?"

"Saddam Hussein. The men were ordered back to the room, thinking they were safe. They were expecting someone to show up and tell them what to do. But they were tricked."

"Tricked? Tricked by whom?"

The answer was becoming obvious. "The fourth kidnapper. The one who triggered the crisis. The one who couldn't speak the language well. The one who disappeared into the lobby as soon as they reached the hotel," I said.

Massoud had caught on the minute I'd said it. "Yes, yes. I see. But who was he working for?"

"Someone or something that wants to create a crisis and use it to destroy U.S./Soviet relations."

The name of the Safari Club had come to mind the minute Massoud asked the question but I kept it to myself. To my knowledge at the time, Massoud was not aware of the Safari Club and its connections. I'd only just learned about it myself and was in no position to speculate, but all the pieces seemed to fit.

***

157

I'd already completed all the groundwork for Roger's arrival that I could do on my own. What might I have overlooked? What question would I kick myself for not asking once I got back to the U.S? I pulled out my notebook and thumbed through and all I saw was the name Dubs, Adolph Dubs. The U.S. embassy crowd claimed his abduction and death made no sense unless you blamed the Soviets. I thought his death made no sense *if* you blamed the Soviets, but it made perfect sense for a third party like the Safari Club. They got to remove the major stumbling block for their drug operation while getting to blame the Soviets for their complicity in the death of an ambassador.

Dubs was the key to the Soviet invasion. His murder tipped the scales in Brzezinski's favor. Made the Soviets look like everything Team B wanted them to look like, and then some. Swayed American public opinion that the Soviet Union was an outlaw state run by KGB thugs. Enabled Carter to turn one hundred-eighty degrees from peacenik to Cold Warrior and launched the U.S. military into exactly where Team B and the Priory of Sion wanted them – the Middle East.

It was Brzezinski's narrative that didn't make any sense. If Amin was a Soviet agent why had the Kremlin thrown the SALT treaty and détente out the window and come down there to kill him?

The Soviets invaded because Amin was a gangster, working with the CIA's favorite holy warrior and drug dealer, Gulbuddin Hekmatyar, who was going to turn Afghanistan over to the United States the way Sadat had done in Egypt. He'd murdered the royal family, destroyed the Peoples' Democratic Party, killed the leader of that party and murdered thousands of Afghans. Brzezinski's case was beyond sloppy. It wasn't credible. It was based on ideology, not facts. Amin's behavior had benefitted the CIA and Team B, not the KGB, but absolutely no one was calling *him* on it.

***

The rest of the day was light. I'd done most of what I could do to assure a smooth week for Roger and the crew after they arrived. I'd learned to trust Massoud. His face told me everything I needed to know – I thought. I'd hoped he genuinely appreciated what I was trying to do.

Saturday afternoon we killed time and did all the things an American was allowed to do in Kabul. The antique jewelry, fur, and rug vendors on Chicken Street were glad to see me. *Roll on up cause the price is down.* Things had been slow since the Soviet invasion and the Russians didn't have dollars to spend. Rubles were worthless outside the Soviet bloc. I used the calm before the storm to take as many pictures of Kabul street life as possible; merchants, vendors, street scenes. I got the perfect shot of a grocer sleeping amidst his bounty of potatoes, carrots and beets. I didn't get ten yards down the street before the other vendors started shouting and waving at me.

"He woke up," Massoud said, laughing. "He wants you to go back and take another picture of him awake." I went back and found the man sitting up proudly and smiling. It was a great bookend to the first shot and said a lot about the state of the war. The produce stalls were packed with fresh fruit and vegetables. At the butcher shop, a dozen carcasses swung from meat hooks out front. The streets were crowded. The shopkeepers were calm and friendly. An occasional Russian civilian mixed with the Afghan shoppers and there was no hostility shown towards them. Soviet soldiers were nowhere to be seen. This was *not* the picture the *New York Times* or CBS News wanted the world to see.

Saturday evening after dark the bustling streets cleared quickly. By eight o'clock they were uncharacteristically quiet. You could feel the tension in the air. Word must have spread to stay indoors. Off toward the southeast, behind the Bala Hissar I can see bursts of bright light from explosions. They continued and intensified for an hour as if the city was under siege. At first I heard no sounds, but later I could hear faint rumblings from off behind the mountains. I tried taking pictures with my Nikon but it was a waste of film.

I pulled out my Sony Walkman and started playing Billy Joel's *Nylon Curtain*. The songs were moving. They got me thinking about the unseen war that was going on at home right under people's noses. Big business was closing factories in Allentown and throwing people out of work. Filling out forms in Bethlehem where they used to make steel. American industry couldn't compete with the Germans and the Japanese because American's money went into MX missiles and Trident submarines justified by the Soviet occupation of Afghanistan. It was another self-fulfilling prophecy. The Reagan administration had embraced workers in Poland, not Pennsylvania. American resources went to drug dealing Freedom Fighters in the mountains of Afghanistan not job creation in Pittsburgh. But the clincher was in Billy Joel's song *Goodnight Saigon*; helicopters over the city; scaled chord progressions signaled the sad tragedy of America's imperial dream going down in flames.

159

They heard the hum of the motors.
They counted the rotors and waited for us to arrive.
And we would all go down together.
And we would all go down together.

It was an epiphany. I could hear it and feel it and see it all before me. I was alone on a Saturday night in Kabul watching Jimmy Carter's "Greatest Threat to Peace since the Second World War" and it was utter bullshit. Afghanistan was a diversion created to cover up the transfer of power and wealth away from the American people to a global elite, and nobody but a handful of creatures in some thousand-year-old secret society understood why.

CHAPTER 34

I needed to get some air and crashed a wedding downstairs in the ballroom. An Afghan soldier stood guard at the door and laughed as I danced the Attan, an Afghan dance, past him to the music. The band was good, and I mean good. I wished I'd had these guys at my wedding.

After dinner I encountered one of the East German radio guys sitting alone in the hotel's small café.

"Will you join me?" he asked, offering me a cigarette.

After a week on my own it was a relief to have someone other than an Afghan to talk to. So I sat down and took a cigarette from his pack.

"You're here for the anniversary of the revolution?" I asked.

"Revolution? There was no revolution," the German sniffed.

This was a media guy from a Communist country. I was taken aback. "You don't think this government is revolutionary?"

The young man grimaced. "This government is a farce. The Parcham controls some ministries, Khalq the others. There is no unity. They each struggle for power inside and outside their factions. They are so busy shooting at each other in the hallways they have no time to fight the rebels."

Jesus, it was that bad – just the way Louis Dupree, the CIA's anthropologist described it. Dupree had tried to convince Washington that the PDPA wasn't Communist, but they just hadn't cared.

We exchanged small talk. I asked the man his name but he shook his head no. "No names," he grumbled as he glanced over his shoulder.

"I am with a team from Rundfunk DDR – Deutsche Demokratische Radio. I'd hoped to do a documentary about building socialism in Afghanistan," he said. "But it's pointless from that perspective. They don't even know what socialism is."

The exchange ended suddenly when his colleague poked his head into the room. The man eyed me suspiciously, and my new German friend begged off. "I must go," he said abruptly.

That was quick.

A week's worth of Kabul's dust and high desert climate had my vocal cords in shreds. Pulling smoke across them was probably the worst thing I could do, but at that moment I really didn't care. I took the last few drags on the cigarette outside to the patio and stared up at the night sky. The rumbling was now closer than it had been all week. Shells burst over the hills just a few miles away. I tried to imagine what the reaction would be from Liz and the crew when they finally got here, but I came up dry. I had come to enjoy my own private Afghanistan and I wasn't sure I could explain what I knew to anyone else. Or why I knew it.

"It's growing on you, isn't it?" said the now-familiar voice of Desmond FitzMaurice.

My mood had turned sour. "It's the nihilism. I'm drawn to the spectacle of human failure."

"The spectacle of human failure?" FitzMaurice repeated as he emerged from the dark fringes of the patio. "Now that *is* nihilism."

"No. Nihilism is when an American ambassador gets killed so some very old French noble can be crowned the king of the world."

FitzMaurice feigned curiosity. "So you've figured it out, have you?"

"Bear with me. A Polish noble, Brzezinski, gets a French noble, de Marenches, to get a Saudi noble, Kamal Adham, to destabilize the Russians in Afghanistan. Count de Marenches then sends his cousin, the Belgian noble Arnaud de Borchgrave, to paint the Russian response as Communist aggression, when it's actually just a reaction to what the other nobles have done. The destabilization kills three birds with one stone. It weakens the Soviets whom all four despise. It acts as a cover for moving the heroin business out of Vietnam/Laos and Cambodia to a safe haven on the Pakistan frontier with Afghanistan – a trade that propped up the British Empire financially for over a hundred years. And it makes all the parties involved fabulously rich, enabling them to operate against the Soviet Union without having to account to anyone. Adham then gets Afghan drug dealer and CIA asset Gulbuddin Hekmatyar to organize a deal with the renegade gangster, Afghan prime minister, and possible CIA asset Hafizullah Amin. Amin plots to get the Soviets out of Afghanistan and make Kabul the center of the world-heroin trade. The deal gets everybody excited. Adham pays for the off-the-books operation with drug money brought in by Hekmatyar and laundered through a Pakistani bank set up by the CIA and Adham known as BCCI. Everything goes smoothly until the new U.S. Ambassador Adolph Dubs launches a campaign against the destabilization and starts advising Amin how to keep the Russians from overreacting."

I'd paused to see if FitzMaurice was still with me.

"Go on," he said, quietly.

"I'm speculating of course, but the ambassador had his own connections to the Soviets. He served as counsel at the embassy in Moscow in the early seventies and was stationed in Moscow during the Cuban Missile Crisis. He probably had his own contacts with the Soviet military, too. He knew their people in the Interior Ministry and the GRU, military intelligence. He knew how to keep a cool head and how to keep them cool. I know his objective was to maintain the established policy of détente with the Soviets and find a way to make it work in Afghanistan. I assume Brzezinski, de Marenches and Adham didn't. Am I right?"

FitzMaurice rested against the low garden wall of the patio, listening quietly. "And you're implying?"

"That the ambassador had worked out a deal with the Russians that ran counter to the Safari Club's deal with Gulbuddin Hekmatyar and Amin. The people that abducted him were Tajik Maoists from Badakhshan in the north on the Soviet border. I've learned that the ambassador knew these people, and that he may have been conducting some kind of business transaction with them. But what I don't know is why."

FitzMaurice hadn't wasted a second. "Early in the Cold War Kabul CIA station was looking for ways to do cross border raids into the Soviet Union, turn the populations of Tajikistan, Uzbekistan and Turkmenistan against the Kremlin. They tried to get Afghan Uzbeks and Hazaras to work together. The Mogul band, they called it, but the Uzbeks were Sunni and the Hazara were Shiite so it didn't stick. What did stick was a Tajik-Maoist connection in Badakhshan."

"So therein lays the key to the mystery?" I asked.

"On one level," FitzMaurice said, thinking carefully about it. "The U.S. embassy had a longstanding relationship with the Tajik Maoists as a backdoor to Beijing. The OSS worked with Mao against the Japanese during World War II. The Tajiks despised the Pashtuns, the Maoists despised the PDPA. The embassy supported them with cash payouts under the cover of drug enforcement."

"And the only cash crop around here is opium." I declared.

"And such is how covert action is paid for," FitzMaurice replied, smirking cynically as he continued.

"The U.S. has been working directly with the Chinese since Nixon. Henry Kissinger worked out the details. Just after Dubs arrived in 1978 Mao's intelligence chief made a deal with the Shah to wage war against the Soviets in Afghanistan with SAVAK. SAVAK used the Tajik Maoists as their agents and everybody used the BCCI bankers as their laundry. The Tajik Maoists hated Amin because his drug police were shutting them down and scooping the profits. They wanted to overthrow him but couldn't do it without SAVAK's help."

"And that's where it gets complicated, doesn't it," I added.

FitzMaurice gazed into the darkness as he thought about it. "Dubs didn't want Amin destabilized, and with the Shah about to be expelled from the region, SAVAK was finished. Kamal Adham needed a replacement. So he reached out to the up-and-coming Saddam Hussein to get Amin in line with the Safari Club plan."

It had all began to make sense to me. "So he sends his ambassador to Kabul to meet with Amin and offers him a deal he can't refuse."

"Billions in aid from Saudi Arabia channeled through Baghdad, a huge cut of the proceeds from the heroin trade out of the Hindu Kush, and millions more as a conduit for South American cocaine which the BCCI wants to smuggle into the Soviet Union through their connections with the Soviet Mafia."

I was stunned by the idea. "Jesus Christ, South American cocaine in Afghanistan?"

FitzMaurice's argument was persuasive. "To fund the Contra war against Rome's Liberation Theology in South America."

"No wonder Amin couldn't leave the meeting with Saddam's ambassador. He must have been staggered."

"Unknown to most of the embassy staff, Dubs had been meeting with Amin secretly in the backseat of his car. The ambassador signaled his readiness by removing the American flag from the right front bumper of his Oldsmobile. Before every meeting Police Chief Lal Mohammed quickly swept the car for weapons and bugs, and then signaled Amin."

I realized the connection. "So the ambassador signaled for a meeting. A policeman stopped the car and Dubs opened the door. It's the men Dubs had met with the day before. They got in and drove to the Kabul Hotel. Only this time one of the men was a Safari Club agent working security with the Iraqi delegation and it turned into a kidnapping."

FitzMaurice completed the follow up. "Dubs thought he had shut down the Tajiks with a payment the day before. The Safari Club agent convinced the others it wasn't enough. He leads them to believe that someone would be waiting for them in room 117 then lights the fuse by sending the driver to tell the U.S. embassy what they've done. He then disappears in the confusion of the lobby before anyone realizes what's happening and leaves the other three with the ambassador to face Lal Mohammed's police. He's never even missed until one of the Americans asks Lal about the fourth kidnapper, but nobody knows what he looks like, or where he went. Later in the day he leaves the hotel with the Iraqi delegation and joins the Iraqi ambassador at the airport for the trip home."

"So it *was* the Safari Club that ordered Lal Mohammed to put four .22 caliber bullets into the ambassador's head."

"The Safari Club was already embedded with the Afghan police at the hotel coordinating security for Saddam Hussein's delegation and advising Lal Mohammed backstage. Amin, Lal Mohammed, police commissioner Sayed Taroun and Interior minister Major Saifuddin were all directly involved in the narcotics trade. The Interior Ministry was in charge of drug trafficking in and out of the country and Lal was the contact man for drug traffickers. His nickname was "Land and Load." Taroun's was "To You Run." Major Saifuddin was a pilot. They were Amin's point men in Kabul and the surrounding countryside. The Tajik Maoists were already on Lal's drug hit list and political enemies of his boss Hafizullah Amin. The American ambassador had been caught meeting with said enemies while transacting a "business deal" in addition to interfering with the Safari Club's plan to make Afghanistan the capitol of the world heroin trade. Adolph Dubs was also interfering with the deal to bring Gulbuddin Hekmatyar to Kabul and transform the Safari Club into "The Base" (Al Qaeda) for Saudi Arabia's religious and economic expansion into Central Asia. Do you get the dimensions of this picture?"

I struggled with the immensity but the meaning was clear. "Dubs was set up for an ambush. Like JFK."

"And Amin was set up as the fall guy like Lee Harvey Oswald."

My mind was blown away as Desmond continued.

"JFK was stage one of the enterprise. In 1963 an alliance of forces coalesced to seize control of the U.S. government; Cuban exiles, the China Lobby, old OSS China hands, Meyer Lansky's mob syndicate, CIA hawks, and a radical Zionist political movement known as neo-conservatism. Everybody involved had three things in common; Asian opium, a fascist worldview and the willingness to eliminate anyone in the way."

"And JFK was in the way."

"JFK was born to be in the way. Whether he appreciated it or not, his lineage went back two thousand years to Rome, not London. His mother's family had been at war with London for eight hundred years."

"His mother's family? You mean the Fitzgeralds?"

"Your very own. The OSS was groomed by London's MI-6. The CIA was its step-child. Wild Bill Donovan referred to his OSS agents as Knights Templar. The loyalty of the Knights Templar was to *Zion*, not Rome. *Old Testament*, not new."

I couldn't help but be cynical. "But the Templars were burned at the stake weren't they? Jacques DeMolay?"

"The United States is a Templar creation kept alive through Free Masonry. MI-6 has always used Masonic lodges to recruit their agents. November 22nd is the Masonic Day of revenge for Jacques DeMolay. Dealey Plaza is a Masonic shrine named after Thirty-third-degree Scottish Rite Mason, Knight Templar, Shriner and member of the Red Cross of Constantine, George B. Dealey. Need more evidence?"

He turned toward the dark sky illuminated by the bursting shell fire.

"What you're looking at is the Templar's *Old Testament* project. Purify the material world of everything in it through war. The war against matter. The White Knight's War. The Puritan war."

CHAPTER 35

The idea had struck me like a blast of stale, cold air from a crypt. Puritans. This was where I'd crossed Theodore Eliot – the Puritan white knight riding to the rescue of a fallen world. He hadn't taken me on that night at the Parker House for what I'd done. He'd taken me on for who I was in some past life as an Irish Catholic who didn't know his place in God's order. By going to Afghanistan I'd entered his Manichaean war of light against the dark. And "if" Theodore Eliot and Richard Pipes and Team B had convinced themselves they were the White Knights by destroying a material world corrupted by Rome that made me the Black Knight for trying to save it.

The war against matter was old; at least as old as Afghanistan's Indus Valley civilization. It went by many names – Manichaean, Gnostic, dualist, heretical, Cathar, or just plain good and evil. All I could think of was Hiroshima and Nagasaki – Oppenheimer and his *I am become death* from the Bhagavad Gita. The Puritans had hit a home run for anti-matter that day. Oppenheimer had shown the world what a Gnostic future looked like.

"They call this place the graveyard of empires," FitzMaurice said, now exuding the presence of a ghost. "But this war will make Afghanistan the graveyard of graveyards because it's all going to end here. Imperialism itself will end here."

"So is this where the war of light against dark ends?" I asked. "The return to where it began? The place Fyodorov considered the Garden of Eden?"

"If you look hard enough here you'll find your own connections to the past. Knighthoods continue to exist. The Templars see themselves as the White Knights protecting the Grail and the Black Knights as their enemies. Royal bloodlines still battle for influence in the game. Publicly they run corporations, direct armies – make foreign policies. Unseen, in the background, they adhere to a calling that came before."

I struggled with the idea. "And I'm one of those?"

FitzMaurice snorted a laugh. "*Everyone who comes here* has been called. You think it's about the narrative. It is. But the narrative was written down in the *Old Testament* long ago and you can't change it."

"Don't be so sure," I said in a fit of hubris. "I brought back-up this time. He's arriving by plane tomorrow along with my wife and crew. We'll see how that old Puritan bastard Theodore Eliot deals with that."

FitzMaurice smiled coldly. "And how do you think the CIA will react to your rewriting their dream of fulfilling Old Testament prophecy?"

FitzMaurice's comment had almost knocked the wind out of me. "The CIA," I said, absorbing for the first time who exactly I was up against. "Can there be such a thing as Central Intelligence?"

"The insiders call it Mother," he said coldly.

"How very Gnostic," I responded.

FitzMaurice looked at me thoughtfully as the light show rumbled on over the horizon.

"You will learn before long that the White Knight's obsession with 'Mother' has made them mad," he said, sighing deeply. "They are locked into their dualism. By fulfilling the prophecies they actually believe they are hastening the arrival of the Redeemer. The Dad who'll come down off the mountain and straighten it all out."

"And who's the Dad?"

"Yahweh. Of course. Yahweh will restore the King of Jerusalem to his rightful throne and rule the final empire. When all the nations will pay tribute to the house of the god of Jacob. For the nation and the kingdom that will not serve you will perish and the nations will be utterly destroyed," FitzMaurice muttered pensively as the rumble of the guns grew closer.

"But they've forgotten that in reality the Father and the Mother must come together in their Son to escape their dualism. For without the Son incarnating, there can be no Trinity and without the Trinity there can be no Resurrection."

FitzMaurice turned back one more time to the chaos over the ridge.

"And that is the narrative you must be prepared to deliver."

***

I had arrived at a place of "ancient prophecies and the like" where I could no longer discern whether I was awake or in a dream. FitzMaurice and the patio had seemed to melt away and without realizing it I'd found myself at mass in the central nave of a large medieval cathedral, steel torchiers blazing halfway up the steep stone walls. It was then I realized I was surrounded by men dressed from head to foot in black Nazi uniforms – an army of them.

The place, hazy with smoke, seemed familiar to me. The mass that had been in progress was coming to a close. The priest on the altar in his cassock and surplice raised his arms to which all the figures bowed their heads and repeated, "Amen" then turned in unison toward the aisle. I could hear their steel-boot-heels clicking on the gray stone floor, their dull black helmets shielding their faces as they filed out of the pews.

I'd felt as one with these men but as I turned with them toward the aisle I realized I was dressed in the off-white woolen suit I'd brought with me on the trip. Then suddenly the lead Stormtrooper who'd been in the front row removed his headgear and said to me, "So, what do you think? Are you ready to join us?"

The man's face was so gentle, so full of color against the stark black and white background of the Cathedral it had taken me by surprise. Was that what I was there for? To join with this black legion?

"I suppose I was trained for this somehow," I said, fumbling for an answer. "The sisters that taught me were always looking for a few good men. But I never saw myself becoming one of you."

As we progressed up the aisle toward the back of the cathedral, we'd come to a group of nuns sitting in a circle on the stone floor quietly examining a large pile of books, almost as if my comment had invoked them.

"Those are my nuns, the Sisters of Providence, the ones who taught me as a boy," I said to the black-suited Nazi as I watched each nun select a book, briefly scan the pages, and then discard it on the pile. "What are they doing here?"

The man was smiling now. "They're here to remind you that it's not too late to change your mind."

The sight of the nuns first made me uncomfortable, then angry. At that moment I realized it was them that had brought me here. It was them that had trespassed on my inner life, narrowing my choices before I'd even known what choices were to be had. They were more than just symbols of the powerlessness I felt as a boy in Catholic school. They were the acrid smoke of the torchiers in my lungs; the mindless cruelty of blind obedience; the source of the nihilism that had followed me through life. And they were still at it. I wanted them gone, and at that moment I turned toward the roof of the Cathedral and shouted in as loud a voice as I could, "I renounce you!"

The call echoed off the walls and up to the steeple. I could see the black Stormtroopers leaving by the main door. My opportunity to reconsider was slipping away quickly but I had no intention of joining them. The show was over. I would escape this place on my own through the side door, until I realized the path was blocked by a large black dog.

The renunciation had brought me face to face with a demon – my demon staring back at me and snarling. The only way out would be to face him down. But as I bolted through the door I realized there was no escape. The alley outside led nowhere and the black dog had followed me into it … as the door slammed shut behind us.

CHAPTER 36

Sunday Morning May 8, 8:30 A.M.

y eyes were already open when I woke up. It was another bright Kabul morning. Looking down to the hotel garden helped shake off the dream. But the feeling lingered. Afghanistan had opened a door to something that was once only vague. Dreams with Catholic nuns and Nazi Stormtroopers, and a phantom I knew only as Desmond FitzMaurice. Some might've called them nightmares. But a voice told me they were not.

Downstairs, Massoud and a new man named Daoud joined me for breakfast. I told them about the rumbling and the lightshow from the previous night. I asked what it was all about and Daoud responded.

"It's nothing," he said dismissively. "It happens all the time. Young party members signaling each other with flairs and anti-aircraft beacons. Young party members fooling around."

I tended to think it was more like rebels fooling around with young party members, but I just smiled. It was obvious by his expression that Massoud was ill at ease with Daoud's fiction, but said nothing. They both seemed to believe they could tough it out and put on a good front. The world-class test started that day with the arrival of Liz and Roger Fisher.

The difference between then and two years before was striking. The Afghans were more confident but they'd obviously lived in fear of outside infiltration. Abdullah Shadon at Afghan TV had told me the terror bombs were the most feared. The randomness shattered the public's sense of security and gave the rebels an image of power that was clearly beyond their actual strength.

After confirming the plane was on schedule, we headed over to the airport to welcome the flight from Prague. Daoud had arrived with the second old white Peugeot I'd managed to rent. I took it as a sign of good luck having once had a similar old Peugeot get me out of a jam in the middle of Yugoslavia.

It was a beautiful day. No wind blowing out of the east and no signs of any trouble. I managed to get a spot at the railing on the second floor observation deck just as the blue and white Ariana Boeing 727 made its descent onto the runway and taxied to a stop in front of the terminal building.

The sun was shining, the air was warm, and my wife Liz and her companions were the first ones off the plane – Roger Fisher, his wife Carrie, Tom the cameraman and Mark, the M.I.T technician. What a relief.

"Welcome to Kabul. How was the ride over?" I asked, following a speedy trip through customs.

"We got stuck in Prague. Ariana had to fly a part in from somewhere so the Czechs put us up overnight at a hotel in Kladno, the Hotel Kladno. It was the worst hotel I've ever been in," Liz said.

"The Soviets must have used it as a bunker during World War II," Mark chimed in.

Despite our cut-down expenses we'd managed to hire an Emmy Award winning cameraman out of New York and our favorite technician from Boston. Tom was a veteran cameraman with lots of overseas experience who brought his own Ikegami HL-79 with film lenses. He was an artist. Mark was a teacher and full blown M.I.T. electronics and computer genius. I had no personal experience with Tom. He came by recommendation and with a fabulous reputation. He also arrived with a bad eye infection and carrying a copy of *Penthouse* magazine under his arm. Coming on the heels of the U.S. diplomat's expulsion for brandishing a copy of *Playboy*, this was a problem I'd never anticipated. I hoped nobody noticed.

"Oh God, ditch the magazine," I told him without trying to raise a fuss. "And don't let anybody see you do it."

Tom took my request in stride, and after getting all the equipment packed into the two Peugeots we headed off to the Kabul Hotel at which point Roger, without saying a word, walked out the front door, hailed a cab and disappeared.

Now we had an additional mystery to add to the lobby of the Kabul Hotel. It wasn't until later, after shooting all afternoon on the streets of Kabul, that we discovered what he'd been up to.

"I set it up with the Soviet embassy before I left New York that I'd come in for a rundown on the situation as soon as I got here," he said when Liz and I stopped by his room on the way down to dinner. "I thought I'd meet with their ambassador but Andropov sent down his top man, Stanislav Gavrilov to meet with me."

Yuri Andropov? Really. Yuri Andropov was the former head of the KGB and General Secretary of the Communist Party of the Soviet Union.

It was nice to know somebody cared that we were there. The news was unexpected and Roger was very impressed. "And how did it go?" I asked.

"It was amazing, really. I started doing my usual routine for *Getting to Yes*. You know, listing all the positive reasons for a Soviet occupation then the negative ones and at that point he stopped me."

Roger's genuineness was enthralling. "And?"

"And he said 'Roger, you're leaving out the spiraling cases of drug addiction and typhoid fever not to mention the demoralization of the military. Our boys came here to fight fascism, not to kill impoverished peasants fighting to protect their villages. We want to get out. Please, go back to New York and tell your people we've had enough. We make mistakes, but we're not stupid. Give us six months to save face and we'll leave the Afghans to settle their own scores.'"

And there it was. Kabul, May 8th 1983. Roger wasn't in town for an hour and he'd gotten the whole Soviet position straight from the horse's mouth.

"What about Karmal?" I asked.

"I got the impression they're willing to sacrifice Karmal," Roger said. "They may even accept a coalition government."

"That confirms what I was thinking." I replied. "I was over at Afghan Television the other day and Karmal was not on the reviewing stand for the 5th anniversary parade. I'd say that's a big signal. The Soviets aren't committed to the revolution because there was no revolution."

After dinner Liz and I escaped to the patio and got up to speed on my week alone. "If Andropov sent his top man down here to meet Roger, then we've got it. This trip is more important than we realized. This is huge. The Russians really do want to get out of here."

"But will Reagan let them?" Liz asked.

"That's what we're going to find out when we get back to New York. The bleeders and the dealers, remember? The dealers want to get them out. Vance proposed a peace plan to Carter right after the Soviet invasion, but Brzezinski got Carter to kill it."

"And Casey wants them to bleed."

"I'm beginning to think it's more than that. There's been this man hanging around out here every night since I got here. British, sixtyish, spooky, if you know what I mean. He's confirmed the story we heard about Adolph Dubs and the drug deal."

"You're kidding."

"No. It explains everything. But it's not what we thought. This is opium country. It could become the opium capital of the world. The DEA was active here before the Soviet invasion. They worked out of the embassy and paid informants and drug dealers. But the CIA also used drugs as an exchange for guns and paying off terrorists. And who knows what the Russians do."

Liz was with me instantly. "So the DEA operation is a cover?"

"And a very good one. D.C. politicians get to look tough on crime. The CIA gets all kinds of intelligence. But they aren't stopping the drug trade. They're using it to fund a covert war, and nobody back in Washington notices the obvious. The CIA and DEA people work together. Their jobs overlap. The CIA guy and the DEA guy came to the hotel together the day Dubs was killed. They were both the first to reach him after the shootout. And they were the ones instantly pushing the "Russians did it" narrative. They must have been the unnamed source for the *New York Times* article implicating Soviet advisors. Not long after Dubs was killed the U.S. put Afghanistan's biggest known drug dealer, Gulbuddin Hekmatyar, on the payroll to keep destabilizing Hafizullah Amin's regime. Afghan heroin has been flooding the U.S. since the summer of '79. The labs were running at capacity by the time the Soviets invaded. It's financing the insurgency and Gulbuddin Hekmatyar gets the biggest chunk of American weapons deliveries."

"And Dubs had opposed destabilization," Liz countered.

"But a lot of people wanted it, not just Brzezinski and the CIA. This whole operation had been in the works for years before Dubs was killed, and even before 1978 when Daoud was overthrown by Amin. It goes back to when Daoud overthrew the king in 1973. That's six years."

"And that's when Eliot was ambassador here," Liz said as the lights went on.

"Pakistan always wanted control of Afghanistan. The Chinese were brought in by Kissinger early in the 70s and eventually came to work with the Shah's SAVAK when Brzezinski took over. SAVAK works together with the Tajik Maoists and the U.S. embassy but there's another group, something called the Safari Club that's been operating as a privatized version of the CIA. They were used to get around the oversight imposed by the Church Committee."

Liz realizes. "And they were the ones who pulled it off. Of course. Outsource it. Plausible deniability."

"Add in a CIA ringer like Hafizullah Amin and you've got your fall guy. Brzezinski blames him and the Russians for killing Dubs but they're both being played off against each other by a third party."

"And this guy helped you figure this all out?" Liz said.

"That and a few other things."

Liz was now concerned. "Other things like what?"

"That Afghanistan will change everything but not in the way we think."

"You mean the war?"

"No, not just the war. All wars. So much history has passed through here. The Harappan civilization is five thousand years old – Alexander the Great and Genghis Kahn. The British East India Company was here before the U.S. was even colonized."

"Then this is the place, isn't it? The location at the beginning of everything," Liz said.

"But it's also at the end. This isn't just a story about Dubs or the Safari Club. This is the alpha and omega. And nobody in the U.S even knows about it."

"It's only been a week and it's already affected your thinking, hasn't it?" Liz said as she stared at me with a peculiar grin.

"It's gotten into more than my thinking. It's gotten into my dreams."

CHAPTER 37

Monday morning May 9, 8:00 A.M.

Much to my relief, word came at breakfast that we'd been scheduled to interview the foreign minister, Shah Mohammed Dost. We spent the morning getting cover shots in the bazaar and at 1:00 P.M. the interview went off as planned.

The Foreign Ministry sat amid a beautifully manicured estate of modern government buildings in the center of town and an easy walk from the Kabul Hotel. Roshanrowan greeted us in the lobby and escorted us all upstairs into a large, palatial conference room with high ceilings.

As Mark and Tom set up for the interview, I went over my concerns with Roger. I emphasized the issue of Afghan press censorship and Roger agreed to bring it up. Within fifteen minutes we were underway.

Dost is a formidable five feet, ten inches. Well-built, almost athletic, nearing sixty – with short gray hair and a mustache. Like many of the other Afghan officials I'd met, he was a holdover from Mohammed Daoud's regime – which meant he was a nationalist – and apparently had little problem making the crossover to working for the PDPA. However, he *was* better dressed in a fashionable dark blue pin-striped suit, vest and expensive shoes. He would easily pass for a wealthy businessman at St. Moritz, or even a banker on the streets of Zurich. I could see that Roger was in his element.

"Your Excellency, we're most grateful for your welcoming us here in your Ministry of Foreign Affairs to help the Americans and others understand the present situation. In the United States we tend to see it as a hundred thousand Soviet troops fighting some Afghan resistance. That's not the way you see it. In a word, how do you see the situation today?"

Dost was formal, diplomatic, and spoke perfect English. "Well, first let me say that I am very pleased that you are here and have this opportunity to talk to you."

And that was as much as Roger Fisher and Shah Mohammed Dost could agree on.

"Let me say you referred to the number of Soviet troops. That's not correct, actually," Dost said, shaking his head. "We do not agree on that number. And you mentioned the term 'Afghan resistance.' I must say that that is not correct at all."

The interview was off to a bad start. Dost considered the Afghan resistance to be "counterrevolutionary bandits and highway robbers" which many of them were. And when Roger asked him to clarify the number of Soviet troops fighting them, he literally didn't know. "But I must say that this is just that number, which is able to help the Afghan armed forces to repel or ward off any threat coming from abroad, mainly, of course, from Pakistan, and to some extent Iran."

Translation: to Dost the exact number was not important. What was important was that the Soviets were there legally according to a treaty signed in 1970, their numbers were limited to the task at hand, and more importantly, in his opinion they were only in Afghanistan temporarily.

But Roger's Harvard courtroom-lawyer style loomed over the moment. And when he challenged Dost's fumbling attempt to minimize the size of the resistance, the interview descended into chaos.

For a few tense moments the two men stared at each other in confusion until Roger realized he had to get down to business.

"And how do you see the future going forward? How do you want to see it? Through negotiation?"

To which Dost replied, "Definitely."

And everyone in the room had breathed a sigh of relief.

The interview lasted for over an hour. Roger covered the bases, asking Dost if he saw the Soviet Union as a threat to Afghanistan's independence, (Not at all); to Afghanistan's "non-alignment," to whether Afghanistan looks forward to closer relations with the United States, (Afghanistan would like to have normal relations with all the countries of the world, including the United States).

After which Dost turned the tables and asked, "But would the United States actually like to have normal relations with Afghanistan?"

I'd already given my Conrad Ege *Counter-Spy* analysis to Roger. Ege argued that the U.S. media were intentionally suppressing information and slanting Afghan coverage in favor of the Pakistan-based rebels, but Roger had outright rejected it. Now Dost was blasting him with the *New York Times* article Roshanrowan had harangued me about on my second day here. And I could see Roger was uncomfortable with it.

"You are aware the administration clearly admits that they are providing military assistance to the counterrevolutionary elements – bazookas, mortars, antiaircraft rockets? This shows clearly that the United States is involved in these activities against our country."

Roger responded, "Yes, but as the United States…" just as the tape ran out. It was a pity. It almost sounded as if Roger was about to venture to where no interviewer ought to go. His preconceived bias was that the U.S. was practically neutral in this case. The Soviets were the perpetrators. His whole prescription for *Getting to Yes* rested with the assumption that both sides had to give something to get what they wanted. But Dost was making it clear. Roger was not going to get anywhere if he thought the so-called Afghan resistance had any legitimate role to play.

After a new tape was loaded, Roger asked Dost whether Afghanistan would go to war with Pakistan if negotiations failed. But when Dost responded that, "We are not that pessimistic that negotiations will fail. It is our intention to solve our problems peacefully at the negotiating table." A surprised Roger shifted to a more conciliatory tone.

"So what do you want us to see and report?" he asked. "What could we tell Americans about your revolution that you want them to know about?"

For once Dost smiled. "They should know that here has been a revolution. And they should know the background of how it came about, that the motive behind it was that Afghanistan was living in a feudal, even pre-feudal tribal system. And despite all the problems and difficulty, we have made some headway in different fields, culturally, socially, politically, economically."

Dost's summary of the Afghan government's progress was just what I'd been looking for. But when Roger broached the sensitive issue of filming the Soviet role in gaining that headway, Dost got defensive again.

"We are not hiding the Soviet presence here in Afghanistan," he said. "But let me tell you, in what country can you go to these barricades and take pictures of soldiers?"

Now it was Roger's turn to be defensive. "I was not asking for permission to film inside a Soviet base. I am impressed with how few Russians I have seen in my brief stay in Kabul. But if a Soviet helicopter flies over, if a thousand people can see it, may we not film it? We would like to go home and say we had the freedom to film whatever the public could see, including the Soviet friends who are supporting your revolution."

Dost was completely bewildered with the concept and continued to struggle with the request until we ran out of tape again. Having been made aware by Peter Larkin of the Afghan censor's willingness to black out anything remotely Soviet, I felt compelled to cut in.

"Excellency, you know that we have come to explain the situation here fully to the American public. In order to do that, we must view things on the streets as they are. Unfortunately, if our film of a Soviet citizen, or a technician, or soldier is censored when we return home we will be told that your government has something to hide."

Dost shook his head unhappily. "Well I don't know exactly what the policy is of the Department of the Press, you know, the State Committee for the Press and Publication. Do you know that there is something? Or are you just imagining?"

I tried to stay calm. "We know! We have requested permission to film in the city and the countryside. And in order to keep on the program I requested that we not be censored."

Dost was confounded. "Have you contacted these people?"

"Yes," I said. "Unfortunately, the State Committee prohibits showing Soviet citizens, Soviet technicians, or *any* Soviets helping the revolution."

I leaned forward. "The last time I was here two years ago I was not censored. I showed the occasional Soviet citizen or army personnel carrier. We got back to the United States and they said where are the Soviets? We thought that this was supposed to be Russia's Vietnam. And I said, well there they are, there's one at the bazaar buying a melon, that's a Soviet truck over there, and that was the extent of it."

Dost stared silently at me. And at that moment I knew I'd managed to find a way through the labyrinth. "Then I don't think if it is just anything normal and routine, if somebody walks somewhere, nobody will prevent you actually taking a picture of them. I don't think."

Roger jumped on Dost's comment. "We'll quote you on that," he shouted.

And we were good to go. Everyone, including Dost, laughed and the two continued for the final twenty minutes as best friends with the details of how an agreement could be constructed and what it should include. Dost spoke of the controversial land reform program that had brought on the insurrection. He maintained that it was the real basis for a social transformation of the whole country, and was very much needed.

"And I must say that at a certain stage, there was some wrong implementing in the matter. But now those things have been corrected. We have the cooperation of peasants themselves and have started a second phase of the land and water reform. We are now distributing property documents to the peasants who have acquired land and it is continuing. Perhaps it is something that will take time but we have proved that when done in the correct way it works, whether you believe it or not, for the Afghan people."

CHAPTER 38

It was a good day. Despite Dost's bouts of confusion, he had a chance to get his side of the story on the table and Roger had a chance to showcase his methods. We'd successfully laid the foundation for a second Afghan documentary and perhaps a whole new approach to Cold War journalism, not to mention blowing a hole in the Reagan administration's Afghan narrative.

Roshanrowan took our talk of filming Soviets helping Afghans seriously. He'd sent us straight out from the Foreign Ministry to the Macroyan housing project to interview Soviet engineers in the process of piling concrete boxes on top of concrete boxes. It was a crude way to build housing, but it was fast and cheap and the finished apartments were the nicest in Kabul.

The place was a crazy madhouse of mud and men. Gangs of laborers and uniformed Afghan soldiers mud wrestled a thick black electric cable into a freshly dug trench. Soldiers laughed and shouted as they crowded around us. The workmen stared at us suspiciously. We were the most interesting thing they'd seen in weeks. The Afghan foreman led us across the muddy courtyard to a building under construction. We climbed the prefab stairs and I recognized some of the Soviet engineers I'd seen hanging around the hotel. An Afghan laborer in a blue cap thumbed his nose behind their backs, then gave the thumbs down in an absurdist pantomime. I got the message.

A Soviet engineer struggled to communicate with Afghan laborers attempting to lower a prefab third story onto the second floor. It seemed like no use. I struck up a conversation with a Soviet engineer named Boris as Afghan workers started to crowd around again. Boris wore the signature white Ben Hogan golf cap and pink shirt. After the usual back and forth he told the translator he'd been on the job for a year and planned to stay for two more after that.

I was impressed. "So he likes it here," I remarked, trying to think of something interesting to say. "He's too young to retire. What will he do when he goes back to Moscow?" I asked.

Daoud's translation was a dull thud. "He works the same. He'll go back and be an engineer."

The interview was dying from boredom so I tried shaking up Daoud's predictably uninspired translations by reaching out and pointing to the man's growing paunch.

"Tell the man it looks like the Afghan food is agreeing with him," I said. "I have the same problem."

All the Afghans stared in confusion until Daoud translated. When they realized what I said they all broke out laughing.

The Russian replied with a big laugh, "It's not me. The shirt is big!"

My little joke changed the mood. Daoud was unnerved but Massoud got it and lightened up. We stayed on a few more minutes to watch the crane lift the prefab sections of concrete wall up to the third story and the Afghan workers setting them in place. Afghanistan was the poorest country on the planet. This project would add hundreds of new apartments with running water and electricity. The Soviets had done the major building in Afghanistan since the 1950s, including housing, factories, and roads. The Indians were building a new hospital and training school for doctors and nurses. The Swiss were here with an electrical power project. The Japanese had signed a cooperative venture agreement and some European countries had small scale irrigation projects. All the Afghans I met wanted to see the U.S. step back in and help the way it did under the king. But the U.S. was now occupied helping the Mujahideen to blow up power lines and burn down schools.

After an hour of shooting we thanked our hosts and finished the day back on the streets.

Tom and Mark spent the last of the daylight capturing Kabul's rush hour traffic and last minute shopping in the medieval bazaar down by the river. The whole picture came across like a three dimensional painting. The river was high that year and flowed through the center of the city in a torrent. Small children and women, some in modern dress, others in full chador, rushed by on their way home. Men labored with their wooden carts stacked high with bales of wool or boxes of produce. The sky was clear and a deep blue, the air filled with the smell of charcoal roasted meats. Friends met on the street and kissed on the cheek. A soldier in the green uniform of the PDPA Army stopped to buy a bag of almonds. There was something deeply human and appealing about all of it – an ephemeral unhurried elegance. Then you realized it had been happening on these streets this way for five thousand years and you couldn't help but gasp. I could never have imagined I would be drawn to this – to the magic of it. As the sun set over the ancient city the war was a thousand miles away, and the sights, smells, and tastes of the old world revealed themselves. It all seemed more authentic than the world I'd come from, and made me realize that we in America had lost something sacred and given over to the profane.

***

We spent the next few days getting shots of the city and filming interviews as Roger made the rounds of the foreign diplomatic missions. I did my best to educate him on the gaping holes and outright fabrications in the American narrative, but I got the feeling he didn't want it to be true. In his mind the solution here would come between the two superpowers, and the Afghans would just have to take what they could get.

Liz and I speculated on the outcome as we walked the busy streets of Kabul.

"As I see it, Roger is too trusting of the authorized version of events and not skeptical enough of U.S. behavior," I said.

"I talked to him a lot on the flight. He will listen if we give him the facts."

"Then we should start at the beginning. The Carter administration had excellent intelligence on the events that triggered the Soviet invasion but ignored it. Beginning in June of 1979 both the East German ambassador and the special Soviet emissary openly informed the U.S. embassy of Soviet intentions. They wanted two things, to get Amin out and avoid a military intervention."

Liz finished the thought. "But Brzezinski and Carter encouraged the destabilization."

"And when they did intervene, even Cyrus Vance joined them in acting as if they were all caught by surprise," I countered.

Liz hadn't had to think about it. "That was just posturing. They had to look tough on the Soviet Union going into the election year," she said, shaking her head in disgust. "You know the fear of appearing soft on Communism always rules. It's the way the American government works. The CIA baits the Soviets into doing something against their interests, and then capitalizes on it when they react."

"But what if it wasn't the CIA? And what if Washington wasn't really in control? What if the administration was just reacting to events somebody else created for them. Like that guy FitzMaurice told me about!"

We turned left and headed toward the bazaar. "I've been thinking about Carter and the Democrats," I said. "It was Clark Clifford who got this whole Safari Club business started because of the Church Committee hearings. Here's a guy who's supposed to embody the Democratic Party going back to Harry Truman and he's undermining the whole purpose of the hearings? And then there's Carter himself."

"What about him?" Liz asked.

"He comes across as a simple Georgia farmer but he's working with Brzezinski on Rockefeller's Trilateral Commission to rearrange the global economy. He's a front for the global bankers and the Bilderbergs. His brother Billy is up to his ears in debt to the Saudis and his financial advisor Bert Lance is fronting the Saudi's illegal takeover of an American bank in Atlanta."

I saw the light go on in Liz's eyes. "The same Saudis that are behind that other bank you told me about. The one that's financing the drug industry and supplying the holy warriors with the weapons to tie down the Soviets in Afghanistan."

I tried to settle down to the business at hand.

"BCCI – the Bank of Crooks and Criminals. Look, I know Roger is a very good guy but I think his obsession with numbers instead of politics is a mistake. Does it really matter to the negotiation if the Soviets have a hundred thousand troops or seventy-five? It was so unimportant Dost didn't even know it. I know he's the expert but unless he starts looking at the American motives behind the Soviet occupation, he'll fail."

CHAPTER 39

Thursday May 12th 8:00 A.M.

It was another beautiful day in the neighborhood. We mounted up in our two old white Peugeots and clunked out beyond the Bachad Bal, the mountains that ring the city. Liz and I traveled in separate cars just in case. It was a precaution. Danger was something I took for granted.

I took the front seat of the second car. Tom the cinematographer sat in back and within five minutes we were in the war. Outside the city was another world. Flat plains, dirt road – dry, dusty, and bright. Just as a HIND MI 24 gunship passed overhead, we encountered a big eight-wheeled Soviet BTR 80 armored personnel carrier heading towards us. The two Russian soldiers sitting on top waved as we passed in a cloud of dust and I broke out laughing. This was exactly what I had asked Roshanrowan and Dost to give us, but Emmy-Award-winning cameraman Tom was still fumbling with his camera in the back seat.

After a fifteen minute drive we reached a two story mud-walled military compound. Upstairs we found ourselves in a local PDPA command center with bandolier belts, radios, all sorts of weapons, and pictures of engaging young women hanging from the walls. That was a surprise. A tall muscular Afghan commando holding a Kalashnikov came forward. By his side was a smaller, younger man whom I immediately recognized from the news footage at Afghan TV as Malang. I offered my hand. The big man's was well-calloused and the size of a ham. The small man's was a pair of scissors, grown hard from squeezing off Kalashnikov rounds at young Soviet recruits.

It was getting interesting. Standing next to the commando, Malang looked like a scrawny underfed runaway. First impression said the big commando was guarding him. But the wooden handle of the automatic pistol sticking out of his belt said otherwise. Malang was a master killer, now in the service of the PDPA.

Another young soldier eyed us suspiciously as he talked under his breath into a walkie-talkie by the window. He got the all-clear and we headed back down the stairs. Outside we strolled across the empty terrain

toward a larger compound in the distance where I heard the sound of soldiers drilling. And I remembered reading Kipling's *Gunga Din*.

I shan't forgit the night,
When I dropped behind the fight,
With a bullet where my belt-plate should' a' been.
I was chokin' mad with thirst, An' the man that spied me first,
Was our good old grinnin', gruntin' Gunga Din.

We were all at risk of taking a bullet on this one, and I was leading my
wife and a Harvard Law professor and his wife into the thick of it. How
bizarre.

Inside the fort was a wide, barren parade ground surrounded by thick,
mud brick walls. I had asked to see what the war looked like and it looked
like a 1930s movie set.

A squad of local soldiers drilled two by two, or at least tried to. Fighting
came natural to Afghans. Marching didn't. Arms swung out of time and
out of sync. Bodies collided. It was a great show.

Massoud brought Malang over and introduced him.

"Malang fought with the counterrevolutionaries but turned himself in
under the Kabul government's amnesty program," Massoud explained.

"I know who he is, Massoud. What's he doing here?"

"He trains with these men and helps protect the village."

Ah. Based on the film I'd seen at Afghan TV, Malang's defection was a
big sign the government was getting the upper hand with the rebels. And
if the government was getting the upper hand with the rebels, then the
U.S. would have to start negotiating.

I asked Massoud to translate. "Why did Malang join the counterrevolutionaries?"

"He joined because he heard that everyone was in danger in Afghanistan."

"Who told him that?" I asked.

"Gulbuddin told him that. He was part of the Gulbuddin band."

This was *really* interesting. "So Gulbuddin lied?"

"Gulbuddin says that he is Islam. But what he does is anti-Islam."

"How did he find out the truth?" I asked.

Massoud translated. "He saw for himself. They were burning schools,
the mosques, the houses. Because of this he knew what he was."

Malang went in depth about his time with Gulbuddin and said that he
killed many innocent Afghans.

"Were you trained to do this?" I asked.

"Yes."

"Trained by who? The Pakistanis?"

"Yes. There were Pakistanis, Chinese and American trainers," he said.

"So he met Americans and Chinese?

"Yes. He has met them. He and his men."

"And where did he meet them?"

"In two secret camps. One in the Sikh lands near India. The other in Parachinar. On the Afghan border."

"And did his men stay with Gulbuddin?" I asked.

"All of the people who were with me have come and joined the government."

I was shocked. "All?"

"Yes. At first it was thirty persons. Then it was eighty-three and now it is about two hundred."

Malang had brought two hundred rebels back to the government and considered Gulbuddin's holy war a fraud. No wonder the Reagan administration was upping the ante and letting the *New York Times* troll the public for support. The official American narrative was failing on the ground in Afghanistan and the U.S. media was propping it up. What would happen when we got back to tell the tale?

Roshanrowan and Dost had come through with my request. We got some great footage of Malang at work as well as clear shots of a couple of Soviet APCs guarding him at a public meeting. At another stop we got a burned-out school and stood amid scattered Kalashnikov shells. All that was left was a broken blackboard on a smashed wall surrounded by snowcapped mountains, punctuated by the roar of jet fighters flying low overhead. It was Dante's *Inferno* and I was standing in the middle of it. It was obvious the Reagan administration didn't want peace in Afghanistan. They wanted this place turned into hell on Earth.

***

Back in Kabul we grabbed a quiet moment with Roger in his hotel room before he left for dinner at the American embassy. He seemed calm, but inquisitive.

"We've been doing the diplomatic circuit since we arrived," he said as Liz and Carrie conversed in the background.

"I thought I'd get a better idea of what's really going on here but I'm more confused than ever. I spoke to the Italian ambassador and he said to talk to the German ambassador. I talked to the German ambassador and he gave me what I thought was a good assessment. Then I mentioned it to Charlie Dunbar at the U.S. embassy, and he said the German didn't know what he was talking about."

I thought about it for a second. "Charlie Dunbar?"

Roger stared without moving his gaze. "He's the chargé at the embassy. I heard you had a great day. The government seems to be giving you the access you wanted."

Was that a note of suspicion I heard in Roger's tone? "I think they're being as open as they can," I said before he threw me a curveball.

"How do you know how to do this?" he asked.

At this late date I was surprised. "I *was* here before," I responded.

Roger scrunched his eyebrows into a question mark as if thinking out loud. "No. It's more than that. They trust you. You don't move so easily in the company you're in without some kind of training," he added, scanning my face hard for an explanation he could believe.

What did he mean by training? Was he saying that if they trust me, he shouldn't? Roger was old line Harvard Square material like "Ken" Galbraith. Younger but of the same stock. Christian missionary parents – onward Christian soldiers. Personable but rigid. I could tell Roger was hiding something. He was trying to disguise it but something had pierced his armor. Then he looked at me with a peculiar frown and delivered the payoff.

"I was at an engagement party for Elliot Richardson's niece a couple of weeks ago. Ted Eliot and his wife were there. When I told him I was coming here with you he went ballistic on me, just the way he did with you that night at the Parker House. 'How dare you go to Afghanistan and talk to those people,' he said."

Ted Eliot had struck again. But this time his target was the patron saint of negotiation and charter member of the American legal establishment. Roger had dismissed Eliot's attack on me back at the Parker House in December of '81 as a spontaneous lapse in protocol. But an attack on *him*, at a moment when the Soviets have made it clear they want to get out, meant something far more serious was afoot and this trip had brought it out into the open.

CHAPTER 40

Desmond FitzMaurice had said it flat out. "How do you think the CIA will react to your rewriting their dream of owning the future?" If Central Intelligence dreamed of owning the future, where did that end? And if they did own the future, would they own the resurrection, too? I mean what was really the plan? And where would they take everyone when they woke up? Up to a Puritan heaven or straight to Dante's *Inferno*? It seemed I wasn't just tampering with the official narrative, I was messing with Yahweh's will and Theodore Eliot was his messenger.

Roger was facing a defining moment in the limits of temporal law and diplomacy at the highest levels of the American government. Being slapped down in front of a room full of Boston Brahmins, including the noble Elliot Richardson, Attorney General to Richard Nixon who'd resigned over Watergate, was a shock and a personal insult to his commitment to citizen diplomacy and decades-long negotiation project. I could only hope that he was up to the challenge.

Liz's jaw dropped when I told her the news. "This is serious," she said, collapsing into a chair by the window. "These people don't break out in the open like that."

"They do when you get them out of the formal and into the real," I countered.

She snickered. "I knew you'd get around to quoting James Burnham."

"When they start screaming like a biblical prophet you know you're getting at the truth. Biblical truth."

"Biblical truth?" she said, shaking her head in wonder.

"Yeah. It's exactly what this guy FitzMaurice told me. The narrative we're experiencing, the narrative being pushed by the neoconservatives, by Richard Pipes and Theodore Eliot together on the stage, was written three thousand years ago. It's prophecy. Isaiah 60-61."

Liz looked stunned. "How can that be?"

"Because the neoconservatives want it to be and the Old Testament Puritans like Eliot at the State Department and CIA and the White House are right there with them. In their minds Afghanistan's secular government stands in the way of the second coming and they want it destroyed. They want Afghanistan returned to God under Israel, not Moscow. And they will do whatever they need to do to fulfill it."

"But the people they're supporting out there aren't Jews, they're Muslims."

"And when they're finished using them, they'll turn against the Christians."

"But aren't Puritans and Christians, the same thing? I'm confused."

"That's what I always thought, but apparently no. Puritans identified with Old Testament Jews. They wanted a state that adhered to biblical law, and that's where we're headed. That's what Christian Broadcasting is all about. Setting us up for the final battle against evil."

I expanded on my meetings on the patio and the strange education I'd received. "I had it explained to me by Desmond FitzMaurice. 'You'll get nowhere trying to change the narrative,' he said. CBS, *The New York Times*, ABC are all working from the same book. *The Evening News* with Dan Rather is just a cipher for the original narrative and that narrative is the Old Testament.'"

"You know, you *were* told you were sent by God when you came here the last time. Remember? The Mullah told you. I can see by your face that God sent you to tell our story," Liz said.

"I did not take that literally."

"Well maybe you should have," Liz said frankly. "Getting that job with Pat Robertson at the Christian Broadcasting Network? You did play Jesus in *Jesus Christ Superstar*, you know. Coming here to ward off the Apocalypse? You've been getting educated in the merger of Christianity and Zionism so you can tell the story of what's really happening. Isn't that what this guy Desmond told you?"

"Yes. But I didn't really know what was happening – until now."

Liz stared at me, stunned at the revelation. "So what do you want to do?"

"I don't know. According to FitzMaurice I can't change the narrative at the end of time. If the Zionists want to destroy the nations that reject Yahweh to fulfill an Old Testament prophecy, what can I do about it?"

"Just tell it as it is."

***

Friday, the Muslim Sabbath - May 13th 10:00 A.M.

Word came at breakfast that we were on at 11:00 for our interview with Afghanistan's Prime Minister, Sultan Ali Keshtmand. Roger would do the interview. I would assist. Sultan Ali Keshtmand was another in a long list of world leaders to enter into Roger's world, but Afghanistan may have been his biggest test. Afghan governments had been laboring to bring Afghanistan into the modern world for a hundred years and had slowly moved the population in the right direction.

The Constitution of 1923 limited the role of the monarchy, guaranteed equal rights to all ethnicities and granted women the right to vote. Poverty, illiteracy, malnutrition and infant mortality were slowly being reversed by education, but Washington was intentionally undermining those efforts.

Roger's goal was to bridge the gap between the warring parties and find a common ground. On the level and on the square, so to speak, in keeping with the responsibilities of a high level Mason. Yes, Roger was a member of the Craft. I'd grown up with many of them in my small suburban Boston town, one of those with an Odd Fellows Lodge. My father had apprenticed the pharmacy to a 33rd degree Mason. DeMolay, Rainbow Girls, and Daughters of the Eastern Star had populated my youth, all dedicated to the Wisdom of King Solomon. I recognized the telltale signs. Roger was applying Masonic harmony to an out of balance world. It made Theodore Eliot's shrieks all the more troublesome. Roger had already found common ground with Afghanistan's Foreign Minister Shah Mohammed Dost and I was guessing he'd find it with the Sultan Ali Keshtmand. But what about the people who were tearing up the countryside? And what about the people who were paying them? Roger was working from the assumption that the United States had the responsibility to use its unrivaled power to bring warring parties together to make peace wherever they lived. The U.S. could pressure, cajole or threaten, but the end result would be something everybody could live with. But what if there were parties that didn't want a settlement? What if there were malign forces bent on discord that would reject any negotiated settlement? Could Roger make that adjustment?

We tackled the Pul-e Khishti Mosque immediately after breakfast and witnessed the Sabbath spectacle of religious observance as men poured into Kabul from the countryside for worship. The display of devotion was massive. The Reagan administration liked to declare that the Afghan government was oppressing Islam, but that too was obviously just anti-Soviet propaganda. Huddled at the gates was an example of exactly what successive Afghan governments had been slowly working to change. Tom and Mark panned and wheeled amongst the worshippers to record the spectacle of crippled beggars, deformed children, blinded men and destitute women covered head to toe in full chador. It was a scene out of *Jesus Christ Superstar*. But this was not the Broadway show. This was the real thing in all its biblical glory. And just then I realized Roger had joined us on the street, clutching a handful of small stones.

"I found these in the market," he said, proudly pointing to some deep grooves in the surface. "They're counterweights for balancing scales. I have a collection from all the places I've travelled around the ancient world. Marrakesh, Jerusalem, Baghdad. These are particularly good. Look how they're worn smooth."

"Funny you should bring them here, to the grand Mosque," I confessed in a fit of morbid self-reflection. "I was in a show once, *Jesus Christ Superstar*. The Temple scene is a pivotal moment. Jesus throws out the merchants and nearly gets swallowed by the needy crowd. He wants to help but there's just too many. He ends up screaming at them, 'Heal yourselves,' and runs away. It's his moment of doubt and pain. He wants to help but he knows what he's doing will never be enough."

I could almost hear Roger groan as he reflected solemnly on the idea.

"I had the chance to talk with Ariel Sharon when we were filming *Arabs and Israelis* back in '74," he said thoughtfully. "The Israelis didn't want us doing the series at all. They were convinced I favored the Arabs and was just doing it to make them look bad. Sharon wouldn't admit to whether Israel would withdraw from the conquered territories or even whether Israel really wanted peace. He stonewalled me. So I finally asked him whether he would allow the Palestinians to remain on the West bank. And he said, 'Sure, but by the time I'm done with them, they won't want to stay.'"

Roger's way of keeping sane was to collect ancient weights that had been handled by merchants and traders over centuries. It was a thoughtful way to maintain balance in a world full of imbalances. There were always adversaries that would put their weight on the scale or cheat to win a victory, but without the balance, their victory would never hold. And Roger knew it.

CHAPTER 41

I compared notes with Roger as we waited outside the Presidential Palace to interview Afghanistan's Prime Minister, Sultan Ali Keshtmand. "Everything I've heard indicates Babrak Karmal is on the auction block," I said. "The Afghans don't want us talking to him, and I'd say their failure to produce him is proof. They're giving us Keshtmand instead."

Roger agreed. "The Soviets are letting everyone know they want desperately to get out. Karmal is being sacrificed to enhance the seriousness of the Soviet's offer. But none of the foreign diplomats I spoke to can explain why the U.S. isn't encouraging peace talks."

"There's a simple explanation for that," I responded.

Roger's face was a mask of doubt. "Tell me about Keshtmand," he said.

"Keshtmand was one of the original PDPA members along with Karmal. He was tried for treason by Amin and found guilty. He's probably close to the Soviets, but he doesn't have the stigma of being installed by them."

"But will he go along with a Soviet withdrawal?" Roger asks. "I've been hearing a lot of talk the Soviets want to replace the PDPA with a coalition government and bring back the king."

I'd heard rumors of that as well. "Keshtmand and his faction might go along but I don't think Amin's faction, the Khalq, would accept it. Khalq murdered most of the royal family in 1978 and then bungled the land reform. You heard Dost explain how they've corrected those mistakes. But they can't correct for the murders, and the party is still deeply divided."

It took an unusually long time but we were finally ushered inside the Palace and greeted by Keshtmand's special two-man security unit. These men seemed much more serious than any of the Afghans I'd met and I decided to take a photo as they frisked Roger. It was a mistake.

They glared at me and immediately shouted at Daoud.

"It is forbidden to take pictures of the Prime Minister's security. They want your camera," he said.

"They want my camera?"

"They want the film in your camera, to wash it."

I had to pause and think, but there was no time to think. I'd been pushing myself as far as I could on adrenalin for over a month. I was stretched to the limit. I stayed calm and tried to argue the case I'd been arguing since I got there.

"I was told by your U.N. ambassador and your foreign minister there would be no censorship," I said. "Taking the film is censorship."

Roger looked over at me and shook his head no. "It's normal, Paul. No security would allow you to photograph them. It doesn't qualify."

There was no point in objecting further. I rewound the film, popped the back of the camera and handed the roll to Daoud. He smiled for the first time.

"We will wash," he said.

"Great." I'd just lost all my shots with the Afghan commando out in the countryside.

As we entered a large ornate meeting room we were told Prime Minister Sultan Ali Keshtmand was a busy man and the interview must be brief. We set up quickly. Unlike the Pashtun officials I'd met, Keshtmand was a fifty-year-old ethnic minority Hazara. His oriental features were highlighted by his large round glasses and comb over, but his pudgy appearance disguised a tough political survivor. Keshtmand joined the Parcham faction of the PDPA early in the 1960s and served as minister of planning until imprisoned and tortured by Amin. He was first and foremost an Afghan nationalist. If anyone knew what was going on, it would be Keshtmand. Roger asked his first question, and *he* got right down to the shocking details.

"We have seen evidence of the guerilla fighting in the countryside. How extensive has the damage been?"

Keshtmand didn't need to think. "We have given a figure ... around twenty-four billion Afghanis have been caused by the bandits and the terrorists here in our country. And that is only the governmental institutions. There are many other damages that have occurred in the lives of the people. They have had so many losses."

The opening exchange was hopeful as Roger continued. "The report said that maybe half of the schools were destroyed."

Keshtmand nodded emphatically. "Yes. Yes. Almost half of the schools have been destroyed and almost half the hospitals also have been burned and destroyed."

Roger followed up with, "That is surprising. Is this because some of the rebels are hostile to education?"

"Yes, they are really," Keshtmand replied. "Because they don't want that the children, that the people should know the realities. They want people to know nothing in order to deceive them."

Once again Roger engaged a contentious issue – the definition of terms. "Is this the so-called Islamic party, the fundamentalist Islam that's fighting?"

"No, their actions are against Islam," Keshtmand insisted. "And now everybody in our country knows that these bandits are against Islam's rules."

Roger's first few questions were just the warm-up before he closed in on what he'd really come to find out.

"How do you reconcile Islam with the Socialist or the Marxist? Are you a Marxist?"

Ah. There it was. Keshtmand was polite but ignored Roger's question. "And anyway we have declared so many times that our revolution is a national democratic revolution, and we are working for that. Such a kind of revolution is for the progress and the development of our country and economy and for the welfare of the people."

"But what about Islam?" Roger persisted.

"In Islam, the fundamental rules are social justice, equality and brotherhood. ... We are in keeping with this, with the fundamental objectives and aims, goals which we are following. It is identical. It is the same that we are following."

Roger continued. "Can you reconcile that also with the Soviet style or do you see your goal as different from the Soviet goal?"

"We are our own style," Keshtmand insisted, frowning in frustration at Roger's attempts to link his goals with the Soviets' goal. "We take our own specific conditions of our country into consideration, and we are building a new society based on equality or brotherhood and based on social justice and for the progress for building a new economy which would serve for the benefit of the people."

And so it went for thirty minutes as one of America's elite top legal minds struggled to reconcile his high minded assumptions with Afghanistan's reality on the ground.

"What countries do you see as a possible model?" Roger asked. "India, Cuba, Bulgaria?"

Keshtmand's frustration with Roger's methods was growing.

"We don't search for any model. We are making our own society. And you know from this or that country there are many differences, so there is no model for us. But we are taking in the experiences of other countries in the way of progress, taking into consideration our own specific conditions. "

"What experience from the United States will you borrow from us?" Roger asked. "Civil liberties, free speech? What American customs do you find you might learn something from?"

Keshtmand could hardly believe the question and his expression showed it. He shook his head at Roger's naïveté and turned combative.

"Americans? They say all kinds of things they don't do. They are talking so much about human rights but unfortunately we don't see that they are following this. The United States is so far from here and is a developed capitalist country and those conditions are not applicable. We are an underdeveloped country and we are working for a new society which is no relation to the road which was taken by the United States."

Keshtmand's rebuffs frustrated Roger. The two struggled over the same material for another ten minutes with Roger desperately trying to squeeze out a number on Soviet troops and Keshtmand stubbornly insisting he was missing the point.

"A war is being waged on Afghanistan from Pakistan by the United States and that's all you need to know," Keshtmand told him. "The Soviets are providing military, technical and economic aid according to need. But every day Afghans are being trained to replace them."

Keshtmand's answer was simple and clear. The U.S. was attempting to break the government's efforts to bring Afghanistan's peasants into the 20th century and evolve its society. Afghanistan's meager infrastructure had suffered massive damage from the U.S.-backed campaign to hurt the Soviets. The rebels were coming over the mountains from Pakistan to burn, loot, and kill, but their real fondness is for burning mosques, hospitals, and schools. By targeting its mosques and its moderate mullahs, the United States was pushing the country into the hands of Islamic extremists.

We spent the next few hours filming the undone odds-and-ends to flesh out the trip.

Tom and Mark took one of the cars and went off to film exteriors of the U.S. embassy and to get some panoramic shots of the city. Tom's Ikegami captured a thriving third world metropolis of broad boulevards bustling with cars and people. From a vantage atop Kabul's highest building, he saw a city that looked surprisingly peaceful and prosperous on the surface; unfazed by the war as the population went about its daily business.

Due to Roger's interaction with the U.S. embassy we were all invited to the official residence for what amounted to the weekly Sabbath dinner.

Due to the fact that we we're just about done filming, I agreed we had nothing to lose by accepting the invitation.

Later that afternoon we all trooped over to the Sharanow section of town and got the shock of our lives as we walked off the poor, dirty streets of Kabul through the gates of the ambassador's residence. Inside was a modern American villa that rivaled anything ever built in Beverly Hills, complete with lush green lawn, water sprinklers and swimming pool. After almost two weeks in Kabul it was a sight for sore eyes, but it also evoked mixed feelings. Inside the gated and diplomatically protected community, the American staff led a charmed life in a surreal fantasy land detached from the outside world as well as the consequences of their policies. Outside the gates, Afghan men, women and children labored through a long-day's work in medieval conditions for the lowest per capita income in the world. The U.S. government was burning down their schools and even their mosques, but inside the residence, it might as well have been Disneyland.

CHAPTER 42

After learning about Theodore Eliot's latest outburst I was on guard to meet Charles Dunbar the American chargé d'affaires. I had avoided the U.S. government at every step on this issue going on three years and I didn't know anything about the guy. But as we made our way through the gathering we came face-to-face. Dunbar offered a smile, a friendly handshake and a welcome to a fellow American. I was glad not to have to fight another battle, at least not today.

Mr. Dunbar was about my height and fifteen years my senior in a gray blazer and slacks. At first glance, he shared none of the devil may care "attitude" of his predecessor, George Byers Griffin. In one sense I found this comforting, but on the other I realized it made Mr. Dunbar a gray blot in the landscape – hard to see and harder to read.

Fortunately our encounter was brief. An excellent dinner prepared by Afghan cooks in white jackets was served and we found ourselves sharing a table with members of a Quaker mission stationed in Kabul.

American Quakers in "Marxist" Afghanistan? I'd bet Peter Larkin at CBS News wouldn't be reading *that* in *The New York Times*. Their head man Jim and his wife Virginia were about thirty-five, Midwestern and exceptionally enthusiastic.

"What's it like living here?" I asked Jim.

"It's the best mission I've been posted to since I've been doing this. The Afghan people are wonderful, and the government has been a great help."

I was shocked. "This government?"

"This is the best government Afghanistan has ever had. They got off to a rough start but they're doing everything a government should do for its people."

Liz looked towards me with a gigantic grin before turning to Jim. "I love it here, too," she said. "The warmth of the people. And the food. But what about the Soviets? Do the people resent them?"

Jim raised his eyebrows. "They're never around. I mean they're out in the countryside and up in mountains supporting the Afghan government, but you don't see them inside the city very much. They keep to themselves out at Bagram airfield."

That was curious. "We just saw a story on CBS News before we left that showed thousands of Soviet troops coming in and out of the city," I told him. "Some freelance guy named Eric Durschmied. Dan Rather made a big deal about it over three nights. *Afghanistan under the Soviet Gun*, big write-up in *Variety*. CBS exclusive. First time ever footage."

Jim smiled broadly. "Oh, that guy. We met him. He was hanging around for weeks waiting for the annual Soviet troop rotation. They do it every March, as soon as the snow melts. Move all the troops from down south up through Kabul and the new units down from the north at the same time. Creates a heck of a traffic jam, but they've been doing it every year since they've been here. He must have claimed it was something it wasn't."

Neither Liz nor I could believe what we'd just heard. "Dan Rather is reporting the Soviets are preparing for an offensive with a massive troop escalation," Liz whispered, turning to me in wonder. "But they're not. They're just pulling troops out and replacing them with others. Wow."

So there it was. We'd had to come all the way back to Kabul just to get that one spot of truth.

"Now we know why we got such a strange reaction from Peter Larkin," she said. "They promoted Durschmied's fake story for three nights as proof the Soviets don't want to leave."

I could hear the voice of Karen McKay shrieking at me from the other end of the phone. "We don't need proof, we know they're guilty." She should have said, "And if we don't have proof, we'll manufacture it for you."

I'd learned all I needed to know. We left on Sunday morning. Flew to Prague and then Frankfurt on Afghan-Ariana Airlines. At Frankfurt we switched to Lufthansa for the flight to New York. While we waited, I called ABC for a customs broker to meet us at Kennedy, but the night desk had no idea who or what my request was about. Why was Bill Lord keeping it a secret?

***

We showed up at the ABC News front desk on Wednesday morning and were greeted as strangers. The secrecy thing had really got to me. Something was wrong. We were kept waiting until a solitary emissary quietly arrived to escort us and our boxes of video tapes up to the *Nightline* offices.

Upstairs was no different. We were assigned a veteran producer, Bob Le Donne, who'd been given the task of pulling the story together. Le Donne was mystified, too. He couldn't explain why our journey was kept a secret. He shrieked when he discovered the tape of our documentary I'd left with Bill Lord three weeks before, sitting unwatched on a backroom shelf.

"I could have started preparing for this a week ago," he moaned, exasperated. "It's just the way things work around here." Fortunately Le Donne was a seasoned pro and quickly got the picture as we sat and reviewed the tapes with his assistant. We shared a laugh as the Afghan recruits attempted to march in formation, and we logged the interviews with Malang, Dost and Keshtmand.

"This is great stuff. You managed to get a rebel leader, a Shah and a Sultan all in one trip. Not bad," he said, laughing.

Bill Lord gave Le Donne a free hand and within a week's time everyone had been interviewed and we'd crafted a ten minute news story to introduce the live segment to follow. I was impressed with the people at ABC. Le Donne and crew were open to what we'd experienced, unlike CBS News which couldn't have cared less. The end result promised to shake the neoconservatives and their Team B narrative to its core.

When word came we were going live on Thursday the 26th, Roger was directed to a studio in Boston to make the case for a Soviet withdrawal from Afghanistan while we buckled down inside a closed-circuit booth somewhere in the ABC matrix of offices.

But unbeknownst to us, the British-sponsored Soviet dissident Vladimir Bukovsky had been brought on live to debate Roger together with an Afghan rebel from the Jamayat-I-*Islami*. And at that moment I realized it was an ambush. Bukovsky's operation Radio Free Kabul was the parent organization to Major Karen McKay's red bating operation and her operation was straight out British intelligence. Choosing Bukovsky instead of a diplomat or well-known American/Soviet expert like a Marshall Shulman or a Gary Sick was a clear case of foreign intervention and a slap in the face to what Roger stood for as an American legal expert.

Bringing on a fighter from the Jamayat-I-Islami, sponsored by Leo Cherne and CIA Director Bill Casey's Freedom House, out of "a concern for democracy" was a joke.

The Jamayat-I-Islami was a well-known extremist organization dedicated to establishing a pan Islamic Caliphate in Afghanistan – about as far from a democracy as you could get.

Ted Koppel began the exchange with the cloak of evenhandedness by asking his guests: "Is there any prospect now for a negotiated settlement and a withdrawal of Soviet troops?" But Bukovsky's outright dismissal of Roger's firsthand observations and the Afghan fighter's ridiculous claims of military dominance over the Red Army quickly reduced the exchange to an absurd parody. Koppel actually made no bones about positioning his guests as fighting the good fight. Bukovsky was there to help step up support for the Afghan resistance while Abdul Rahim of the Jamayat-I-*Islami* wanted America's help advancing the cause of Islamic extremism. It was off the wall. If you could imagine Lucky Luciano on live radio in the 1940s raising money for the Sicilian Mafia to defeat Mussolini, you'd begin to get the picture.

Desmond FitzMaurice had been right. The biblical narrative couldn't be changed. It could only be studied.

I realized right there and then that getting the Soviets out of Afghanistan was a pipe dream. Roger Fisher was my shot at leveling the playing field between me and Theodore Eliot. But if ABC News, Bill Lord, and Ted Koppel were so willing to rally support for the CIA's secret war right out in the open there was no chance Afghanistan would be resolved and we all might as well go home.

One small reward came a week later when Bob Le Donne wrote to tell us, "Your piece received much warm reaction around here. But, as usual, the rebel side and Freedom House thought us biased and unfair and wouldn't have been on the program if they had known about the film. Freedom House called, infuriated me, and got absolutely no satisfaction. The woman stated flatly that the piece we had done was inaccurate and unfair. And after ten minutes of trying to pin down precisely what she objected to I gave up. I thought Freedom House was conservatively oriented, but not quite so stupid from a public relations standpoint."

My second trip to Afghanistan in May of 1983 had confirmed the suspicion I'd felt when I'd first seen Theodore Eliot and Richard Pipes just days after the Soviet invasion. The fix was in. The problem with Afghanistan wasn't with the Soviet Union, it was in Washington and I was just beginning to find out why.

CHAPTER 43

C BS News' Peter Larkin called the first week in June to find out whether we'd gone to Kabul. I told him about *Nightline* and delivered the news that there were hardly any Russian soldiers to be found on the streets.

"That's because they were being so bad they were all confined to their bases," he replied. "It was just like Saigon."

"That's not what we heard. There were no troops on the streets because they'd already gone back to Russia. Durschmied had filmed the yearly Soviet troop rotation."

Larkin greeted my message with a long silence until he asked, "Can I get a copy of the show?"

I offered to send Larkin a tape but he said he'd call *Nightline* himself and that was the last I heard from him.

Getting the first documentary up and running was a singular act of time, money and some meager backing from the PBS flagship WGBH. Instead of the momentum I'd expected to gain from bringing Roger Fisher to Kabul, we were facing a brick wall. Roger wrote up a proposal for a *New York Times Magazine* article based on our ground-breaking experience, but the proposal was greeted with disdain. "You can write the article," Roger was told. "But we won't necessarily print it."

Roger was shocked by the mugging he'd received at *Nightline*, and then the *New York Times* had shut him out. His opinion had always been welcomed with a high degree of respect. As a World War II citizen-soldier who'd helped fight a war in Europe, he prided himself as an American citizen-diplomat helping to bring peace. Roger was asked to help formulate President Carter's position on the Camp David Accords, schooled Secretary of State Cyrus Vance on negotiating techniques, and was asked to work back-channels to resolve the Iran hostage crisis. But for some reason he couldn't get anywhere with Afghanistan.

I could see then that Roger had never imagined what he'd be up against when he'd volunteered to help after Ted Eliot threatened me that night in Boston. He'd sincerely believed he and Eliot were on the same side, but

Afghanistan was exposing Eliot's connection to a hidden agenda. I suspected that agenda involved Eliot's association with Richard Pipes and Pipes' leadership of Team B. Team B's massive military agenda was apocalyptic and a full mobilization for war. It had imposed a secret parallel government that operated behind the scenes. But until the Afghanistan trip I had never imagined that secret government might be part of an ancient plan to rebuild the kingdom of Jerusalem. The neoconservatives had always lingered on the outside of legitimate debate in Washington. But because of Afghanistan they were now on the inside and using the Soviet occupation to legitimize Old Testament prophecies which they wanted fulfilled.

Roger had mentioned his revealing encounter with Ariel Sharon, but he hadn't spoken of Israel's animosity toward his seven-part PBS series. I soon found out that the Israelis viewed Roger's objectivity as "disturbing" and had pressured to have him removed from the project. When that failed, they had worked with the local Jewish community to control it from within WBGH. In the end Roger won out and the series broke new ground. But when it came to Afghanistan Roger's enemies were making sure he had zero impact.

Over the next months we followed up with an array of proposals for articles and television programs about a Soviet willingness to withdraw, which went nowhere. *National Geographic* followed the Reagan administration line without question. They rejected the idea and wrote back that "State Department officials suggest that both the Russians and the freedom fighters are prepared for an extended conflict." Case closed. *Mother Jones* found the possibility interesting but couldn't "fit it in with our projected editorial plan." NBC News and CNN were interested to hear about future plans, but when asked, couldn't support going further. PBS expressed hope that a project could be funded but the Corporation for Public Broadcasting found it more suited for a standard commercial television documentary than for PBS. And so it went.

Roger wanted to believe his ideas were universal and acceptable to anyone willing to talk. But Afghanistan was defying his theory and he didn't like it. It hadn't occurred to me before the trip that I was dealing with something so much deeper. But after three nights with Desmond I was starting to realize that Roger was up against something that neither Theodore Eliot nor Richard Pipes or the Reagan administration would allow him to interfere with.

***

As bad as they were, I hadn't realized that the implications surrounding Afghanistan were broader and more ominous than I'd imagined. Afghanistan seemed to allow things inside the system to happen that hadn't happened before. A phone call to my old friend Ron in Washington told me everything I needed to know but was afraid to ask.

"You remember Keith Paine and Colin Gray?" Ron asked.

"Of course. *Victory is Possible*. I read that Gray is working for Reagan."

I could almost hear the helicopter blades whirring in Ron's mind. "He's working on Carter's old 'Plan for nuclear war.' It's called Able Archer."

"Able Archer. You mean it's operational?"

"Because of the presence of Soviet troops in Afghanistan. Why else? The administration is operating under the assumption that nuclear war is inevitable, and working with NATO to win it."

The December 1979 Soviet invasion had given Zbigniew Brzezinski the opportunity to activate a doomsday machine that couldn't be turned off. Through a series of Presidential directives 56-57-58-59 President Carter had ramped up America's strategic nuclear capability and set the stage for a nuclear first strike because of a fallacious Team B claim that the Russians were gearing up for an imminent attack, and the American public was clueless.

"He's insane," I responded. "Gray wrote that nuclear war could be limited to twenty million US fatalities."

I could imagine Ron's eyes bugging out from their sockets. "They don't want to limit it," he said. "I spoke to someone at the White House. Reagan believes the world is coming to an end and sees himself fulfilling biblical prophecy."

Not that again – back to the bible. After my time at Christian Broadcasting I should have known what was coming. Afghanistan had justified putting U.S. troops into the Middle East. The U.S. was fighting alongside Israeli soldiers in Beirut. Christian Zionists and Jewish Zionists were calling the shots inside the administration, and on March 8 Reagan delivered his Evil Empire speech dividing the world between good and evil. Had Reagan just transformed American foreign policy into a gnostic struggle between light and dark? Or had I just realized something it had been all along?

It didn't quite sink in until after the *Nightline* piece, but I was beginning to understand. Radio Free Kabul, Margaret Thatcher and Lord Nicholas Bethell. The world was up against an alignment of World War II fascists and old European royal families thrown out of work by the Enlightenment, and they had played a magical card in Afghanistan.

It was a war to roll back history, and we'd had too much invested in it to stop. Roger had introduced us to the Undersecretary General of the United Nations, Diego Cordovez. Cordovez offered us exclusive coverage of the peace talks in Geneva. We got to fly with him on his private jet and lean in on the inside story. We knew firsthand the Soviets wanted to get out of Afghanistan but it was clear the Reagan administration didn't want them going anywhere. We drafted numerous proposals and made dozens of inquiries, but a new character had arrived on the scene. His name was Texas congressman Charlie Wilson and it seemed he had been inspired by none other than Dan Rather to make sure the Soviets couldn't leave their Vietnam. Over the next four years we exhausted every route trying to move the story forward but got nowhere. By 1987 we had reached the end of the road when a call came in from Farid Zarif.

"Foreign minister Dost is replacing me at the UN," he said. "I'm returning home to become his deputy next week and I would like you and Liz to join me when I get back to Kabul. I will act as your personal guide and get you the permission you need to see anything. We want to show the world what we are trying to do here. You can even ask Dan Rather to come with you if you want. We have nothing to hide going forward."

The idea of asking Dan Rather to share in such an incredible opportunity was of no interest to me or Liz, so we went to Peter Jennings at ABC News who immediately said, "Yes, I'll take it."

It appeared that after seven years we would finally be able to break the Afghan story wide open. But as we prepared to fly to New York to sign the contract a call came in from ABC that the deal was off.

"The Afghan government announced this morning that they have lifted the ban on the western media," an ABC staffer said. "Peter Jennings wanted you to know we are sending in our own team and thanks you for your offer but he is no longer in need of your services."

The receiver on the old black rotary phone was suddenly very heavy as I laid it back in the cradle. "Thank you for your services," I found myself mumbling.

Liz squeezed her eyes shut. "That wasn't ABC was it?"

"The Afghans opened up to the press. No exclusive, no deal."

She stared at me and froze like a statue before muttering "Oh. Well, you knew they had to open up eventually."

"But not now, not fucking now."

I gazed around at the few pathetic sticks of cheap furniture we'd cobbled together to make a dining-room-set during our seven years trying to make this thing work. I wasn't angry. I was disgusted.

"You can't blame the Afghans," Liz said, shaking her head.

"I don't blame the Afghans. They're just trying to survive. But so are we."

"So what do we do now?" she asked.

"I don't know. It's been seven years. I'll have to sleep on it."

CHAPTER 44

Sleeping wasn't something I could do when planning for a trip to Afghanistan. In the run-up to my first two trips I'd gone into some kind of weird metabolic overdrive; an adrenalin rush. I'd shed twenty pounds just thinking about what I had to do. That night I went to bed wanting to sleep a deep sleep, trying to forget. Instead I found myself dropped into another war.

I was hiking through a cold slushy forest in the dark somewhere in Germany. I had just been dropped there with a band of British and American commandos but I didn't remember why. Up ahead I could see the dim glare of headlights. I dove for cover. Damn. Wet snow. The water was freezing and my tweed pants were soaking it up. I was awake. This was real. A line of 1930s Mercedes Benz comes up the road headed towards me. I crawled behind some bushes for cover but I couldn't avoid the procession. Young men and women in uniform waving red and black banners parade beside the cars. Was that music I heard? They'd spotted me. Overhead floodlights flipped on and I was exposed. What the hell was this? I waved as they sang a song of welcome. Black uniformed men exited the cars and hustled me into a back seat.

Suddenly I was inside a rustic Westphalian inn crowded by German, British and American commandos. I was acutely aware that this was a secret "signing" ceremony and I was helping to make it happen. Some of my colleagues who'd dropped in with me for the occasion stood with a high-born German officer in a formal turquoise/green uniform at the front right corner of the dining room. An angry German man sitting next to me on a stair railing overlooking the room tried to burn me with his cigarette while saying something about my pants. "You English and those twill pants. Don't those pants of twill burn you when you walk? Want to feel them burn?"

I ripped off my right leather glove, exposing a twisted finger on my hand and yelled at him that he had already broken my finger with his stupid tricks. He had now gone too far. "You fucking Nazi sadist," I said as I knocked him off the railing onto the floor. Just then I was called to the front of the room and had to face the German officer shuffling documents in his hands. He was looking for something he couldn't find, but the imputation was clear he didn't believe I was credentialed enough to be there. Ignoring me, he turned to his right and asked some of the assembled military officers whether I should be allowed to sign. I responded angrily that I was the great, great, great, great, great, great grandson of Desmond Fitz-Maurice Fitzgerald, Hibernian and Norman King of Ireland.

An apparent colleague of mine who stood next to the German, dressed in wool cap and trench coat, stated without emotion, "It doesn't matter what he thinks. You've convinced us. Sign it."

I had waved my hand across the page, yet I didn't remember the name I'd signed. I looked at the glove in my left hand and saw that it had writing on it. Was I to sign the glove, too?

Liz shook me awake from the dream.

"What's going on? You were shouting."

"I just yelled at a German officer that I am the great, great, great, great, great, great grandson of Desmond FitzMaurice Fitzgerald, Hibernian and Norman King of Ireland."

Liz was already awake but now she was stunned. "Desmond FitzMaurice Fitzgerald? The guy you met in Kabul?"

"I don't know. But it was like the Black Knight dream that last night I spoke to him. The night before you got to Kabul four years ago."

"Didn't FitzMaurice ask you what drove you to do this? Well I think you're getting the answer."

"Yeah, but what's the answer?"

"Your family. Something they were trying to do. Lowenstein said it that night two weeks before he was killed. Your family is talking to you and you'd better listen."

Listen? Listen and do what? What was I supposed to do about a dream that I'm the King of Ireland when my family had never become the kings of Ireland?

I drifted back to sleep but the night wasn't over. My chest was heavy. I could barely breathe. I found myself struggling through some dark suffocating tunnel. I broke out into a large darkened hall illuminated only by torches, but I was choking on the smoke. The hall was circular and draped in dark red cloth. The ceiling was domed and the aisles steep, like some kind of medieval amphitheater punctuated by twelve stone pedestals. To my left there was a pulpit with high officials dressed in Nazi uniforms gathered around it over which hung a huge black swastika on a white background. Faces could be seen by the light of the burning torches. The air was thick, the sound deadened by blood red drapes covering the stone walls from floor to ceiling. I couldn't bear it. The air was so close and oppressive I could barely breathe. I woke up choking.

Liz was already downstairs waiting.

"That was quite a dream."

"It didn't end there. There was another place."

"What kind of place?" Liz said, placing a cup of coffee onto the table.

"Some kind of smoky crypt-like place. I had a sense I was there once, a long time ago. It was that feeling in my chest. It brought back a memory."

"A memory of what?"

"Death. There was something I wanted to remember the last time I felt that near to death."

Liz stood frozen in the bright light of the morning sun coming through the kitchen window.

"And this crypt was a clue?"

"You said something last night about my family. There was something they were connected to that's still alive."

"You said your aunt Mary was the family historian."

"The BBC interviewed her about it once. But they never aired it."

"Why?" Liz asked with growing intrigue.

"I think the royal family is a little insecure when it comes to the Fitz-geralds."

Liz was aghast. "The royal family insecure?"

"We think of England as the British Empire, but in 1169 that empire was four hundred years in the future. Henry II wasn't all that confident of his hold on things. Rebellious sons, rebellious barons. Strongbow had just married the Irish king's daughter. He had holdings in France and an army of his own, led by the Fitzgeralds."

"And they had just conquered Ireland," Liz responded.

"Something even the Roman Legions didn't attempt. Strongbow died shortly after the invasion, leaving the Fitzgerald family in charge of the oc-cupation. You see the picture? Henry II is so nervous he spends the winter in Dublin laying claim to what the Fitzgeralds are sitting on."

"And so the grudge begins."

"From that moment on, the Fitzgeralds are at odds with London. Mary used to say the British Empire began the day the last Fitzgerald Earl of Desmond died."

Liz's curiosity was piqued. "Another Desmond? When was that?"

"In 1583. He wrote his last letter from Abbeyfeale, my grandfather's village. He had a castle there. The castle of the three enemies."

"Three enemies? Sounds like you," Liz replied sarcastically.

"Not funny. Mary said there were books but I've never seen them."

"What kind of books?"

"Family histories."

"Well maybe we should find them," Liz suggested.

***

The last place I'd expected to connect my involvement with Afghanistan was to a 12th century Norman/French invasion of Ireland. What did my work on CBN and CBS and ABC have to do with the history of my family?

When Liz produced *Strongbow's Conquest* and the *Twilight Lords* from the Boston Public Library I knew we'd found an answer.

"*Strongbow's Conquest* is about the beginning. *Twilight Lords* is about the end," Liz said solemnly.

"The end. At least the verdict is succinct."

Liz was a little breathless. "The original invasion in 1169 was chronicled by a grandson of Windsor named Gerald de Barry in a book called the *Expugnatio Hibernica*. It's a whole personal history of the Fitzgerald's coming into Ireland written in Latin."

"Expugnatio?"

"The assault! The storming of Ireland," Liz said with a glint in her eye.

"Storming. So the Fitzgeralds are the Riders On the Storm?"

"Into this house we're born. Into this world we're thrown. Why not?" she finished with a laugh.

Jesus. Desmond FitzMaurice had opened my eyes to the hidden currents swirling around the storm in Afghanistan. Clans of European elites had the crazy idea they could rule the world by reestablishing the Kingdom of Jerusalem and restoring God's laws. The operation had started out with the Crusades and slowed with the Enlightenment. But after World War I and the Bolshevik revolution the movement to roll back the modern world had come roaring back with calls for a one world global government. And with the advent of Ronald Reagan, the New World Order of strict monotheism had moved on to the next level. One world, one rule. Organizations like Theodore Eliot's Bilderberg Group and Zbigniew Brzezinski's Trilateral Commission were modern day fronts for the operation. But when FitzMaurice had asked point blank why I'd put myself into this fight, I'd had no answer. But now I had clues.

A light went on somewhere. The link between Afghanistan and me was a 12th century overt act of imperial hubris called the invasion of Ireland. *Expugnatio Hibernica* and where that led, I was about to discover.

END OF BOOK I

Epilogue

I'd plunged myself into the Afghan enigma thinking I'd get the answer and a career to go with it, but instead I'd found myself on the other side of the mirror.

Trapping the Soviet Union in Afghanistan freed America from its Vietnam guilt trip and bought the U.S. military time to recover. But instead of healing a wounded nation, it merely authenticated the fictional narrative that ideologues like Zbigniew Brzezinski and Richard Pipes were using to push their globalist agenda. There was obviously a deeper political story being covered up, and so began our shift from news to the telling of that story by writing screenplays. Hemingway had done it and so had Fitzgerald. It couldn't be duller than writing stories for the evening news with Dan Rather, so I gave it a try.

The move away from journalism was a welcome relief. That was until we realized bringing our experience to the big screen came with even bigger problems. The L.A. scene wasn't just about glamor and money. L.A. was about framing a reality for the masses and that's where some very strange things began to happen. In late 1987 we'd tagged along with some Hollywood-types on a trip to the Soviet Union and saw with our own eyes what the Soviets had been trying to achieve all along. The Soviet bureaucracy had been desperate to get out of the Cold War for decades but Hollywood could have cared less. Our Soviet guide was astonished by the American naiveté and told us in no uncertain terms.

"People come here from all over the world," she said, shaking her head in disbelief after a few days of pointless conversations. "They come from capitalist countries and communist countries and tell us what life is like where they come from. Only the Americans brag to us about how free they are. But as far as I can see Americans are the most conformist and narrow minded people I've ever met."

I wasn't surprised by what the woman said and I often thought of the comment over the next few years as we struck out time after time in our effort to circumnavigate the Hollywood narrative-creation machine.

Our 1988 screenplay on the Soviet Union's coming collapse was rejected because it was viewed as "unimaginable." Our 1989 screenplay about the emerging dangers of genetic engineering was greeted as out of touch with where the human race was headed. And our 1990 screenplay about the use of Vietnam Veterans as test subjects for developing a "brave pill" was first received enthusiastically but then rejected once Hollywood embraced the drumbeat for war in the Persian Gulf. Hollywood appeared to be a deader-end than the news business dominated by fossilized World War II archons who were blind to what we'd come face to face with in Afghanistan. As the new decade progressed we realized we had nowhere else to turn but the personal, and as we dug into the Fitzgerald family history we stumbled upon a hidden link to the assassination of John Fitzgerald Kennedy in the 12th century politics of the Norman invasion of Ireland. In the nearly thirty years since the assassination, no one had ever considered the cause might lie outside the intrigues of 20th century American politics. But as we followed the trail of revenge and retribution down through the centuries we realized a more ancient vengeance may have played a role. We titled our discovery The Voice in honor of its calling to us from the past, and that's when the voice began speak to us in ways we could never have imagined.

First published in January of 2001, The Voice lays out an understanding of how we got to where we are through a story that is more relevant today than when it was originally published.

– Paul Fitzgerald and Elizabeth Gould

THE VOICE — Paperback is Available at Amazon
https://www.amazon.com/Voice-Elizabeth-Gould/dp/1439212015

- The Voice: An Encrypted Monologue, EBook and our 2017 interview about the story creation process is available at ForbiddenKnowledgeTV.net

  https://www.forbiddenmedia.com/product/the-voice/
  https://forbiddenknowledgetv.net/the-voice-an-encrypted-monologue/

- Background on the creation of The Voice is at our website. https://grailwerk.com/

- We incorporated our multidimensional understanding of the narrative creation process in a 2012 presentation titled, Afghanistan and Mystical Imperialism, An expose of the esoteric underpinnings of American foreign policy. https://www.youtube.com/watch?v=XB-brZLTdTBQ

PHOTOGRAPHS

PHOTOGRAPHS

Paul Fitzgerald at WXNE (CBN) Channel 25 1979.

John Galbraith and Paul from *Arms Race and Economy*, 1979.

Paul Interviews SALT Negotiator Paul Warnke for *Arms Race and the Economy*, 1979.

SALT Rally Hyannis, Paul Fitzgerald interviews Ted Kennedy, August 1979.

Paul and Henry Cabot Lodge at Hyannis, August 1979.

Paul – Afghanistan – Outside Kabul, 1981.

Paul and the Mullahs, 1981.

Paul Fitzgerald interviews Afghan President Babrak Karmal – Arg Palace, May 1981.

Paul Interviews General Gul Aka at the Dar Ul Uman Palace, 1981.

Richard Pipes, Theodore Eliot – *MacNeil/Lehrer Report,* January 1, 1980.

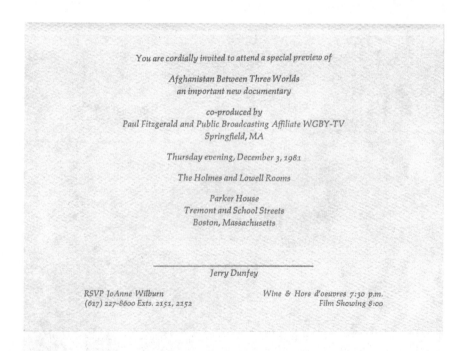

Invitation to *Afghanistan Between Three Worlds,* Parker House, December 1981.

Parker House, Paul and Jerry Dunfey, December 1981

Parker House, Mark Erstling WGBY, Kay Dunfey, Paul Fitzgerald – *Afghanistan Between Three Worlds*, December 1981.

Parker House, Paul and Liz standing next to her mother at *Afghanistan Between Three Worlds* preview, December 1981.

Parker House, Paul Meets Roger Fisher, December 1981.

Afghan Commando, 1983.

Afghan Mullah Malang demonstrates his marksmenship with Kalashnikov, 1983.

Mullah Malang, 1983.

ROGER FISHER
HARVARD LAW SCHOOL
CAMBRIDGE, MASS. 02138

617 495-4615

June 6, 1983

Mr. Martin Arnold
New York Times Magazine
229 West 43rd Street
New York, NY 10036

Dear Mr. Arnold:

Enclosed is a short memorandum sketching out the points about the Afghan situation that I think might be made in an article growing out of last month's visit that Paul Fitzgerald and I made to Kabul.

Let me clarify. I am not a specialist on Afghanistan and I do not speak the language. My specialty is negotiation and other ways of coping with conflict. Although I have made several trips to Pakistan and the Middle East, this was my first trip to Kabul. Fitzgerald, a filmmaker, was there two years ago and spent more time there than I did on this trip.

To give you the best up-to-date understanding on the situation that I know of, I am enclosing a copy of the page proof of Selig Harrison's forthcoming article in Foreign Policy. I would not propose that we cover the same ground, but rather analyze the interests of the parties and the mediation process.

Yours,

Roger Fisher
Williston Professor of Law

RF:abm
Enclosures-2

cc: Paul Fitzgerald

Roger Fisher proposal to *New York Times Magazine,* 1983.

Roger Fisher, Shah Mohammed Dost and Paul at Foreign Ministry, 1983.

Roshanrowen, Dost, Paul, Roger and Liz at Foreign Ministry, 1983.

Kabul, 1983.

Kabul, Mark Abbate photo, December 1981

231

Afghanistan – Old Fort outside Kabul, 1983.

Cameraman Tom Hurwitz and our trusty white Peugeot, 1983.

Kabul – Foreign Minister Shah Mohammed Dost and Roger Fisher, 1983.

Kabul – Roger Fisher interviews Prime Minister Sultan Ali Keshtmand, 1983.

Kabul – Kabul restaurant, Lunch with Roger Fisher, 1983 .

Afghanistan – Roger joins us in the field, 1983.

Kabul – Soviet Engineers working at Macroyan Housing Project, 1983.

Kabul – Sleeping Grocer, 1983.

Liz and the crew stopover in Prague, 1983.

Liz and Paul

Elizabeth Gould, 1970

Closeup Paul as Jesus Christ - January 1972.

SPRING 2022

THE
VALEDICTION

RESURRECTION

Desmond's Castle Askeaton Co.Limerick.

Paul Fitzgerald
Elizabeth Gould